D0497902

DATE DUE

DE 10'82			
AP 17 87			
JA 5'98			
JA 29'98 RENEW			
JA 29'90			
FE 26 98			
DE 23'94			
JE 18 '12			

JC481
G692

1976

RIVERSIDE C C LIBRARY

Interpretations of Fascism

A. JAMES GREGOR
University of California, Berkeley

GENERAL LEARNING PRESS
250 James Street
Morristown, New Jersey 07960

Riverside Community College
Library
4800 Magnolia Avenue
Riverside CA 92506

*This book is dedicated to M.—
without whom my life would
have been different.*

This study was funded by the Institute of International Studies,
University of California, Berkeley.

Copyright © 1974 by General Learning Corporation, Morristown, New
Jersey, 07960. All rights reserved. No part of this publication may be
reproduced or transmitted in any form, or by any means, electronic or
mechanical, including photocopy, xerography, recording, or any information storage and retrieval system, without written permission from the
publisher.

Manufactured in the United States of America.

Published simultaneously in Canada.

Library of Congress Catalog Card Number 74–75727

Preface

This volume constitutes a survey of social science efforts to "explain" the fascist phenomenon. Attempts to adequately interpret fascism have involved an inordinate number of social scientists and historians for an inordinate amount of time over the past half-century. For all that, we still find ourselves without a compelling account of the entire complex sequence.

Fascism—whether conceived as an inclusive phenomenon involving two or more related political regimes, or as peculiar to Italy between 1919 and 1945—constitutes a significant concern for students of contemporary politics. To develop an intellectually defensible explanation of the nature, origins, and development of Italian Fascism and/or fascist systems in general has been, and is, a responsibility that is still outstanding.

This book provides a brief review of the efforts that have been made to date to interpret and explain the phenomenon. It addresses itself specifically to those efforts undertaken to provide a social science explanation of Mussolini's Fascism. Dealing with the special application of social science techniques to a special problem—and within the broader context of that problem to deal with a specific instance (Italian Fascism as a paradigm case of generic fascism)—hopefully provides the opportunity of learning something about both social science and fascism. This book should be useful for such college courses as political theory, political behavior, political sociology, political psychology, comparative politics, democracy and dictatorship, economic and political development, social and political philosophy, and modern European history. I hope also, that it will be rewarding reading for the many citizens interested in re-thinking the problem of fascism.

Should this book succeed in accomplishing, even in part, its purposes, it is probably the consequence of insights and criticisms of such colleagues as Professors Martin Landau, Carl Rosberg, Robert Scalapino, Ralph Retzlaff, and Peter Sperlich. My graduate and undergraduate students, too numerous to mention, have also assisted me in untold ways. Dr. John Bowling, Program Coordinator of Political Studies of the Foreign Service Institute, Washington, D.C., provided friendly criticism and support. The works of Professor Renzo Di Felice inspired, in large part, this undertaking. The responsibilities for whatever shortcoming this exposition contains are, of course, my own.

Finally, I should like to thank Professor Ernst Haas of the Institute of International Studies for the support that made much of this work possible and the University of California, Berkeley, for providing me so attractive an intellectual home.

A. J. G.
Berkeley, California

Contents

CHAPTER ONE
On "Understanding" Fascism

During the past decade there has been a renewed interest in the interpretation of fascism. Historians, political scientists, sociologists, psychologists, and journalists have all tried their hand at providing some kind of "understanding" of the complex of phenomena we loosely identify with "fascism." For all the enterprise, for all the time and critical intelligence devoted to the undertaking, we really have little purchase on "understanding" "fascism." Why this should be the case is very difficult to say—but certainly our inability to specify what "understanding" is supposed to mean, or how we might come to competently "understand" something as complicated as "fascism," constitutes a good part of the problem. More than that, even if we were prepared to lay claim to some kind of "understanding," we are not all agreed upon what might constitute its compelling public evidence. Even if such issues did not trouble us, we would still face a major difficulty: there is no consensus among social scientists and/or historians as to the meaning of the term "fascist." Professionals have not even agreed upon the question of whether Hitler's National Socialism should be included as a member of the class of "fascisms."

As a consequence of at least these preliminary difficulties with the *definition of critical terms* and the *evidence conditions* governing truth claims, both students and professionals have been largely unable to come to grips with some of the most important political phenomena of the twentieth century. We not only do not know what is to count unambiguously as a "fascism," but we have very few empirical or theoretical generalizations about "fascism" (however the term is understood) in which we can invest confidence. When we maintain that we "understand" some complex sequence of events, we can be understood to mean that we are prepared to say something about the causes that produced the sequence. Providing a convincing account of a complicated phenomenon in terms of causation is largely what historical or political "interpretation" is all about.

To provide a competent causal account of such a sequence is a demanding task. Undergraduates have perhaps learned, somewhere, that to identify the "cause" or "causes" of any event requires a "regularity analysis." What this seems to mean is that one can identify a cause if event B is always and invariably preceded by event A. If A is antecedent in time and invariably precedes B, then it is conceived that we have some justification for asserting that A is the "cause" of B.

It is not our purpose here to attempt to analyze the notion "cause." The topic is introduced to suggest several things: 1. That to "understand" a complex event generally implies we have some notions of its cause or causes. 2. To say that we can identify the cause or causes of an event or complex of events necessarily implies that we can unambiguously identify the event or the complex of events with which we are concerned. To say A invariably precedes B requires that we can invariably identify B. To say that we understand "fascism" is to say that we know something of the causes that "give rise" to "fascism"—and this, in turn, requires that we can unambiguously identify instances of "fascism" whenever "fascism" makes its appearance. Unhappily there is no agreement about which political movements and political regimes should be included in the class. If we are in doubt about whether National Socialism is a "fascism," [1] is it possible to talk with any conviction about prewar Japan as a "fascist" state? [2] Is Peronism a "fascist"

----

[1] Cf. A. F. K. Organski, "Fascism and Modernization." In S. J. Woolf, ed., *The Nature of Fascism* (Random House, 1969).

[2] Masao Maruyama, *Thought and Behavior in Modern Japanese Politics* (Oxford University Press, 1969), chaps. 2 and 5.

movement? [3] How much "fascism" is there in Franco Spain? We are not in the least surprised to find Daniel Fusfeld [4] identifying the United States as a "fascist democracy." Now that Maoist China has identified the Soviet Union as a "fascist state," and Soviet sympathizers have characterized Maoist China as a "military-fascist" dictatorship, we are embarrassed by a collection that is unmanageably large. We have very little hope of identifying "invariant" causal connections between such an array of complex phenomena. Certainly there is no hope that we can proceed by a simple inductive inspection of all the available members of the class.

Before we can identify all the members of the class "fascisms," it would seem that we must have some reasonably clear idea of what we are looking for. But to know what to look for is to presume much of what we are trying to discover. Given the present state of our "understanding" very few strategies are open to us. Under such circumstances the strategy that recommends itself to us, intuitively, is one that corresponds closely to the actual manner in which the study of Fascism (and, by implication, "fascism") was undertaken.

The study of "fascism" began with the intensive study of that system that lent its name to the more inclusive phenomenon: the political movement and the regime led by Benito Mussolini. The intensive "clinical" study of a single case can, and has, suggested the *defining properties* (or "criterial attributes") that one will use to define an *entire class* of related instances. Such a study can, and has, suggested

----

[3] Gino Germani, "Fascism and Class." In S. J. Woolf, *Nature of Fascism*.

[4] Daniel Fusfeld, *Fascist Democracy in the United States* (Union for Radical Political Economics, 1968).

explanatory generalizations that might serve to explain not only the case under inspection, but any other cases that develop under similar circumstances. Employing such a strategy to either begin the study of complex political and historical phenomena or to assess the competence of available explanatory efforts, means that Mussolini's Fascism will be treated as the "model" or "paradigm" instance of "fascism."

To utilize such a working strategy does not commit one to any specific conclusions. In fact, at the conclusion of one's efforts it may be decided that there is no such thing as "fascism"—there was only one Fascist Regime—that of Benito Mussolini. (Renzo De Felice comes to something like that conclusion[5].) Alternatively, it may be concluded that Mussolini's Fascism was actually only one (and perhaps a minor) member of a more inclusive class of movements animated by an "ideology of retarded or thwarted industrialization," [6] or one of a number of "mass movement regimes," [7] or "totalitarianisms." [8] But for the purposes of commencing inquiry or assessing proposed explanations the employment of an unambiguous instance of "fascism" recommends itself. Mussolini's Fascism is just such a case.

If an effort at explanation fails to plausibly account for Italian Fascism its credibility will be considered compromised. Furthermore, the treatment of the various attempts

---

[5] Cf. Renzo De Felice, *Le interpretazioni del fascismo* (Laterza, 1969), part II, chap. 5.

[6] Mary Matossian, "Ideologies of Delayed Industrialization: Some Tensions and Ambiguities." In John H. Kautsky, ed., *Political Change in Underdeveloped Countries* (Wiley, 1962).

[7] Robert C. Tucker, "Towards a Comparative Politics of Movement-Regimes." *American Political Science Review* 1961, 55/2: 281–289.

[8] Carl J. Friedrich and Zbigniew Brzezinski, *Totalitarian Dictatorship and Autocracy* (Praeger, 1956).

at explanations will be conducted, by and large, from the point of view of contemporary social science. The reasons for that are fairly obvious—but it would serve some purpose to rehearse them here.

Contemporary social science has become explicitly and self-consciously concerned with the production of, and the public evidence for, competent explanations of complicated historical and political sequences. Social scientists no longer have confidence in the discursive narratives, the "connected accounts" that used to characterize the literature of political and social analysis in the past. Social scientists recognize that competent explanation requires recourse to "theories" —however one understands "theory." Even historians have become increasingly self-conscious and talk of writing "new histories" that exploit "testable empirical hypotheses," derivative of an "established" body of "theory," and confirmed on the evidential basis of "hard data." [9]

Social scientists are involved in a systematic effort to come to grips with the entire problem of "understanding" complex political and social phenomena. The age of innocence, when men could "intuit" what "understanding" or "explaining" might be understood to mean, is now far behind us. "Understanding" and "explaining" have so many fugitive and ambiguous meanings that the claim that one has produced or enjoys intuitive "understanding" or possesses a commonsense "explanation" of any complex social phenomena can only provoke, at best, immediate and irrepressible scepticism.

We are no longer particularly satisfied, for example, by "commonsensical" historical narratives that "explain" complex behaviors by appealing to the "psychological quirks"

---

[9] D. C. North, *Growth and Welfare in the American Past: A New Economic History* (Prentice-Hall, 1966), pp. 1ff.

of political leaders—or to their "instincts"—or their "un-wavering" dispositions.[10] "Instincts," "quirks," and "unwav-ering dispositions" require serious evidence to warrant their employment in the effort to explain complex political sequences. Most social scientists are prepared to grant that the appeal to such dubious explanations is a last desperate effort to "understand" obscure historical and political events. The fact that this particular strategy has been regularly invoked in the case of Fascism—and "fascism" in general—is a prima facie indication of how little in the way of comprehensive and competent explanation we have of the entire phenomenon.

The fact is that the most modest and commonplace claims concerning anything other than the simplest social and political phenomena necessarily involve one in issues of compelling complexity. To attempt to conceal the complexity under the guise of seeming commonsense and narrative confidence is to deceive. The most elementary account of any historical or political sequence harbors a tissue of problems that are not easily unraveled. Any narrative historical account, for example, necessarily reflects selective reporting. The complexity of any historic sequence is filtered through selective criteria that are often only half-consciously entertained by the author and rarely explicated to his audience. Moreover, the "reality" of any sequence of historical events often survives only in the most fragmentary traces. Out of these fragile elements, and under the tacit or express controls of sometimes ill-defined sorting criteria, the historian or social scientist provides an account of some sequence he deems significant. Under such circumstances, historians or

----

[10] Cf. Alan Cassels, *Fascist Italy* (Crowell, 1968), p. 21; Richard Collier, *Duce! A Biography of Benito Mussolini* (Viking, 1971), pp. 37, 45.

social scientists cannot "recapture" or "reconstruct" social reality—they can only "interpret it according to surviving evidence and conceptual frameworks." [11] "Theory," in the most general sense of the term, becomes critical to the collection, processing, and interpretation of data—it provides a handle on "understanding" and "explaining"—and it constitutes the foundation for the ultimate defense of the entire effort.

The historian who, in his account of Fascism, recounts an anecdote from the childhood of Benito Mussolini—in which the young Mussolini is reported to have revolted against a refectory system that invidiously divided the pupils into grades according to wealth—does so because he implicitly or explicitly assumes that such behavior is symptomatic of Mussolini's general behavior. Such knowledge provides a foothold on prediction and explanation. The historian who has recorded the incident concludes his account with the claim that "from this moment until the very end Benito Mussolini was a man in quest of an equalizer, seeking to annul the bitterness of childhood hurts." [12] The suggestion is that such an incident is illustrative of a sustained and confirmable behavior pattern—and Mussolini's subsequent behavior is "explicable" on the basis of such a behavioral tendency. It is obvious that such a judgment rests implicitly on some general (if vaguely formulated) theory of human behavior. Whatever "understanding" we derive from the sequence is the consequence of having tacitly accepted some notion of the causes that govern complex human behaviors.

----

[11] Robert F. Berkofer, *A Behavioral Approach to Historical Analysis* (Free Press, 1969), p. 23.

[12] Collier, *Duce!*, p. 37.

Thus, even the most elementary judgments about complex historical events, implicitly or explicitly, invoke a body of related empirical and logical propositions that together pretend to explain an occurrence or a sequence of occurrences by conceiving them to be the probable result of a set of causal factors. If "fascism" is "typically" bestial, for example (as some historians seem to contend), one could argue that such was the case because the men who composed its leadership or rank and file were bestial. If men are bestial it seems plausible to argue that they are bestial because of personal disabilities of an innate or an induced sort—they each may suffer genetic handicap, or their collective disabilities could be the product of their social environment, or individual disabilities could be compounds of personal and collective disabilities and environmental pressures. Whatever explanatory strategy one chooses, one becomes inextricably involved in "theory."

The Problems of Definition

However one chooses to construe "understanding" and "explaining," what is involved, minimally and in the first instance, is appropriate definition. Thus one may be considered to have "understood" or "explained" "fascism" when one rehearses a *lexical definition* of the following sort: "The Fascist movement in Italy was a spontaneous movement of large masses . . . directed and financed by big capitalist powers." [13] Such "understanding" is the consequence of hav-

---

[13] Leon Trotsky, *Fascism: What It Is—How to Fight It* (Pioneer, 1944), p. 11. A *lexical definition* is provided when the meaning of an obscure term or phrase is given via more generally understood terms or phrases.

ing "explained" what "fascism" might be conceived to be or to have been. The request for "explanation" frequently can be satisfied with such definitions, but almost invariably such "understanding" prompts questions that demand an account in terms of *how* and *why* "fascism" came to be what it was. If "large masses" in "spontaneous" movement are necessary to the prevalence of "fascism," one seeks to "understand" the processes involved in "moving" masses. A typical response to this suggests that "fascism" (in whatever variant form) arose because of "frightful economic misery." [14] Implicit in such an account are generalizations about the behavior of large numbers of political actors under crisis conditions. An explanation that accounts for the spontaneous movement of masses in terms of economic "misery" rests on a collection of empirical claims that relate the overt behavior of men to a set of supposed psychological states: a sense of insecurity, frustration and/or anxiety, which are, in turn, the product of a real or fancied threat and a real or fancied downward socioeconomic mobility. Thus David Shermer, in his effort to explain whatever recruitment success British "fascism" enjoyed, referred to the "short-term and localized problem of unemployment combined with economic uncertainties, poor housing and amenities [and] low wages . . . ." [15] Such an explanatory strategy is generalized over the entire generic fascist phenomena by others in judgments like the following: "In general it is to be observed that the middle classes were attracted to fascism as the threats to their social

---

[14] Heinrich Bennecke, *Wirtschaftliche Depression und politischer Radikalismus: Die Lehre von Weimar* (Olzog, 1968), p. 229.

[15] David Shermer, *Blackshirts: Fascism in Britain* (Ballantine, 1971), p. 154.

position mounted . . . . Acute economic crisis mobilized
fascist potential . . . ." [16]

Such generalizing knowledge claims necessarily imply
the availability of a general theory of individual and collective motivation. Such a theory might maintain that when
men are threatened and anxious their behavior tends to be
violent. They characteristically seek to offset threat and reduce their anxiety. The generalizations concerning individual and collective psychological dynamics, logically related,
constitute a general theory of behavior. "Explanatory" definitions that attempt to competently characterize what a phenomenon might be are either parasitic upon some one or
another theory or theories, or they are suggestive of a theoretical orientation that awaits articulation and confirmation.
Most historical accounts of complex phenomena provide
explanatory definitions supported by commonsense generalizations that could, in turn, only be supported by a competent social science theory. Usually, narrative accounts leave
the theory that supports them interred—such accounts remain content to allude to "commonsense" generalizations.
Historians, as a case in point, tend to remain satisfied with
"explanations" formulated in terms of vague but commonsensical propositions that maintain, for instance, that "the
first of the causes that make for Fascism is in certain events
like wars or depressions which cripple human personality . . . ." [17] The exploitation of metaphors, such as references to "personalities" being "crippled" and the like, indi-

----

[16] Reinhard Kuehnl, *Formen buergerlicher Herrschaft: Liberalismus-
Faschismus* (Rowolt, 1971), p. 83.

[17] Max Ascoli and Arthur Feiler, *Fascism for Whom?* (Norton,
1938), p. 324.

cate that whatever cognitive strength such accounts might enjoy derive from some general but half-articulated theory or theories concerning individual and collective psychology. Metaphors generally conceal gaps in argument and the absence of supportive evidence. Narrative historical explanations, can, as a consequence and in general, legitimately be spoken of as elliptical and partial. They are elliptical because the theoretical foundation that supports the surface propositions of the account remains unexposed. The explanation remains partial because most historical accounts refer only to some of the necessary conditions and contingent circumstances governing the entire sequence. Few historians or political analysts, for example, pretend to be in a position to predict events. At best they offer plausible accounts of past occurrences—which more than suggests that what they offer is, at best, elliptical and partial explanation. Such accounts are, however, enough to considerably reduce our puzzlement and confusion—and, as a consequence, we often feel we "understand" a complex sequence of historical events.

We are all aware, in our more critical moments, that the reduction of individual and collective puzzlement can very often be the consequence, not of serious "understanding," but rather of the availability of "convincing" commonplaces. We also know that such commonplaces sometimes turn out to be empty formulations, sonorous phrases and, not infrequently, simple stupidities. We are all too frequently satisfied by inconsequential accounts. To maintain that we "understand" or can "explain" a complex historical or political sequence requires in its support considerably more than the possession of a sense of psychological satisfaction. To insist that we have adequately "understood" and can effectively "explain" events can be taken to mean that we have at our disposal at least a minimally competent theory covering that aspect of the universe of inquiry with which we are concerned.[18]

Empirical Theories and the Problem of Moral Judgments

To "understand" and "explain" requires, minimally, the possession of definitions that identify, with as little vagueness and ambiguity as the case allows, the objects of our inquiry. We can identify, for example, instances of "fascist" as distinct from "nonfascist" systems. This kind of "nominal scaling" provides an elementary classificatory schema. Such a schema, in turn, implies (in principle) the possession of a collection of defensible general knowledge claims, which in its turn, and at its best, implies the possession of a competent general empirical theory or theories.

Most contemporary historians and political analysts are prepared to grant as much. When they allude, on the other hand, to an "understanding" that transcends adequate definition and competent empirical theory they can generally be taken to be concerned with moral or normative issues. When Gilbert Allardyce insists that the task of the historian or the political analyst is to "fully understand" "fascism"—an obligation difficult to discharge because in the course of analysis "historical discourse" must "inevitably" become "moralistic" —he can be understood to be alluding to this normative dimension of "understanding" or "explaining." Allardyce maintains that "moral involvement is inseparable from an understanding of fascism, for the fascist era can be inter-

---

[18] A. James Gregor, *An Introduction to Metapolitics* (Free Press, 1971), chaps. 7 and 8.

preted in a general sense as a study in the moral collapse of Western civilization." [19]

This kind of "trans-scientific understanding" is, in fact, a concern with moral argument. The concern is, in effect, a preoccupation with the moral dimensions of the fascist phenomenon. Such a preoccupation is frought with complex problems. That "violence" was "typical" of "fascist" movements can be conceived, for example, either as an empirical or a moral concern. To distinguish between the two is, in no sense, easy to accomplish. That the Fascist movement in Italy came to power over the bodies of hundreds and perhaps thousands of individuals can be conceived as either the consequence of tactical necessity—there was no other way in which political victory could be achieved—or it can be conceived as evidence of moral perversity. Furthermore, the goals of Italian Fascism can be conceived of either as responses to economic, social, and political necessities, or the commitment to inhumane and immoral purpose, or both. In fact, it would seem that the distinction between empirical and moral considerations can be successfully drawn only when one possesses a competent empirical theory of one's range of inquiry. Whether Italian Fascism served the interests of the "privileged classes" is an empirical problem. Once the empirical problem is resolved one can address oneself to the moral issue of whether such defense is to be the object of approval or disapproval. Can, for example, the defense of "privilege" ever be conceived as productive of social "good"?

Even more complex is the discussion of the massacre of the Jews at the hands of National Socialism. We are all prepared to insist that the massacre of innocents is immoral, but the question to which we are compelled to address ourselves

----

[19] Gilbert Allardyce, ed., *The Place of Fascism in European History* (Prentice-Hall, 1971), p. 3.

in this context is whether National Socialists conceived themselves as massacring innocents, or whether they were convinced that they were performing an "historical task" in the service of mankind by destroying what they took to be a threat of unparalleled magnitude. Nearly all the internal evidence indicates that National Socialists were persuaded that in destroying "human animals" they were "bravely" performing a public service by protecting "German culture" for posterity.[20] If we grant that such was the case, are we dealing with a moral problem or one in psychopathology? Are we dealing with a question of a "crisis in morals," cognitive failures, collective pathology, pathogenic social and political circumstances, or what? It would seem that before one could embark on "trans-scientific" inquiry or exclusively moral assessments one would have to begin to resolve a great many essentially scientific questions. No one would be content with an analysis of "Marxist socialism" that conceived it to be essentially or exclusively a "moral problem" because Stalinists massacred millions in death camps. There seems to be no immediate reason why the analysis and interpretation of either generic fascism or Italian Fascism should be any more amenable to such a strategy. It would be difficult to compare meaningfully the degrees of suffering generated by Stalinism or Maoism and that generated by Hitler's National Socialism or Mussolini's Fascism, but there seems to be no prima facie plausibility in insisting that generic fascism constituted a "moral crisis" while Stalinism did not—that the former requires a "trans-scientific" or moral "understanding" while the latter lends itself to exclusively "objective" inquiry.

----

[20] Karl D. Bracher, *The German Dictatorship* (Praeger, 1970), pp. 420–431.

Four Bases for "Understanding" Fascism

In effect, "understanding" and "explaining" political phenomena as complex as "fascism" seem to invoke four kinds
of constituent propositions taken separately or systematically
arranged: *adequate definitions* that serve to unambiguously
distinguish elements within our universe of inquiry; *empirical generalizations* that explain complex events and support
classificatory strategies; *general empirical theories* in which
both definitions and generalizations can be housed without
contradiction and with mutual support; and, finally, some
moral judgments concerning the actions of individual and
collective political actors and the nature of entire political
systems. Only the confident possession of all these sorts of
propositions, systematically integrated into an intelligible
whole would seem to provide purchase on cognitive "understanding" and "explaining."

Of all the constituent components that contribute to
"understanding" the easiest to coin and the hardest to publicly warrant are *moral judgments*. Ascriptions of "evil," "inhuman," and "perverse" can be made with the same ease as
attributions of "idealism," "self-sacrificial," and "noble."
Certifying such ascriptions and attributions, on the other
hand, involves very complex and sophisticated argument.
Unhappily, while we are all prepared to admit that competent definition, valid generalization, and effective theory
construction require special skills and public strategies,
many of us remain convinced that moral judgments can be
conjured up, employed, and certified by anyone possessed of
"moral sense." As a matter of fact, it seems that moral judgments, of all explanatory locutions, are the most difficult to
competently formulate and publicly vindicate. Any serious

scholar who insisted that "communism" was "intrinsically evil" would be dismissed as one afflicted with "cold war hysteria" or "anticommunist paranoia." And yet "fascism," a political phenomena easily as complex and inclusive as "communism," is regularly so characterized. Only in the immediate past has it become possible for scholars to entertain the possibility of a " 'good' fascism." [21]

More significant than the simple recognition of such a possibility, and the implication that competent analysis and historical reconstruction require a studied measure of objectivity and detachment, has been the evidence that the literature that sought to "understand" "fascism" all but exclusively in terms of "moral crisis" is largely incompetent. Omnibus moral judgments generally do succeed in affording one the subjective sense of "understanding"—but such judgments regularly fail to meet the requirements of any confirming public test. As the subsequent discussion will indicate, there has been a significant decline in the efforts to "explain" "fascism" in moral terms. One can, and is perhaps required to, tender moral judgments of so significant an historic sequence, but such judgments are most responsible when they are subsequent to adequate definition, the public pursuit and confirmation of empirical generalizations, and the possession of competent explanatory theory.

For about a half-century men have sought to provide a competent interpretation of the "fascist" phenomenon. To date contemporary social scientists remain prepared to admit that "despite all the literature that has . . . been written to explain the movement, few scholars are convinced that they fully understand it. Fascism remains the most difficult and perhaps the most important historical problem of our

---

[21] Allardyce, *Place of Fascism in European History,* p. 5.

time." [22] Almost all scholars admit that "it is certainly difficult to define with precision what is fascism . . . ." [23] Because adequate definition has apparently escaped us, commentators on the entire sequence have delivered themselves
of the most paradoxical generalizations in the effort to characterize "fascism." "Fascism" has been spoken of as a "mass
movement of reaction" [24] that was not "conservative," but
"revolutionary." [25] "Fascism" was, apparently, a noncon-
servative, revolutionary mass movement of reaction. Moreover, it was a "reactionary" movement that created a "new
type of state structure." [26] "Fascism" was apparently a reactionary movement that did not look backward in order to
restore an antecedent state structure—it created a *new*
type of state structure." Furthermore, "fascism" is understood to have ministered to the needs of "both social and
economic conservation, in the interests of bourgeois capitalism" [27] and in doing so "discarded" its "conservative patrons" and made them its "prisoners." [28] "Fascism" served
the interests of the conservatives and at the same time discarded them and made them its prisoners. In pursuing these
ends, we are told, "fascism" in Italy "slowed down" and
"severely repressed" the rate of economic growth until in-

----

[22] Ibid., p. 1.

[23] S. J. Woolf, "Introduction." In S. J. Woolf, ed., *European Fascism*
(Random House, 1968), p. 1.

[24] Ibid., pp. 9, 17.

[25] H. R. Trevor-Roper, "The Phenomenon of Fascism," in ibid., pp.
31ff.

[26] Woolf, in ibid., p. 40.

[27] Ibid., p. 45.

[28] Trevor-Roper, in ibid., pp. 32, 33.

dustrialization came to a "virtual halt in the 'thirties," [29] but at the same time Italian Fascism is understood to have pursued the "development of the economic and military strength of the state." [30]

In substance, the literature devoted to the interpretation of "fascism" is incredibly rich in paradox and seeming confusion. To "understand" "fascism" we require reasonably precise definition, plausible generalizations, and a body of substantive theory. To date, unfortunately, there has been very little effort to bring any order out of the mass of materials devoted to the interpretation of "fascism." Almost every specialist has his own interpretation.

These are some of the disabilities and difficulties that attend the efforts to "understand" or "interpret" "fascism." We shall consider the various accounts, employing Mussolini's Fascism, and the wealth of historic evidence now available, as the test case of interpretive adequacy. Wherever appropriate we will pursue the analysis into the treatment of the putative "generic fascism."

The Four "Classic" Interpretations of Fascism

The first major attempts to interpret Fascism, in any serious "theoretical" sense, made their appearance during the two decades prior to the outbreak of the Second World War. Out of the welter of efforts undertaken during the interwar years four "classic" candidate interpretations emerge:

----

[29] A. F. K. Organski, *The Stages of Political Development* (Knopf, 1965), pp. 37ff.

[30] Woolf, *European Fascism,* p. 10.

1. The interpretation of Fascism as the consequence of "moral crisis"
2. The interpretation of Fascism as the consequence of psychological disability
3. The interpretation of Fascism as the consequence of the intrusion of "amorphous masses" into political life
4. The interpretation of Fascism as the product of "class struggle."

We will select those efforts at interpretation that have been given the widest circulation and make their case most explicitly. Most historians and political analysts generally are eclectic—they conceive historical and political events to be the consequence of a wide and often indeterminant number of "causes." For the purposes of analysis we will survey those attempts at interpretation that seem to make the case for one or several specific causal factors. Almost all "theories" of "fascism" incorporate a variety of "contingent" causes in their account, but those that we shall review will characteristically select some one "cause" or "causes" as "primary" or "determinant." Unfortunately, most accounts are never explicit about the claims they entertain. "Causes" interact in many complex ways—and most historical and political science accounts of involved events do not clearly specify how the causal factors they identify are related. At best our judgments concerning which factors one author or another considers primary or determinant must be made on the basis of emphasis and general impressions. In the treatment of the various interpretations of "fascism" such judgments about emphasis must be made. Those authors who argue that "fascism" was the product of "moral crisis" seem to argue that "moral factors," the "ideas" entertained by political actors individually or collectively, were of "fundamental importance" in "giving rise to" "fascism." Similarly, the interpretation of "fascism" that conceives it to be the consequence of the psychological disabilities caused by the "family sexual drama" cite "sexual repression," lasting perhaps "thousands of years," as its "real" cause. As will be suggested, we are never quite sure whether the "real" or "fundamental" cause is to be understood as a necessary or sufficient "cause" or both. A necessary cause of something is that factor without which something could not happen—but given the presence of the necessary cause one cannot argue that the event must, in fact, occur. We all know, for example, that the necessary condition for passing a course is registering for it. We all know, equally well, that registering for it is not sufficient for passing. Without having registered, however, one could not pass. Similarly, having suffered "sexual repression" might be necessary for making one a "fascist"—but it might not be sufficient. In effect, the analysis of the various interpretive theories is very difficult because frequently the authors of such accounts are not very specific about their claims. As a consequence each analysis should be understood as provisional and corrigible. The analysis offered is only a beginning—but it is a beginning that characterizes any serious study of complex historical and political events.

The four interpretations that surfaced during the period between 1922 and 1945 are considered "classical." They constitute the foundation for the subsequent and more "contemporary" efforts. The notion that "fascism" was a product of the intrusion of "amorphous masses" survived the war and has developed into its more modern variants. Similarly, the interpretation of "fascism" as the product of "class struggle" has more modern variants. On the other hand, the remaining two "classic" interpretations, the one that conceives "fascism" as the product of "moral crisis" and the other that imagines it to be a function of "sexual repression," have not produced any notable modern versions. The two modern interpretations—one that conceives "fascism" to have been a function of some special stage of economic development, and that which conceives "fascism" as a "totalitarianism"— had their roots in the interwar years, but only became explicit and popular notions after the war. In effect, we shall be dealing with six reasonably distinct discursive theories of "fascism." These six are "fascism" as:

1. the product of "moral crisis"
2. psychological disabilities
3. the intrusion into history of "amorphous masses"
4. "class struggle"
5. a function of a special stage of economic development
6. as "totalitarianism."

What will be attempted here will be an exercise in stocktaking, a brief analysis of the theoretical accounts advanced as efforts at "understanding" and "explaining" Fascism. Such stocktaking is calculated to reduce the necessity, on the part of each student and scholar, to review a vast amount of literature in order to obtain some cognitive foothold on a complex and protracted historical and political sequence. There is little in English available to the student or the scholar that affords critical insight into the candidate interpretations of Fascism. Aside from Allardyce's[31] brief comments on the contending interpretations of Fascism, and John Cammett's[32] short article on "Communist Theories of Fascism," there is nothing in English to compare with Ernst

---

[31] Allardyce, *Place of Fascism in European History.*

[32] John Cammett, "Communist Theories of Fascism, 1920–1935." *Science and Society,* 1967, 31/2: 149–163.

Nolte's introduction to *Theorien ueber den Faschismus*[33] or Renzo De Felice's *Le interpretazioni del fascismo*.[34] As a consequence, one is left to contend with a mass of literature, the bulk of which is devoted to historical narratives, often mutually exclusive, each parasitic upon some "theoretic insights" that are rarely ever disinterred or provided public review. Few have the time or resources to pursue an analysis that might reduce the perplexity such literature generates. The study of Fascism involves too many significant concerns to be left in such disordered and parlous circumstances.

---

[33] Ernst Nolte, ed., *Theorien ueber den Faschismus* (Kiepenheuer & Witsch, 1967).

[34] De Felice, *Le interpretazioni del fascismo*.

CHAPTER TWO

Fascism as the Consequence of "Moral Crisis"

The renewed interest in the interpretation of Mussolini's Fascism as a complex historical and political phenomenon has been marked by the impressive work of men like Renzo De Felice and Ernst Nolte.[1] It has also seen the republication of some of the "classic" interpretations of Fascism that came out of the interwar years. American students and academics have, for example, rediscovered Wilhelm Reich's *The Mass Psychology of Fascism,* which was written in 1933.[2] Erich Fromm's *Escape from Freedom,* which was originally written in 1941, still remains a standard reference in any course in contemporary political history.[3] In 1967 a new edition of Emil Lederer's *State of the Masses,* which first appeared in 1940, was issued. In 1965 a new edition of Sigmund Neumann's *Permanent Revolution,* originally published in 1942, was made available—and in 1969 Harper published a new edition of Peter Drucker's *The End of Economic Man,* originally written in 1939. In 1956 Daniel Guerin's *Fascism and Big Business,* which originally appeared in 1937, was published in an Italian edition. Not only has there been a revived interest in the interpretation of Italian Fascism, but there has also been a resurfacing of "classic" texts that seem to have contemporary relevance and significance.

Such texts and the literature they have generated in-

----

[1] Renzo De Felice, *Mussolini il rivoluzionario* (Einaudi, 1965); *Mussolini il fascista: la conquista del potere* (Einaudi, 1966); *Mussolini il fascista: l'organizzazione dello Stato fascista* (Einaudi, 1968); *Le interpretazioni del fascismo* (Laterza, 1969); Ernst Nolte, *The Three Faces of Fascism* (Holt, Rinehart & Winston, 1966), *Die faschistischen Bewegungen* (Deutscher Taschenbuch Verlag, 1966).

[2] Wilhelm Reich, *The Mass Psychology of Fascism* (Orgone, 1946). A newly translated edition appeared in 1970 (Farrar, Straus and Giroux) translated by Vincent Garfagno.

[3] Erich Fromm, *Escape from Freedom* (Avon, 1965).

volve a vast collection of material. Only those works that
are "theoretical" in character, and have enjoyed reasonably
wide exposure will be treated in the subsequent considerations. Many of the more eclectic narrative accounts will pass
unnoticed, not because such accounts are necessarily defective, but simply because we will direct our attention to attempts that specifically make an effort to "understand" the
Fascist phenomenon in some broadly conceived "theoretical" sense. It is obvious that much historical substance is lost
by such a restriction.

We shall be concerned with the discursive "theories" of
Fascism that made their appearance during the interwar
years, and have resurfaced in the postwar period. Even if
attention is limited to the more popular attempts at interpretation, there remains an inordinately large body of material at our disposal. Students and colleagues attempting to
come to grips with such abundance have little to guide their
enterprise. What will be attempted here constitutes an effort
at stocktaking and appraisal—in order to reduce the amount
of unnecessary labor that too frequently attends preliminary
study in this area. One of the central contentions of this survey is that much of the material devoted to the interpretation
of Fascism is deficient in many respects. It is safe to say that
we simply do not have, as yet, a compelling interpretation
of Fascism. What serious interpretation requires is a comprehensive theory that provides retrodictive, predictive, and
explanatory yield. Social science, in general, has few, if any,
such theories at its disposal. The best we have, concerning
phenomena as complex as Italian Fascism, are histories en-
joying varying degrees of plausibility. As a consequence the
best we can do, for the time being, is to sort out the plausibilities. We may never have a fully comprehensive theory of
Fascism, but we can surely begin to distinguish qualitatively
between available plausible accounts. If we are compelled

to satisfy our interests with plausibilities, it seems reasonable to attempt to identify those accounts that make less demands on our credulity and traffic less on our ignorance.

One of the prima facie evidences of credulity and ignorance is a dependence on general and vague normative and empirical ascriptions. Assertions such as "Fascism was the product of a wave of barbarism and immorality" may do a great deal to steel our resolve to resist Fascism, but they do little to enhance our serious understanding. Moreover, the tendency to make such judgments is frequently conjoined with an irrepressible impulse to attribute moral frailties or behavioral traits to entire classes, whole nations, and heterogeneous populations. Almost all the accounts of Fascism articulated before World War II are characterized by such generalizations—and all are, as a consequence, equally impaired. There are ways in which evidence can be collected about the moral, behavioral, or interest properties of large groups of political actors. None of those accounts employed any of them. Any account employing broad and unsupported generalizations to make its case is suspect. Omnibus moral and empirical judgments may well be true, but we rarely have opportunity to establish their truth with any credible evidence. Some accounts, such as those that analyze Fascism as a consequence of class struggle, are less defective in this regard because of their exploitation, for instance, of available data on income distribution, economic plans, financial policies, and tax structures—that is to say, because of their dependence on public data that can be, in some sense, reviewed, assessed and perhaps rebutted. The difficulty with such data, of course, is that we have no complete and universally acceptable body of information. Economists will continue, for the foreseeable future, to argue about the nature of "Fascist economic and social policies." The interpretation of Fascism is subject to all the disabilities of any interpretation based on dubious data and information short-fall. In many cases, we do not have enough data. Further-more, what we do have is both of doubtful authenticity and highly selective. As a consequence there is inordinate room for subjective interpretation to fill in the gaps.

For all that, we are compelled to make an effort to begin to understand one of the most fateful sequences of political events in the twentieth century. Fascism was an important phase in the history of European and world poli-tics. It involved an entire "epoch" that may not be entirely behind us.

What is offered here is a first and very general assess-ment of those interpretations of Fascism that conceived it to be the consequence of "moral crisis." Such an interpreta-tion, largely produced during the years before World War II, recommends itself to our consideration not only because of its popularity but because of its seeming "relevance."

For all their popularity and apparent relevance such accounts, in fact, provide scant intellectual satisfaction. At best they offer a plausible "explanation" post factum, but they can marshall little supporting evidence in their own behalf, and afford little, if any, predictive leverage on po-litical or social events. As we shall argue, they are invariably tendentious, and all but irreducibly subjective. Whatever constituent elements survive the most rudimentary analysis are generally borrowed from more sophisticated empirically oriented historical and sociological appraisals.

In terms of analysis, it is significant that the interpre-tation of Fascism as the consequence of moral crisis origi-nates among both Fascist and anti-Fascist authors. At their worst such interpretations maintain that Fascism was the product of individual or collective perversity and moral disability—or alternatively (if one is sympathetically dis-posed), that Fascism was the consequence of a struggle of young and heroic idealists against a superannuated and materialistic social order. Those accounts that have been reduced to print are generally a trifle more sophisticated— they are all, nonetheless, afflicted with the same cognitive impairments that earmark the worst.

Contemporary students of Fascism will be most familiar with that interpretation of Fascism that conceives it to have been the product of moral perversity. Such an interpretation was given wide currency during the years of anti-Fascist struggle. Its principal spokesmen have been scholars such as Benedetto Croce and Peter Drucker.[4] There have been any number of lesser luminaries who have employed the same interpretative strategy (e.g., Kohn, von Mises, and Einaudi[5]), and elements of this interpretation resurface in any number of accounts—but Croce and Drucker have provided its most forthright spokesmen. Less familiar to students is the interpretation of Fascism that conceives it to have been a victory of "idealism" and "morality" against the "materialism" and "immorality" of liberalism and socialism. These latter interpretations derive from Fascist or philo-fascist sources and may be found in the works of such prominent Fascist ideologues as Gentile, Dino Grandi, and Ugo Spirito.[6]

---

[4] Benedetto Croce, "Il fascismo come pericolo mondiale," and "La libertà italiana nella libertà del Mondo," in *Per la nuova vita dell'Italia* (Ricciardi, 1944); "Chi è 'fascista'?" in *Pagine politiche* (Laterza, 1945); "Il fascismo come parentesi," in Costanzo Casucci, ed., *Il fascismo* (Mulino, 1961). Peter Drucker, *The End of Economic Man: The Origins of Totalitarianism* (Harper & Row, 1969).

[5] Hans Kohn, *Revolutions and Dictatorships* (Harvard University Press, 1943), *Political Ideologies of the Twentieth Century* (Harper & Row, 1966). Ludwig von Mises, *Planned Chaos* (Foundation for Economic Education, 1947). Luigi Einaudi, *Il buongoverno* (Laterza, 1954).

[6] Giovanni Gentile, "Origini e dottrina del fascismo," in Casucci, *Il*

What will be attempted here will be an exposition of these interpretations, followed by what are taken to be substantive criticisms of all such efforts. We will commence with the anti-Fascist accounts.

Benedetto Croce

Immediately after the fall of Mussolini in 1943 Benedetto Croce felt free to deliver himself of an analysis of Fascism that he thought capable of accounting for "the forces and conditions" that gave rise to Fascism in Italy. According to his interpretation, the principal factor that made Italians susceptible to Fascist mobilization was the "corruption" among them of the "consciousness of liberty" brought about by "materialistic" influences (particularly "Marxist materialism"). Marxist and Nationalist ideas had worked their influence, and Italians were flawed by a "lack of faith in the principle of liberty." As a consequence of "anti-idealistic" ideas, Italians had begun to become enamored of "heroes," of government conducted by men of will and determination. This corruption of conscience, conjoined with the erosion of the "concept of liberty," produced a disposition to return to "absolutism."

Already with the coming of World War I, Croce contended, Italian advocates of intervention in that war had begun to speak of the population of Italy in terms of "mobilizable masses," and of "heroes" and "elites" who might invoke them. The war itself produced hundreds of thousands

---

fascismo. Dino Grandi, "Le origini e la missione del fascismo," in Renzo De Felice, ed., *Il fascismo e i partiti politici Italiani* (Cappelli, 1966). Ugo Spirito, "Il corporativismo come liberalismo assoluto e socialismo assoluto," in Casucci, *Il fascismo.*

of recruitable young men who were possessed of a "collec-
tivistic" turn of mind. These were men who had lived for
years with their every need serviced by others who stood
"behind or above them." They had grown accustomed to
command or to being commanded. They had unlearned how
to attend to their own wants and well-being. To this was
added their general readiness to solve problems with violence—to undertake risk and adventure. They were infected
with a "war psychology." In peacetime, they sought to live
in the style of life to which they had become inured while in
the trenches.

During the years of World War I, to continue Croce's
account, Italian political life had significantly altered. Italian electoral reform and proportional representation introduced new and immature population elements into the political contest. The result was incompetence in governing
circles and an increased incidence of factional and counterproductive parliamentary strife. At this juncture the Fascists
made their appearance and found a recruitment potential
among the masses of demobilized and displaced survivors of
the trenches. Not that Fascism was a movement exclusively
composed of war veterans. Fascism was not, Croce insisted,
a "class or category movement." It received support and sus-
tenance from all classes. "Whoever imagines that Fascism
was a movement of a single class or some determinate classes
against others is in error," Croce maintained. Fascism was a
consequence of a kind of "moral or intellectual morbidity"
that afflicted all classes and reflected a "lost faith not only
in rational liberalism but in Marxism as well." [7] The critical
factor in the rise of Fascism was the "debasement of the idea
of liberty," and the collective infatuation with "heroes and
supermen." Fascism had been the product of a kind of moral

---

[7] Croce, "Chi è 'fascista'?" *Pagine politiche,* pp. 49, 51.

contagion, an epidemic moral corruption. What followed in the train of such moral disease was Fascism—the Fascism that constituted a "parenthesis" in the healthy history of Italy and its pursuit of "liberty and equality."

This kind of interpretation found its echo in, or was anticipated by, a great deal of literature in English. Perhaps the most prominent exponents of these views included Hans Kohn and Peter Drucker, both of whom had articulated these notions either prior to, or during, the Second World War.

Hans Kohn

Kohn, for example, had argued that Fascism found its origins in the "disillusionment . . . , the social unrest and moral confusion which followed the war of 1914–18." The "deep social unrest" that prevailed gave Mussolini his opportunity. His "squads of violent young men" seemed to offer the "frightened upper classes the guarantee of security." Thus with the "connivance of the army, Mussolini's followers set for themselves the task of 'restoring order' . . . ." With what Kohn called "boastful ruthlessness" and "a sacrifice of all ethical scruples," the Fascists imposed themselves on Italy. Fascism, Kohn went on, "rejected contemptuously all ethical motives as weakening the resoluteness of will. Fascism is power politics and *Realpolitik* in their most naked form." It was facilitated by the "growing complexity of life in the age of masses and machines and by a feeling of disillusionment and cynicism in the postwar generation after 1914." It opposed itself to "democracy," with democracy's "emphasis upon individual responsibility and individual decisions"—responsibility and decisions that require "human maturity." Fascism provided an "escape" from such responsibilities by promising the "masses" "social security and economic progress."

Mussolini, Kohn maintained, did receive the assistance of the king, the Church, the Italian army and Italian big business, who saw in him a paladin against the threat of socialism, but Mussolini "did not rely solely or even mainly upon them, but upon a private army of his own, created by him and directed . . . against the existing order." Part of the intelligentsia, enflamed by "nationalism" and Italian idealism "gave his actions the background of a new and messianic 'philosophy' of life. Without such a philosophy, and without the new propaganda techniques for regimenting mass opinion, modern dictatorships are impossible." Kohn anticipated Croce by maintaining that "it is an oversimplification to interpret Fascism only from the economic standpoint, as the last stage of decaying monopoly capitalism." Fascism was a consequence of moral failure, the advent of a new irrational and unethical conception of life that ruthlessly imposed itself upon the nation.

Peter Drucker

All of these accounts explicitly or implicitly trafficked on what was perhaps the most sophisticated statement of these views, Peter Drucker's *The End of Economic Man,* which originally appeared in 1939. Drucker advanced all the principal theses, with minor variations and differential emphases, to be found in the work of Croce and Kohn.

Drucker charged himself with the obligation of providing an "explanation and interpretation of totalitarianism which [was] valid and adequate." It is clear from his book that the principal form of totalitarianism with which he chose to deal was a generic fascism that included both Italian Fascism and German National Socialism. Drucker, however, devoted enough space to Mussolini's Italy to render his account a "classic" candidate interpretation of Italian Fascism.

Drucker maintained that Fascism could only be adequately explained by coming to grips with the critical problems that subtend every "fundamental change" in man's social organization: "a revolution of man's concept of his own nature, of the nature of his society, and of his own function and place in this society." "[The] . . . true cause, the only possible cause," Drucker insisted, "of a revolution is a fundamental and radical change in the order of values, especially in that most important sphere, man's conception of his own nature and of his place in the universe and society." [8]

Although Drucker insists that his account is based on sociological and economic factors, his central thesis sounds very much like that of Ludwig von Mises:

> The history of mankind is the history of ideas. For it is ideas, theories and doctrines that guide human action, determine the ultimate ends men aim at and the choice of the means employed for the attainment of these ends. The sensational events which stir the emotions and catch the interest of superficial observers are merely the consummation of ideological changes.[9]

Drucker, and those in this tradition, seem to imagine that "man's conception of himself and his place in the world" function in some critical way as determinants of individual and collective action. While all grant that socioeconomic

---

[8] Drucker, *End of Economic Man,* pp. xvii, xviii, 5, 10.

[9] Von Mises, *Planned Chaos,* p. 62.

and political circumstances condition the acting out of political beliefs and ideas, their corruption, enhancement and/or change, seem to be privileged causal agents. Since this seems to be the case, interpretations of this sort are prepared to dismiss alternative candidate explanations of Fascism. Drucker, for his part, dismissed, in serial order, the notion that Fascism was a "primitive outburst of barbarism," that it was "capitalism's defense against socialism," or that it was the product of propaganda. Fascism, according to Drucker, was the consequence of *moral malaise.* Europe's "basic spiritual ideas ever since the introduction of Christianity" have been "freedom and equality." Unhappily Europe had reached a point in its development where it was unable to "develop [these] basic concepts any further in the direction in which they had been moving the last few hundred years." As a consequence of this failure, Fascism made its appearance. The failure of the European tradition "must obviously be the fundamental cause of fascism." Because Europeans sought "freedom and equality," and neither traditional religion, liberal capitalism, or Marxian socialism appeared capable of providing them, the "masses" were driven to "despair." These "despairing masses" provided the human materials for the growth and prevalence of Fascism. "Fascism [was] the result of the collapse of Europe's spiritual and social order."

The masses, hitherto sustained by the ideals of "freedom and equality," were disillusioned by the failure of the Marxist experiment in the U.S.S.R. Their experience with liberal capitalism similarly left them exposed to the "demonic forces" of an inexplicable and irrational war and equally inexplicable and irrational economic dislocations and insecurities. Neither capitalism nor socialism produced the freedom and equality the European masses sought. Both

produced massive inequalities and failed to enhance "freedom." Both were attended by conflicts of an unanticipated
magnitude.

The "European masses" came to realize that "their
dream of equality through economic freedom had been shattered . . . ." The effect was to impair man's fundamental
conception of himself and of his function and place in society. "The masses . . . realized that the exercise of free
economic activity [would] not and [could not] lead to the
establishment of the free and equal society." Since "it is
the very essence of Europe that it conceives man as free
and equal," the recognition that neither a "capitalist" economy nor a "Marxist" economy could produce freedom and
equality drove the European masses to despair. That despair,
compounded by the presence of the "demonic forces" of war
and economic insecurity, deprived the "European masses"
of their faith in rationality. "The function of the individual
in society [became] entirely irrational and senseless"—men
became isolated atoms in a society that ceased to be a community bound together by common purpose. Men lost their
faith in "freedom and equality," the "two cornerstones" of
European social order. The European masses languished in
the belief that "existence in society is governed not by rational and sensible, but by blind, irrational, and demonic
forces." In the effort to lay those "demons," having lost
faith in the real possibility of "freedom and equality," the
European masses gave themselves over to Fascism. What
they sought was "security—security from the depressions, security from unemployment, security from progress . . . ." [10]

Fascism was the consequence of a search for security in
circumstances of disillusionment and despair. Men lost faith
in the ability of the social order to produce the freedom and

---

[10] Drucker, *End of Economic Man*, pp. 21, 24, 49, 50, 55, 58f., 76.

equality that had characterized European history since the commencement of the Christian era. Fascism promised to exorcise the demons of the modern world. It promised security and order. For that security and order the masses were prepared to surrender freedom and equality. But Fascism was, for Drucker, a negative creed. It offered no moral rationale for the exercise of power—nor did the "despairing masses" demand one. It did not offer a progressive development of the concepts of freedom and equality. It offered nothing but a tissue of contradictory policies, designed to maintain the productive system in operation and provide for full employment. The "masses in their great majority," Drucker maintained, would "continue to worship their self-invented demon out of sheer despair as long as the only alternative is the vacuum." What was required to excise the moral cancer of Fascism was "a new noneconomic concept of a free and equal society." [11]

Since the object of Drucker's analysis was the "European masses," he appended special qualifiers to his general account in the effort to explain the appearance of Fascism in only some of the European communities. Italy and Germany, as cases in point, did not have mature middle classes —that is to say, their bourgeoisie did not wield the same measure of political power as the bourgeoisie of other European nations. Italy and Germany, as a consequence, were more susceptible to the "disease" of Fascism. The principal causal factors, however, remained the lost faith in freedom and equality, and pervasive insecurity and despair.

----

[11] Ibid., pp. 235, 242, 268.

Fascism as a Remedy for "Moral Crisis"

Fascist interpretations, with their emphasis on "moral crisis," share some remarkable similarities with those advanced by analysts like Croce and Drucker. Giovanni Gentile, Dino Grandi, Gioacchino Volpe, Ugo Spirito, and Sergio Panunzio[12] have all left accounts of Fascism that conceive it to have been the consequence of moral crisis, of a conflict between divergent concepts of "liberty" and the role of the individual in society.

Giovanni Gentile

For Gentile, Fascism was the resolution of a conflict that afflicted the Italian "spirit." Gentile insisted that prior to, during, and after World War I "two distinct moral currents coursed through the Italian soul." One found expression in a disposition to involve Italy in the great world conflict—for "moral reasons." Those who would involve Italy in World War I saw the war as an occasion for creating among Italians the consciousness of nationhood—a consciousness that hitherto had been absent. Neutralists, in turn, opposed the war because of their calculating indifference to the "spiritual reality" of nationality, the "true foundation of ethical personality." Neutralists were essentially "materialists," measuring policy against a system of involved and egoistic cost-accounting. The interventionists, on the other hand, opted

---

[12] Gioacchino Volpe, "Genesi del fascismo," in Casucci, *Il fascismo*; Sergio Panunzio, "Teoria generale della dittatura," *Gerarchia*, 1935, 14/4: 228–236, 1935, 14/5: 303–316.

for the conflict because of "intangible, impalpable and immaterial moral concerns." Interventionists understood that men could attain the fullness of self, and enjoy concrete liberty, only within the complex of relations we identify as an autonomous political community. Gentile argued that Italians were embroiled in the working out of two distinct conceptions of liberty: the "materialist" conception opposed the individual to the state and the political community of which he was a member, and the other, the "idealist" conception, conceived the individual as achieving the fullness of personality only when he is intrinsically involved in the state and his community.

The former conception of man and society was materialist and individualist. The "individual," for this conception, was understood to be the empirical self, moved by material interests and driven by selfish motives. The latter conception was wholly "spiritual," and conceived the "individual" and the "community" as an "organic unity," each finding fulfillment in the other. The former conception found expression in Marxist socialism and bourgeois democracy. The latter conception found expression in Fascism—that is to say, in idealism, syndicalism and nationalism. The former was activated by material preoccupations and individual welfare and the latter by "moral and ideal realities."

According to Gentile's account, postwar Italy was torn between these two conflicting moral conceptions of man and his place in society. Mussolini and the Fascists defended the "moral values" of the world conflict of 1914–18. They collected to their standards the young and the idealistic and gave expression to "an effective and profound national will." Fascism manifested itself as a result of "the spiritual and political crisis" that settled on Italian life after World War I. Fascism was a cry for "spiritual rebirth," an injunction that men become "involved" in their community and abandon their individualistic "political apathy." To those ends Fascists deplored detached intellectualism and advocated an intense and moral activism. Out of this "moral crisis," Fascism was born.

Dino Grandi

Essentially the same analysis is to be found in any number of Fascist accounts. Dino Grandi simply dismissed the interpretations that conceived Fascism to be the result of a class action on the part of threatened capitalism. He similarly dismissed that interpretation that read Fascism to be a product of "war psychosis." Fascism was the product of "spiritual and sentimental, intuitive and instinctive" factors. Fascism sought to salvage the "liberty" of the fatherland—not only from "foreign plutocracies," but from the "internal subversion" that threatened the very substance of private and public freedom. The men who returned from the war were possessed of a sure moral intuition that they, their conationals, and their nation, were in mortal jeopardy. They embarked on a "sentimental crusade" governed by three principles: "liberty, the nation and syndicalism." Together they united to form Fascism, a "romantic movement . . . linked to the spiritual tradition of the *Risorgimento*." Against the notions of the state and the political community as an accidental and utilitarian congeries of private and class interests, the Fascists opposed the "idealistic" conviction that conceived the nation to be the "substance of human conscience, the object of selfless commitment and the celebration of the ideals of duty and sacrifice." Fascism opposed itself to those systems of thought that were "devoid of every spiritual and ethical content . . . ." Fascism was a rejection of "mechanical materialism," and a commitment to "a new spiritual consciousness, a definitive formula that satisfies and assuages all inner disquiet." Therefore, according to Grandi, Fascism was the resolution of a "great spiritual problem." It was the victory of a "transcendental and ethical conception" of life over a debased and narrow materialism that understood private and social life only as the arena of conflicting economic and personal interests.

Other Italian Accounts

Essentially the same account, given the variations that distinguish individual authors, is found in the interpretative essays left us by Volpe and Spirito. They all treat Fascism as a "heroic and ethical movement," drawn up against "materialism and selfishness." It was a movement that was heir to a tradition of "idealism," devoted to the "true and concrete liberty" of Italy and Italians. Where both socialism and traditional liberalism had failed to provide the liberty to which Italians aspired, Fascism offered Italians that freedom to "autonomously pursue their own ends, rather than those imposed upon them by others." True liberty can only be found in the equality of an independent political and economic community in which all constituents are "organically interrelated and interdependent." [13]

Such formulations conceived Fascism to be the result of moral or "spiritual" crisis. For the anti-Fascist, Fascism was an "unethical" and "immoral" movement that acceded to power because of men's moral imperfection and/or the spiritual enervation that followed the long and arduous conflict of 1914–18. War and "materialism" had corrupted the conception of "liberty," or men had "lost faith" in "freedom and

---

[13] Spirito, "Il corporativismo," p. 52.

equality" and were beset by "irrational demons." Returning
soldiers were enured to command and obedience. The middle-classes and the "masses" in general were "uncertain and
insecure." So afflicted, they turned to Fascism and surren-
dered their responsibilities to one "demon" that promised to
exorcise their many "demons." Or if one were a Fascist, Fascism was a movement of ethical and ideal purpose, mobilizing the "true idealists" who had fought a war for "moral
purpose" against the machinations of "materialists" devoid
of ethical or spiritual scruple. Fascism was the victory of the
partisans of "true liberty" and "organic equality" over the
debased license that was the product of crass socialism and
egoistic liberalism.

The Flaws in the Moral Crisis Interpretations

What is obvious in all this is that there is no public way to
choose between such "interpretations." That men had motives for what they did is transparent. What those motives
might have been is, by and large, unknown. There are no
surveys, which could pretend to competence, that might tell
us what the "masses," the middle-classes, or the returning
veterans, thought or felt. We know what some of their leaders and some of them as individuals were saying, and we
have some election statistics—but whether returning war
veterans were "possessed" of a "spirit of adventure," and
"irrepressible idealism," or "unethical brutality" is impossible to say. It would be safe to say that some were motivated
by the highest ideals, some by the basest motives and some
were simply carried away in the maelstrom of events.

Any interpretation that makes omnibus ascriptions of
moral dispositions to millions of participants is, on its face,
suspect. Drucker is quick to dismiss explanations of complex

phenomena by recourse to concepts of "national character." Such efforts, he tells us, constitute "the last resort of baffled historians unwilling to admit their inability to explain puzzling events . . . . The national character of every modern people is so complex, seemingly so contradictory and so largely determined by intangibles, that almost anything can be read into it." [14] Having made so astute an observation, Drucker goes on to explain enormously complex political events by attributing universal moral and psychological traits to "European masses" without recognizing that such a candidate explanation shares all the same disabilities of explanations via "national character." If "national character" is "complex and contradictory and determined by intangibles," then the "character of masses," their possession of moral sentiments and psychological traits, must be infinitely more complex and contradictory—and equally susceptible to having "anything read into them." Not only does Drucker pretend to be able to read the behavior traits and moral sentiments possessed by the "masses" in general, but he seems to think he can tell us of what they are both "consciously and unconsciously" aware.[15] Surely few analyses could legitimately make such unrestricted and general claims. And yet all these accounts must inevitably rest on the plausibility of such omnibus ascriptions. While they all specify some of the perhaps necessary or contingent conditions for the advent of Fascism—the dislocations of World War I, the protracted economic crises, the availability of recruitable urban masses—they all ultimately seek the principal cause of political events in pervasive moral sentiments and ethical convictions attributable to millions of political actors. The

---

[14] Drucker, *End of Economic Man,* pp. 113ff.

[15] Ibid., p. 72.

data base for making such judgments is simply unavailable. Consequently anti-fascists can read "uncertainty," "insecurity," "despair," a "corruption of the idea of liberty," a "loss of faith in equality," and a search for "heroes" and "saviors" in the psychology of "masses." Fascists, on the other hand, can read a "desire for true freedom," "moral conviction," "ethical transcendence," "romanticism," and a recognition of the prevalence of the "spirit of the Risorgimento" in that same psychology.

Such accounts are manifestly unconvincing. Moreover, the anti-Fascist interpretations are further impaired by an unrelenting tendentiousness. Drucker can insist that Fascists did not offer any "justification of the social and political system" in terms of "the true well-being of the individual subject to it" when, as a matter of historic fact, we have an inordinate amount of Fascist material devoted to just such an effort.[16] Fascists attempted an elaborate rationale (or rationalization, if one likes) for their revolution and the regime it produced, specifically in terms of the interests of "the true and concrete well-being of the individual." To say that such accounts are inadequate or simple propaganda is one thing—to assert that Fascists offered no such accounts is quite another. To insist, as Kohn does, that Fascism "rejected contemptuously all ethical motives," or that Fascists undertook a "proud sacrifice of all ethical scruples . . . ," may be correct in some interpretative sense. But it is historically false to suggest that Fascists made no effort to support their revolution and their regime with ethical or moral argument. To use the putative absence of such argument to support the contention that the "masses" did not require such arguments, because of a kind of "moral disease" or the "cor-

----

[16] Ibid., p. 11; cf. A. James Gregor, *The Ideology of Fascism* (Free Press, 1969).

ruption of the ideas of liberty and equality," is indefensible. Even Kohn himself admits that the "intelligentsia" employed the arguments generated by Gentile's *attualismo* to support Fascism's "messianic 'philosophy' of life." In effect, there *was* a body of literature devoted to intellectual and moral argument in support of Fascism. We might argue that the "masses" were gulled by it, but we cannot argue that Fascism offered no argument and that the "masses" felt no need of one because of their moral frailty.

The arguments that seek to explain Fascism as the result of moral crisis are hopelessly impaired if they are understood to be accounts of *causal* factors that together provide competent explanation and theoretical understanding. To suggest that Fascism was the result of the "corruption of the idea of liberty" is no more interesting or competent than to suggest that Fascism was the result of the victory of "idealism" over socialist or liberal "materialism." To maintain that men abandoned themselves to Fascism in their search for security and the exorcism of "demons" is no more interesting or significant than to say that the Fascist "ideals" of community, nationhood and selfless commitment to collective betterment "resonated" in the "soul" of Italians. There is little in the way of creditable public evidence that would support either "interpretation." Neither would provide any leverage on prediction and both are so vague and ambiguous in formulation that even their major proponents are diametrically opposed in their interpretation of the entire sequence.

Whenever such accounts contain substantive propositions, such propositions reveal themselves to be, on the most superficial inspection, either trivially true, essentially unconfirmable, or borrowed from empirically based sociological or political studies. To say, with Kohn, that "deep social unrest" gave Mussolini "his chance," is probably true, but trivial. "Deep social unrest" can be generally understood to provide revolutionaries their "chance." The question is not whether there was a "chance" to be had in the post-World War I environment of Italy, but rather why Mussolini was capable of exploiting it while the socialists (of whatever stamp), or the liberals, were not.

To say that Fascism was the product of "mass despair" is a broad empirical judgment that defies confirmation. How does one know if the "masses" were "despairing"—or "despairing" enough to permit the accession to power of Fascists? How much despairing is enough? And when masses despair, why do they choose Fascism and not Marxism, or Zen Buddhism, or drink, or drugs, or suicide? The same kinds of questions might be leveled against the empirical judgment that Fascism was the consequence of "uncertainty and insecurity." How many Italians were "uncertain and insecure"? How many does it take to make a Fascist revolution? Did insecurity and uncertainty affect some more than others? Were those who gave themselves over to Fascism more insecure and more uncertain or more despairing than others?

Finally, to argue that Fascism was either the antithesis of "liberty and equality," or their fulfillment, seems singularly futile and irrepressibly subjective. There is no single concept of "freedom" or "equality" that characterizes European history—even if we restrict our considerations (as Drucker suggests) to the Christian era. Hegel's concept of "freedom" and "equality" is significantly different from that of John Stuart Mill—and Mill's is significantly different from that of Jean Jacques Rousseau—and Rousseau's is significantly different from that of Giovanni Gentile—and so on and so forth. There have been a variety of conceptions of "freedom" and "equality" competing for men's allegiance since time immemorial. To suggest that Europe has been historically possessed of only one concept of "liberty"—and that it "by definition and necessity" involves "the right of the individual or of a minority to behave differently without being outlawed," [17] is historically inaccurate and intellectually privative.

Finally, the whole notion that Fascism was the product of "moral crisis" seems predicated on the counterintuitive assumption that men individually and collectively are in large part, if not exclusively, motivated by moral convictions —that they act out of "moral" or "spiritual" concerns and that those concerns have an objective and public character on which the historian and the political analyst can hang his account. Whatever we know of individuals and groups of individuals seems to indicate that they rarely have a specific collection of well-defined moral priorities that govern their political behavior. Certainly one runs considerable hazard in attributing some specific moral motivations or intellectual properties to entire mass movements or populations. To characterize those motives, furthermore, as "unethical" or "idealistic" is little short of presumptuous—and certainly can hardly provide a factually and cognitively satisfactory account of a complex political movement.

That there are sound elements in such accounts (whether those accounts are Fascist or anti-Fascist) cannot be gainsaid. But it must be seen that such accounts, in and of themselves, can hardly pass as competent. Whatever Fascism was, it was hardly the result, exclusively or predominantly, of "moral crisis," "idealism," or "moral frailty." If it were, we will hardly ever be in the position of affirming that we *know* that to have been the case. If we are anti-Fascist, for whatever reason, we simply "know" that Fascists were morally perverse and unethical. If we are sympathetic,

---

[17] Drucker, *End of Economic Man*, p. 79.

we simply "know" that Fascists were idealists and "defenders of Western morality" against the bestiality of "communism." These kinds of convictions hardly recommend themselves to serious students of complex historical and political phenomena.

CHAPTER THREE

Fascism as the Consequence of Psychological Disabilities

Almost as popular as the interpretation of Fascism as the result of moral crisis is the interpretation that construes Fascism to have been the result of essentially individual psychodynamic problems suffered by large groups of political actors. The form this interpretation takes is almost exclusively psychoanalytic in character. Fascism is understood to be the consequence of problems generated in the psychosexual development of the individual. Many individuals suffering the same process produce the human mass required to support Fascism. Fascism is the product of a "sick society" that is afflicted with the working out of the problems of psychodynamically impaired individuals.

Perhaps the most unfortunate accounts in this tradition are those that are the product of an unrestricted enthusiasm for Freudian analyses conjoined with the righteous indignation borne in the years of conflict against Fascism and National Socialism. Peter Nathan's *The Psychology of Fascism* is just such a book.[1] The remaining major works in this tradition are those by Wilhelm Reich, *The Mass Psychology of Fascism* and Erich Fromm's *Escape from Freedom*.[2] The work of Reich and Fromm differs from that of Nathan in that Reich's analysis involves a "synthesis" of Freudianism and some insights from Marxism, while Fromm entertains some serious reservations about Freud's general analysis. In effect, students of Fascism will be exposed to at least three major variants of the "Freudian" interpretation of Fascism —one that is "orthodox," a second that is an amalgam of Freudian and Marxian "insights," and a third that significantly qualifies the Freudian account. In considering these

----

[1] Peter Nathan, *The Psychology of Fascism* (Faber, 1943).

[2] Page references to Wilhelm Reich, *The Mass Psychology of Fascism* are to the Orgone edition of 1946; the references to Erich Fromm's *Escape from Freedom* are from the Avon edition of 1965.

variants, although they share many significant common features, their differences suggest separate treatment. The discussion here will begin with the work published by Peter Nathan—and then treat those by Reich and Fromm.

The "Little Beast of the Bed" Theory of the Origins of Fascism

Nathan's account begins with the conviction that if "we consider the development of [the] little beast of the bed [that is to say, the average infant], we will learn all there is of importance about government." [3] Since Fascism is a form of government, it follows that if we wish to learn "all there is of importance" about Fascism, we must learn something of the development of the "little beast of the bed."

To begin with, Nathan argues that in some sense or another the life circumstances of the individual produce in him a tendency to somehow *associate* rulers with parents. We are told that the psychodynamics of individual development produce an *identification* in the conscious or unconscious mind of the child between rulers and parents. Then we are told that "our attitude to government is *influenced* by our attitude to our parents." [4] The two claims are obviously different in significant respects, but they do provide at least a toehold on Nathan's exposition. Once we have this toehold, Nathan proceeds to entertain us with a synoptic account of the family drama as some Freudians understand it. If our attitude toward government is in some way influenced by our family relations—knowing something about

----

[3] Nathan, *Psychology of Fascism*, p. 10.

[4] Ibid., pp. 11, 14.

those relations would tell us something about our attitudes toward government.

According to Nathan's account of the family drama, the child wishes to monopolize its mother as its love object and the child's father constitutes a major source of competition. As a consequence, the child entertains ambivalent feelings toward his father. If the ambivalence becomes difficult to bear, the child seeks resolution by repressing his hatred and resentment. We are told that *all* children suffer these intrapsychic tensions.[5] For example, if the child entertains death wishes concerning his father (the rival for the mother's love and attention), his resultant guilt feelings may force him to repress the wishes—but, we are told, not only the buried feelings but the repressed guilt remains. The individual, as a consequence, may become suicidal to atone for his hateful (even if repressed) sentiments. However, "the usual result is that he identifies himself with his father; he becomes conservative . . . . He upholds all that he imagines his father would uphold, he takes root in the past, he stands for tradition . . . . He is opposed to any change, for a change would not agree with these fixed standards; he also cannot tolerate anything new . . . ." [6] Worse than that, since the standards the child has introjected are the standards his father *inculcated* and *not* the actual standards his father *employed,* "the conservative members of the present generation model themselves largely on their grandparents." What such an individual does is to identify "with any established authority and support it strenuously." There are, we are told, "many" such people. "They are terrified of anything revolutionary, anything antiauthoritarian, anything unusual." We

---

[5] Ibid., p. 17.

[6] Ibid., p. 18.

are then provided a seriatim list of conditions that produce these "conservative," "antirevolutionary" individuals who "welcome tyranny." The causal antecedents include "an abnormally strong attachment to the mother . . ."; or circumstances where one's father appears to be "a ruthless rival"; or a household possessed of "a very mild and unaggressive father"; or a history in which one's father suffers some "mishap . . . for which the child feels responsible"; or an "upbringing [that] stresses being good and putting the child on his honor"; or, finally, an environment in which the individual suffers an "education which helps [him] to uphold external authority." People who have lived under the influence "of some or all of these factors will have a tendency to enjoy tyranny." These people suffer "fear," "feelings of inferiority" that generate "rebellion, envy of the feared object [the father], a strong lust for power, a desire to strike fear into the breasts of others, an admiration of authority and force." In other words such persons are "protofascists." Unhappily, these "emotions are probably all necessary parts of our culture . . . [and] these attributes arising out of fear for the father [and associated guilt feelings] are taken over unwittingly towards the government." [7]

All of which leaves us with the conviction that "man is essentially governable; which is the same as saying he is essentially gullible. He is ready to accept any government, provided it has the power and prestige, the insignia and paraphernalia of office, and makes its presence known." In effect, "people get the government they deserve, they would not tolerate them if they did not need them. But saying that they are responsible is not the same thing as saying they are blameworthy. Human behavior obeys natural laws, just like

---

[7] Ibid., pp. 20, 22, 23.

any other biological phenomenon. Free will is apparent, not real." [8]

What is interesting about such an interpretation is not that it fails to explain the advent of Fascism, but that it explains too much. The family drama is apparently an experience that afflicts every "little beast of the bed." How many of us have failed to have either a "strong attachment" to our mothers (it is exceedingly difficult to determine what constitutes an *abnormally* strong attachment"), or (given Freudian postulates) would fail to experience our fathers as a "ruthless rival," or who might have had a "mild or unaggressive father," or one that suffered some mishap which we (in our wishful fancies according to Freud) had reason to believe was our responsibility? Even worse, how many of us have not endured an upbringing that stressed "being good and putting the child on his honor," or one that was "strict," or one that included an education which helped "to uphold external authority"? We should *all,* given this account, be arch conservatives and "protofascists." But there is a form of salvation. Being a conservative and both fearing and being in awe of authority does not, apparently, preclude being "rebellious" and "lusting for power." Being rebellious and lusting for power seems to be, for Nathan, fully compatible with "not questioning the authority of government" and feeling "responsible for the maintenance of people in their predestined places . . . ." [9]

Suffering the family drama can thus make one an arch conservative and a "fascist" who is rebellious, but also one who enjoys tyranny and does not question authority. Such individuals lust for power while being in awe of government; they seek to dominate or be dominated; they strive for posi-

---

[8] Ibid., pp. 25, 26f.

[9] Ibid., p. 21.

tions of authority while working to maintain people in their "predestined" places. Since the individual who suffers the family drama is disposed to act in such fashion—and we *all* suffer the family drama—it is difficult to know what such an account explains. It seems to explain everything: it explains why we are "conservative"; why we are "rebellious"; why we seek change; why we do not seek change; why we are in awe of government, and why we hate it and rebel against it. In effect, we can "explain" everything because we cannot effectively explain anything.

If, as a case in point, an individual adopts Christianity, Nathan conceives the individual afflicted with "strong tendencies to be aggressive, selfish, greedy and lustful." If, in turn, an individual opts for Fascism and "believes in the body and its strength," and enjoys "the pleasures of sexuality," "despises poverty, humility and chastity," abhors "kindness, mercy and pity," it seems safe to conclude that he is no less "aggressive, selfish, greedy and lustful" than the individual who opted for Christianity.[10] All of which should not surprise us, for it appears that, according to Nathan, men are *destined* to be aggressive, selfish, greedy, and lustful. Whether men are Christians, Democrats, Republicans, Fascists, Communists, or National Socialists, they are aggressive, selfish, greedy, and lustful.

According to this account men do not make reasoned choices—they simply act out the consequences of the family drama. Since we all suffer the same Oedipal drama, we are all afflicted with the same psychodynamic disabilities. Since we are all beset with the same impairments, all our behaviors —no matter how seemingly disparate—have the same "meaning" and can be accommodated by the same explanation. Thus, if Fascism was "a masculine homosexual move-

---

[10] Ibid., pp. 118, 115.

ment" that arose out of a fear of impotence generated by repressed feelings of hostility to one's father, much the same can be said of the celibate organization that characterizes Catholicism, the not-so-celibate behaviors of guerrilla bands, the emphatic lustfulness of college fraternities, and the episodic wenching of the Elks. Any organization qualifies as a "masculine homosexual movement" as long as its members pretend to "live for each other"—as long as they advertise "high ideals" and entertain "mysticism"—for a "homosexual culture" is just so characterized. If a "homosexual culture" reveals itself in commitments to "idealism, heroism, war, courage and endurance, loyalty to the death, and self-sacrifice," [11] then the followers of Benito Mussolini would seem to qualify—as would those of Che Guevara, or those of Mao Tse-tung, or anyone who made a pledge of allegiance to the flag. For we really are not told *how much* "idealism, heroism, war, courage and endurance, loyalty to the death and self-sacrifice" are enough to qualify one as a homosexual. If one declared "war" against sin, or poverty or drink or ignorance—would that be enough? When members of fraternities or social clubs vow "loyalty to the death," is that enough to qualify as a homosexual? How much "sacrifice" is necessary to qualify?

We are never quite sure, as a consequence, whether this kind of "explanation" of "fascism" explains too much, explains too little, or explains anything at all. These kinds of universal and cognitively empty ascriptions are the consequence of attempting to explain specific individual occurrences with an explanation that pretends to explain everything. We are given general principles of an order that explain all things but no one particular thing. For example, if one "betrays a strong interest in" anything, this is taken to

----

[11] Ibid., p. 66.

be clear evidence that one desires it. Thus if the Christian betrays strong interest in *suppressing* aggression, he is betraying at the same time a strong "tendency" to be aggressive. If the Fascist betrays a strong interest in *fomenting* aggression, he is betraying, at the same time, a strong "tendency" to be aggressive. This is because "pugnacity, aggression and antagonism are inevitable . . . . [it] has to be reckoned as part of [man's] instinctual endowment . . . . It is in man's nature to be aggressive, wild, destructive, competitive, eager to dominate." [12]

If such ascriptions are not supported by simple appeals to "instinctive nature," they are understood to be the necessary and inevitable consequence of the family drama. Thus we can expect that "the attitude of the follower, the attitude which fascism demands" would be an "attitude which masses of mankind have *always* shown." More than that, whenever we find a "man who gets his own way, undeterred by opposition . . . whether he gets it by bullying and cruelty . . ." we will find that "his opinions and ideas are accepted by the majority of people." Moreover, "man still needs magic, . . . he still needs symbols . . . ." Besides, "as every advertiser knows, it does not take long to make people want what they are told they need." All of which should not surprise us, for "we are *all* deluded, and we do not know it. We have different delusions from those we call lunatics, but ours are not nearer reality. We are deceived *all* the time; for we cannot recognize what is real and what is delusional, what is inside our minds, and what is in the world of reality without." There "is no fundamental difference between lunatics and ordinary people; only a difference of degree." [13]

---

[12] Ibid., pp. 127, 136, 123, 127.

[13] Ibid., pp. 84 (emphasis supplied), 86ff., 117, 85, 51 (emphasis supplied), 41.

So we have purchased an interpretation of Fascism at the price of all becoming homosexuals, potential Fascists, as well as lunatics. But then we really have not obtained an interpretation of Fascism—for as a consequence of "depth analysis" all governments are, in fact, the same. Nathan tells us that his account is an account of why men are "governable"—and in fact all men are governable because they all suffer the same disabilities. Nathan's book is less an interpretation of Fascism than a highly speculative account of why men are "governable." Nathan, in fact, sees no difference between being a Catholic, a Fascist or a Communist. His explanation "explains" the prevalence of "government." When we search for an explanation of why "fascism," per se, manifested itself in Germany or Italy, on the other hand, we are told that it was because "fascism" was in their respective national traditions. "Germany," we are told, "was not conquered by Rome, and thus remained barbaric . . . . Germany understands the forceful argument, not the reasonable one. It has always been anti-intellectual . . . . All this is obvious to anyone who knows Germany." Being so obvious, it is clear that "Nazi ideals are not new to Germany; nor are the Fascist ideals new in Italy. They are in the direct national tradition in both cases. They have never been so blatantly expressed before; but in our age of loudspeakers, both electric and human, every nuance and shade of opinion is shouted abroad and chalked on walls." [14]

Such a candidate explanation of Fascism collapses into a general account of why men are governable and makes Fascism the consequence of a peculiar "national tradition" —some people are bestial, lustful, lunatic, and homosexual in ways that are different from other people who are equally bestial, lustful, lunatic, and homosexual. All of which is not

----

[14] Ibid., pp. 141, 26.

terribly helpful. But more than that, the really critical problem that attends this kind of interpretation centers on how one might establish the public evidence in its support. As we shall indicate, this is the central problem of all psychoanalytically oriented "interpretations" of complex human phenomena. How does one begin to collect compelling evidence of the impairments suffered by children in the family situation? How can we establish that the "average" individual suffers all the trauma associated with the Freudian family drama? If we collect uncontrolled clinical studies of self-selected neurotics can we project, with any confidence whatever, the interpretative findings they contain over the general population? More than that, if *all* our thought processes are indistinguishable from those of lunatics why should we invest credence in one lunatic interpretation rather than another?

These kinds of difficulties resurface in any serious discussion of psychoanalytically oriented interpretations. We will find their traces in the work of both Reich and Fromm.

A "Sex-Economic" Analysis of the Rise of Fascism

Wilhelm Reich's *The Mass Psychology of Fascism*, in its turn, has enjoyed a long life. In 1970 contemporary students of Fascism were exposed to a new edition of his book first written in the early thirties. It is hard to understand why his book has enjoyed so much popularity, but it does pretend to provide a competent and exhaustive account of the rise of fascism.

In his account Reich dismissed available interpretations of fascism. He explicitly rejected, for example, the "economistic" interpretation of "orthodox" Marxist theoreticians. What he offered in its stead was a "sex-economic analysis," an analysis based, in part, on Freud and, in part, on Marx.[15]

Reich addressed himself to the problem of how the "economic base" of society generated an "ideological reflex" and how that "reflex" might "retroact" on the economic base. He suggested that the problem is solved by something he calls "character-analytic psychology." The analysis commenced with the familiar "family drama" involving all the machinery of the Oedipus complex and the infantile guilt feelings toward the father. The critical variable in the analysis turned on "sexual suppression," for "character analytic investigation . . . shows that the interlacing of the socioeconomic with the sexual structure . . . takes place in the first four or five years of life, and in the authoritarian family." The "authoritarian family" is one in which "the natural sexuality of the child, particularly of its genital sexuality" is "suppressed." The result is a child that is

> apprehensive, shy, obedient, afraid of authority, "good,"
> and "adjusted" in the authoritarian sense; it paralyzes the
> rebellious forces because any rebellion is laden with anxiety; it produces, by inhibiting sexual curiosity and sexual
> thinking . . . a general inhibition of thinking and of critical faculties. In brief, the goal of sexual suppression is
> that of producing an individual who is adjusted to the authoritarian order and who will submit to it in spite of all
> misery and degradation. . . . The formation of the authoritarian structure takes place through the anchoring of
> sexual inhibition and sexual anxiety.[16]

Suppression of the natural genital sexuality of children produces fear, frustration, powerlessness, and a sense of in-

----

[15] Reich, *Mass Psychology of Fascism,* p. xix.

[16] Ibid., pp. 22ff., 24ff.

feriority that finds expression in "orgasm anxiety," aggression, sadomasochistic homosexuality, defensive arrogance, and mysticism. Its political manifestation is fascism.

This commonplace account is interesting only in so far as Reich is quick to identify the onset of the "authoritarian family" and its sexual suppression. The suppression of genital sexuality dates from the time when mankind made the transition from a matriarchal to a patriarchal social order —approximately (according to Reich's ethnological speculations) six thousand years ago.[17] "As a consequence of thousands of years of social and educational warping," we are informed, "the masses of the people have become biologically rigid and incapable of freedom. They are no longer capable of organizing a peaceful living together." Men have become "biologically rigid," languishing in a state of "unsatisfied orgastic longing," as a consequence of thousands of years of conditioning in the context of the "patriarchal authoritarian family." "The problem of the Fascist pestilence," according to Reich's account, "is a matter of a development stretching over thousands of years and not, as the economists believe, a matter of imperialistic interests of the past two hundred or even of the past twenty years." [18] Fascism "grew out of the suppression of infantile and adolescent sexuality . . . ." Since this is the case, and since we are concerned with "basic biological functions which have nothing to do with economic class distinctions," we would expect an individual, of whatever class, who has suffered infantile or adolescent sexual suppression, to be fascist.[19] Moreover, since *all* mankind (in varying degrees) has been suffering such suppression for thousands of years, one would expect that

---

[17] Ibid., pp. xxiii, 76, 187ff., 198, 241, 275.

[18] Ibid., pp. 271, 294.

[19] Ibid., pp. 303, 331.

we would *all* be real or potential fascists—and this seems to be just the case. Reich informs us:

> My character analytic experience shows that there is to-day not a single individual who does not have the elements of fascist feeling and thinking in his structure . . . . "Fascism" is only the politically organized expression of the average human character structure, a character structure which has nothing to do with this or that race, nation or party but which is general and international . . . . Fascism is the result of thousands of years of warping of the human structure. It could have developed in any nation. It is not a specific German or Italian character trait. It works in every mortal.[20]

Again we have purchased an explanation of fascism by *all* becoming fascists. We have bought a speculative account of a collection of generic human disabilities. Since all human beings (at least, according to Reich, since the advent of patriarchal society) have suffered sexual suppression, we are all biologically rigid and "enraged" because of "ungratified sexuality."[21] We may now know why we suffer orgastic longing, but since men have been suffering orgastic longing for at least six thousand years, we have not come very close to an interpretation of Italian Fascism.

The best Reich can offer for the advent of fascism in Italy or Germany is a catalog of contingencies. Since everyone is a potential fascist, the Italian Fascists won mass support because they were more emphatic Fascists than their opponents. Then, of course, there was an economic crisis and the "need for coherence during [that time] was so great that the totalitarian and authoritarian state idea could be-

---

[20] Ibid., pp. ix, 273.

[21] Ibid., p. 252.

come victorious with hardly any difficulty." A further factor, it would seem, is the fact that in some countries there were "traditions" that either resisted or fostered fascism. All countries are characterized by a "common denominator: the incapacity of the masses for social self-government," but America did *not* become fascist because America was not "weighed down" by old traditions. Americans entertain "the memory of their own flight from despotism" and therefore resisted fascist blandishments.[22] Why England or France did not become fascist during the economic crisis of the thirties is left to speculation. We find ourselves reduced once again to an explanation of Fascism and fascisms in terms of "national traditions," for we are all biologically botched and bungled and, as a consequence, are all potential fascists.

The best this kind of account can deliver is a statement of the conjectured *necessary conditions* for the appearance of Fascism. In order for there to be Fascism there must be "authoritarian families" that produce children afflicted with a "spastic condition of the genital musculature." But the availability of men so afflicted is not sufficient for the appearance of Fascism—or else there would have always been Fascism. Reich tells us that "fascism" is, in fact, "something completely new" to the twentieth century. Why this should be so is never explained. We have not a clue as to what the sufficient conditions for the appearance of Fascism might be. Reich tells us that Fascist character traits are "manifest in every single individual in the world." [23] And, as we have seen, this has been the case, according to his account, for about six thousand years. Why Fascism waited until the twentieth century to make its appearance remains a mystery.

----

[22] Ibid., pp. 232, 239, 241, 242.

[23] Ibid., pp. 151, xxi, 320.

In effect, Reich's account shares some of the same disabilities that afflict that of Nathan. It is an omnibus account that explains too much. Further there is no way to establish what credible evidence supports Reich's generalizations about *"every single individual in the world."* Such unrestricted generalizations require evidence that is nowhere to be found in Reich's account.

Fromm's Freudian-Marxist Interpretation

Perhaps the most sophisticated explanation of this kind is to be found in Erich Fromm's *Escape from Freedom,* a book that has come to be considered a "classic" interpretation of fascism. Again, Fromm's work is in the Freudian and Marxian tradition. Fromm, however, does make his reservations concerning Freudian analysis quite explicit. Freud emphasized the psychodynamic functions of sexuality to the exclusion of what Fromm takes to be a number of equally significant factors. Fromm maintains that "there are certain factors in man's nature which are *fixed and unchangeable;* the necessity to satisfy the physiologically conditioned drives and *the necessity to avoid isolation and moral aloneness."* According to Fromm, "the *striving for justice and truth* is an *inherent trend of human nature,"* as is "the tendency to grow," which in turn makes "the desire for freedom and the hatred against oppression" natural to man.[24]

Against this background of "necessary" and "inherent human qualities" we are given an account of a process of "individuation" that involves the individual in a process of "severing the umbilical cord which fastens him to the out-

----

[24] Fromm, *Escape from Freedom,* pp. 37 (emphasis supplied), 316 (emphasis supplied), 315.

side world" and to his "primitive community." In the course of human history the individual begins to enjoy "freedom from" nature and a traditionally structured social order. This freedom is a consequence of maturing economic forces. The development of the economic forces of society progressively have liberated man from material want. Economic forces further provide the precondition for the dissolution of "primary ties," ties to a traditionally organized and stable social order. Changes in the economic base of society alter not only its potential to satisfy material needs, but the nature of interpersonal relations as well. What this produces in the individual is an increasing sense of selfhood, but at the same time a growing awareness of isolation, of "aloneness," of powerlessness and insignificance. Only if the individual develops, in the course of this process, an "inner strength" that permits a "new kind of relatedness" to nature and the world of men can he avoid the impulse to "escape" from this new freedom into some kind of association that promises relief from the growing sense of insignificance and loneliness.[25]

For Europeans, according to Fromm, this has been a central issue since the Reformation. He provides a stenographic account of the development of merchant capitalism and the first appearance of industrial capitalism—and suggests that the influence of capital, the impersonal exchanges of the market, and increased individual competition, accelerated the process of individuation and dissolved the ties that had held medieval society together. Out of this period, and in the area where capitalism was developing, various religious movements emerged, among them Lutheranism and Calvinism, that typified the "flight from freedom" with which Fromm is concerned. Luther, as a case in point, exemplified what Fromm calls the "authoritarian personality" who seeks

---

[25] Ibid., pp. 46ff., 52.

to escape the new freedom that economic forces bring in their train. Because Luther had suffered an "unusually severe father" he had not been able to develop "spontaneously"— his "expansiveness" had been thwarted. As a consequence he felt "powerless" and "insignificant." He was torn by a "constant ambivalence toward authority; he hated it and rebelled against it, while at the same time he admired it and tended to submit to it." [26]

Luther represented a character type, those men caught in the trammels of a particular economic development that provided, at one and the same time, release from the negative constraints on freedom, and an increasing sense of insignificance and powerlessness because of a loss in the sense of community involvement. The development of capitalism, particularly its maturation into monopoly capitalism, exacerbated the situation. Men were freed from material constraints and they developed increasing control over natural forces, but they lacked inner ego strength and a sense of community belonging. There was a "lag" between the potential for genuine freedom and its realization. This impairment was, according to Fromm, particularly marked among the "middle class." The great capitalists enjoyed and do enjoy more and more of the creature comforts of the economic system. The middle class, on the other hand, is caught between the developing proletariat and the combined forces of great capitalists. The middle classes find themselves helpless and insignificant, their status threatened, the sense of community hopelessly impaired, their values dysfunctional— they cannot rise to the station of the great capitalists and they loathe sinking into the proletariat. As a consequence, the middle class both admires and fears the great capitalists. It doubts its own significance. It suffers envy and resentment.

----

[26] Ibid., p. 84.

It is lonely. As a class it hates itself and feels itself subject to forces it cannot control. The lower classes, on the other hand, "the poor population of the cities," were "impelled by a new quest for freedom and an ardent hope to end the growing economic and personal oppression." [27]

In general, capitalism

> made the individual more alone and isolated and imbued him with a feeling of insignificance and powerlessness . . . . [It] has made man work for extrapersonal ends, made him a servant to the very machine he built, and thereby has given him a feeling of personal insignificance and powerlessness. . . . Man does not only sell commodities, he sells himself and feels himself to be a commodity. . . . The individual became more alone, isolated, became an instrument in the hands of overwhelming strong forces outside of himself; he became an "individual," but a bewildered and insecure individual.[28]

As a consequence the individual tends to seek recourse in an "escape" from freedom. He becomes submissive to authority in order to find security—or, alternatively, he seeks power to relieve his pervasive sense of isolation. He becomes a masochist, or a sadist, or his character structure reveals elements of both. The German lower-middle class typified this "authoritarian character," and it provided the psychological foundation for the recruitment success of National Socialism. The same analysis apparently would apply to the Italian "middle classes." We are told that "by the term 'authoritarian character,' we imply that it represents the personality structure which is the human basis of Fascism." [29]

----

[27] Ibid., pp. 119ff.

[28] Ibid., pp. 128, 132, 140, 141.

[29] Ibid., pp. 185, 186.

Fromm, in the course of his account, makes a number of empirical claims: 1. There is a growing "feeling" of "insignificance and powerlessness" among men; 2. This "feeling" is particularly characteristic of the "middle classes" at least since the Reformation; 3. These feelings generate a collection of behavioral traits best identified as sadomasochistic and spoken of as "authoritarian character"; 4. That this personality type provides the "human basis" for generic fascism. Fromm clearly recognizes that such claims require evidence in their support. To supply that evidence, he indicates that his studies are based on individual clinical assessments. The result of these "minute" and individual studies, he insists, can be projected to whole populations, classes, and categories. For example, Fromm pretends to know how the artisans of the medieval period felt about the products of their labor, and how the wealthy nobles and burghers of the Renaissance felt.[30] It is difficult, irrespective of Fromm's confidence, to know how the clinical study of a contemporary collection of self-selected neurotics, no matter how "minutely" analyzed, could have produced information that could be projected over whole population categories and classes that lived in medieval or Renaissance times.

Fromm is prepared to grant that his researches do not satisfy the requirements of "academic" or "experimental" psychology, but insists that he invokes a "thoroughly empirical method."[31] Unhappily, after he informs his reader many times that men of various classes "feel" the sense of insignificance and powerlessness that is at the basis of his analysis, he proceeds to qualify that affirmation by insisting that "this feeling of individual isolation and powerlessness . . . is nothing the average normal person is aware of." The

---

[30] Ibid., pp. 64ff.

[31] Ibid., pp. 157ff.

average man is, in fact, "fooled" into thinking he is *not* in-significant and powerless by "advertising and political prop-aganda . . . ." Moreover, individuals, of whatever class or category, who "really" feel powerless and insignificant may effectively conceal it (even to themselves) by "com-pensatory feelings of eminence and perfection." [32]

It is obvious that such an account provides no clear cri-teria for what might count as confirming or disconfirming evidence for the claims that are made. Fromm makes broad attributions of "feelings" to whole classes and entire popula-tions at various historic periods and in various national and cultural circumstances. We are told that "the vast majority of the population was seized with the feeling of individual insignificance and powerlessness" which is "typical for mo-nopolistic capitalism in general." [33] And yet, if we should request evidence to support such a broad empirical claim, we are informed that such evidence cannot be obtained by surveying the *explicit* feelings of populations—because the "normal" individual does not know that he has such feelings. He has either been "fooled" by propaganda or has "com-pensated." We are left with Fromm's insistence that on the basis of his clinical studies of some unspecified number of neurotics *he* knows what the *unconscious* feelings of entire classes, categories, and populations over four centuries might be.

Actually what is at issue here is not an empirical mat-ter at all. There are ways of establishing how individuals and groups of individuals feel. Fromm clearly is not interested in that kind of data. He will "interpret" the feelings of whole populations on the basis of his "interpretation" of the dreams and word associations of some indeterminate number of

---

[32] Ibid., pp. 155, 151, 173.

[33] Ibid., p. 242.

neurotics from unspecified backgrounds, indeterminate age and sex, levels of education and socioeconomic circumstances. On the basis of his interpretations of this kind of evidence, Fromm can insist that "the social character of the lower middle class . . . was markedly different from that of the working class, of the higher strata of the middle class, and of the nobility and the upper classes. As a matter of fact, certain features were characteristic for this part of the middle class throughout its history . . . ." Not only can he tell us what the character traits of the lower-middle class have been throughout its history, but he can make relatively fine quantitative judgments about the frequency of such character traits among other classes as well. We are told that while the "working class" *may* display *some* of these authoritarian character traits they are "typical for the lower middle class, while only a minority of the working class exhibited the same character structure in a similarly clear cut fashion. . . ." [34]

It is more than doubtful whether any of this could pass as empirically based. It is at best speculative. One would have to grant, without demur, all the major premises of his argument—that men have an "inherent" tendency to seek "freedom, justice, truth" and so forth. Further one would have to grant that the "lower middle class" suffers special kinds of vaguely specified economic problems that distinguish them from the "working class." Then one would have to accept Fromm's claim that he has been very "empirical." Even having granted all that one would still have a very fragile base on which to erect his explanation of fascism.

What we have once again is a discussion of some generic human problems—in Fromm's case the putative "inherent tendency" on the part of all men to pursue "positive

----

[34] Ibid., p. 236.

freedom" which, when thwarted, manifests itself in personality impairments. But Fromm admits that men have nowhere and at no time enjoyed "positive freedom"—consequently we are *all* impaired. We are told "nothing is more difficult for the average man to bear than feeling of not being identified with a larger group," and that the sense of insignificance and powerlessness produces in the "normal" individual a disposition to "become an automaton," so that "we have become automatons who live under the illusion of being self-willing individuals." We must therefore recognize that "so-called rational behavior is largely determined by the character structure." It follows that "the phenomena which we observe in the neurotic person are in principle not different from those we find in the normal." Finally, if "modern man," in general, is overcome by "a profound feeling of powerlessness," and the "average person" is "automatized," and "the despair of the human automaton is fertile soil for the political purposes of Fascism," [35] then the question necessarily arises: why have we not all been fascists at least since the Reformation? The only answer Fromm offers is that the special "conditions of monopoly capitalism" produce the protracted crises that make possible the exploitation of the "authoritarian character" in all of us. Why the most advanced capitalist nations did not become fascist on this account is difficult to say. Why did Fascism come to Italy, which was largely agrarian? Why was there a form of fascism in Spain and Portugal, neither of which suffers from monopoly capitalism?

Perhaps more interesting still is the fact that this kind of explanation suggests that wherever there is protracted crisis—given the all but universal personality impairments that follow from "instinctive aggressiveness," or "infantile

---

[35] Ibid., pp. 234, 209, 279, 309, 159, 281f.

and adolescent sexual suppression," of the "feeling of insignificance and powerlessness"—fascism should result. Why should the "working class" or "working class movements" be immune? Both Reich and Fromm wax eloquent about the special personality traits enjoyed by the "working class." For Reich the "working class" is "more internationalistic," "more accessible to internationalism." They are more humane and do not share middle-class attitudes toward sexuality. The workers are, according to Reich's account, "open and matter-of-fact" about sexuality. The worker "is incomparably more accessible to sex-economic concepts than the typical middle-class individual." [36] For Fromm the workers, those at "the bottom of the social pyramid," escape some of the "automatizing" of the middle class. They do not have to conform to prevailing norms. They have nothing to lose and have everything to gain.[37] They see the promise of freedom in the economic changes going on about them.

But the picture is not at all clear. In the course of his discussion Reich laments that the "industrial workers of the 20th century . . . have taken over the forms of living and the attitudes of the middle class," [38] and Fromm grants that the workers have been made into "appendages of machines." So it should not surprise us that both Reich and Fromm discovered that the revolutionary movement of the "workers" which swept into power in Russia degenerated into a perfect analogue of Fascism.[39] We could anticipate what Reich would say about Maoist China, where the peasantry, Reich's "most reactionary class," presumably came to power, where

---

[36] Reich, *Mass Psychology of Fascism*, pp. 49, 55.

[37] Fromm, *Escape from Freedom*, p. 268.

[38] Reich, *Mass Psychology of Fascism*, p. 56.

[39] Ibid., pp. 237, 241, 256, 261ff., 280; Fromm, *Escape from Freedom*, pp. 300ff.

a charismatic "helmsman" rules a state in which nationalism is treated as a special virtue and life is governed by a military style. One could raise similar questions about Cuba and its "agrarian revolution" based on the leadership of a minority of "declassed bourgeois warrior intellectuals" ruling the "masses" through the agency of a charismatic *"Jefe."* In effect, it is difficult to know what such explanations explain. They seem, prima facie, to explain too much—all regimes in general or at least all in which "masses" follow "charismatic leaders"—or they seem to explain too little. Why, for example, if monopoly capitalism is the sufficient condition for fascism, has fascism not come to the advanced industrial nations like England, the United States, and France?

We are all either real or potential fascists and then we have no explanation, or some classes are more potentially fascist than others. Movements that are "middle class" would be fascist, and those that are not would be something else. We have no creditable evidence to support the latter alternative and considerable intuitive counterevidence. The "working masses" of the Soviet Union, China, and Cuba seem as disposed to "escape from freedom" as anyone—and hardly anyone has suggested that Stalinism, Maoism or Castroism are particularly middle-class movements. If people do, in fact, get the governments that find support in their modal character, then the "working masses" would seem to be as "fascist" as anyone. If fascism was the result of impaired personality, such personalities are very prevalent, if not universal. Explanation seems to have escaped us.

The "Authoritarian Personality"

What does survive from all this are the empirical inquiries that these notions stimulated. After World War II a group of researchers and scholars attempted to empirically confirm the existence of an "authoritarian personality." Using an ingenious battery of psychological devices, they began to study subjects to discover if there was, in fact, a syndrome of character traits that could be objectively identified as "authoritarian" or "potentially fascistic." [40] What they discovered was that there were people who appeared to harbor an identifiable collection of behavioral traits that seemed to hang together. They found that those persons who tended to be anti-Semitic were also ethnocentric—that is, they tended to deprecate anything "foreign" or "alien." They also found that such persons tended to be economically and politically conservative. Finally, such persons tended to have "idealized" their parents or had familial relations that could be characterized as "strict" or "authoritarian." This much seems to have survived the extensive criticism to which the quasi-experimental research on the "authoritarian personality" was subjected. [41]

What is perhaps most interesting for our purposes is that the presence of this specific "fascistic" syndrome seems to characterize people who occupy the *lowest ranks* of the socioeconomic scale. Thus, if there is a personality type that could be characterized as "authoritarian" or "potentially fascistic," it probably most frequently is represented among those people with a minimum amount of education, a low intelligence quotient, menial jobs, and low wages. In effect, the "potential fascist" is most frequently to be found among the *working classes*. The "potential fascist" responds, apparently, to "the norms of an underprivileged subculture." The

----

[40] T. W. Adorno, Else Frenkel-Brunswik, D. J. Levinson, and R. N. Sanford, *The Authoritarian Personality* (Harper & Row, 1950).

[41] R. Christie and Marie Jahoda, eds., *Studies in the Scope and Method of "The Authoritarian Personality"* (Free Press, 1954).

"usual thing" found in research with definable economic groups is that the "working class [and] lower education groups [are] exceptionally authoritarian." The highest scores on the F scale, the measure of putative "fascism," have been found among working class groups. Roger Brown suggests that "authoritarianism may be the world-view of the uneducated in western industrial societies." [42]

It seems reasonably clear that if the evidence supporting the existence of a "potentially fascist" personality is used as a partial interpretation of Italian Fascism one must expect to find such personality types more frequently among the working class than among the "lower middle class." If, in fact, anti-Semitism, ethnocentrism, and authoritarianism are generally found to be related behavioral traits, it seems that such a collection of traits is more characteristic of the industrial working classes in the advanced industrial countries than among the better educated middle class. It seems probable that such a personality type is associated with a family characterized by strict, rigid, and punitive discipline. But it is not at all evident that this kind of family is middle class. If, as considerable historic and impressionistic evidence suggests, the middle class provided considerable support for Fascism, it could hardly have been the consequence of an "authoritarian personality" that was "typical" of the class. Certainly we have no creditable empirical evidence to support such a contention.

Postwar research on the "authoritarian personality" "[did] not clearly [show] to what extent 'paranoid' social groups are based on an appeal to authoritarian persons, how susceptible authoritarians are to active participation in extremist movements of any kind, what effects such groups

---

[42] Roger Brown, *Social Psychology* (Free Press, 1965), pp. 521, 522, 523.

have on established social forms and institutions, what . . . the epidemiology of authoritarianism [might be], [or] what modifications of the style are likely under certain social conditions." [43] In effect, psychoanalytically oriented interpretations of fascism were suggestive of lines of research, but the research produced either counterintuitive evidence that the working class should be the recruitment base of fascist movements, or the research has been manifestly inconclusive with respect to the central questions to which the interpretation addressed itself.

Finally, it seems intuitively obvious that as complex and as relatively efficient a movement as Fascism could not have been the simple product of sadomasochistic, latently homosexual personality types characterized by a lack of rational deliberation, an addiction to simple violence, and an irrepressible mysticism. If such individuals are found in fascist movements, it would seem that such movements would also require competent administrators, effective propagandists, planning personnel and rational agents for the formulation of strategy as well. If Fascism exploited aggressiveness and mysticism it could only be *one* of many factors that could explain its advent and prevalence. If the "authoritarian personality" was the "fertile soil" for such exploitation, it probably was not a personality type that was modal for the middle class. Our evidence concerning personality types is, of course, drawn almost exclusively from American samples, none of them representative of the population in general. We could generalize only with hazard. We cannot generalize at all, with any confidence, about Italian personality types whether those types are middle or working class.

----

[43] John F. Kirscht and Ronald C. Dillehay, *Dimensions of Authoritarianism: A Review of Research and Theory* (University of Kentucky, 1967), pp. 134ff.

But whatever the case the psychodynamic interpretation of Fascism is largely inadequate.

In effect, the attempt to interpret Fascism as the exclusive product of peculiar personality types seems hopelessly flawed. The tradition out of which such an account grew, on the other hand, has stimulated a great deal of serious empirical research. The results of that research have not been able to establish definitively the existence of a "fascist personality type." What we have is some evidence that in some environments certain attitudinal traits, which some people think are characteristic of some kinds of fascism, may very well exist in objective fact. But that evidence also indicates that that personality type is probably more prevalent among the uneducated working classes than among the more privileged middle classes. The attempt to explain Fascism as a consequence of individual personality disabilities is inadequate as a general interpretation. At best it suggests that there are some people who might well be attracted to Fascism if Fascism was sufficiently aggressive and authoritarian. But that kind of intelligence does not carry us far. When we review the efforts to explain Fascism via this interpretation we are left with a tissue of unsupported speculation that delivers only a vague sense that we are all lunatics, neurotics, and fascists, and there is little prospect of something better. Such interpretations are not only inadequate, they are irrepressibly pessimistic. Indeed, such interpretations probably tell us more about the authors of such accounts than they do about Fascism.

CHAPTER FOUR

Fascism as the Consequence of the Rise of "Amorphous Masses"

There is an intellectual strategy, easily as old as that associated with psychoanalysis, that has sought to explain Fascism in terms of the collective psychological characteristics
possessed by "mass-man." The traits associated with "mass-
man" are not conceived of as the summated product of many
individual Oedipal dramas, but rather the unique consequence of some special series of events transpiring in society.
Under such special circumstances men in the aggregate
evince "mass behavior"—behavior distinct from any that
might manifest itself under any other circumstances. Long
before the advent of Fascism, the effort to explain revolution
by appealing to the properties of "mass-man" was popular.

One of the first books written in this earlier period—
and certainly one which has remained the most influential
—was Gustave Le Bon's *The Crowd*.[1] For three-quarters of
a century some of the central ideas articulated by Le Bon
have surfaced and resurfaced in a wide variety of places.
Le Bon was among the first to speak of the "amorphousness"
of revolutionary "crowds." He was among the first to speak
of such human aggregates as composed of the residue of all
classes—and to draw the distinction between the rational
behavior of classes, interest groups, and individuals, and the
irrationality of "amorphous crowds." He identified "crowd"
behavior as enflamed by an "exaggeration of the sentiments," by what is now called a "rage for unanimity," by an
"incapacity for moderation and delay," an "absence of judgment" and an "inability to reason." Such a collectivity "in-
stinctively" seeks out a "leader" around whom its sentiments
coalesce. It was Le Bon who was among the first to speak of
a pervasive "thirst for obedience," and a self-effacing, self-

----

[1] Gustave Le Bon, *The Crowd: A Study of the Popular Mind* (New
York: Viking, 1960). Le Bon's work first appeared in 1895.

sacrificial disposition that manifested itself in "mass," as distinct from class or interest-group, behavior.

Robert Merton has alluded to the "prescient" qualities
of these discursive judgments.[2] Merton refers to these ideas
as they appear and reappear in the writings of a subsequent
array of writers who have attempted to explain the rise and
historic trajectory of Fascism: Jose Ortega y Gasset, Emil
Lederer, Franz Neumann, and Hannah Arendt—a list to
which we might justifiably add the names of Talcott Parsons,
Eric Hoffer, and William Kornhauser. Most of the authors
in this tradition have sought to provide a more competent
account of the rise of "amorphous masses" and of the "age"
that Le Bon insisted would be the "era of crowds"—and all
of them have returned to themes first made popular by
Le Bon.

Ortega y Gasset's Theory of Mass-Men

Jose Ortega y Gasset was among the first of those authors
who attempted to explain the rise of Fascism by employing
some of the central ideas of Le Bon. Ortega saw Fascism as
the result of the "intrusion" of the "amorphous masses" into
history. His was perhaps the first, and certainly what appears
to be the least competent, effort in the tradition. Ortega
explicitly maintained that "Fascism . . . [is] the most pal-
pable manifestation of the new mentality of the masses, due
to their having decided to rule society without the capacity
for doing so . . . Fascism," he went on, is "a typical movement of mass-men." [3] Mass-men, according to his account,

----

[2] Robert Merton, "Introduction," to Le Bon, *The Crowd,* p. xxxiii.

[3] Jose Ortega y Gasset, *The Revolt of the Masses* (Norton, 1932),
pp. 10, 134.

are the "automatic" products of nineteenth-century liberalism and technology. They are the product of security and well-being—the consequence of a "self-satisfied age." [4] The "mass-man," for Ortega, is "the spoiled child of human history." [5] According to his account, the "mass-man" possesses an "in-born, root impression that life is easy, plentiful, without any grave limitations; consequently, each average man finds within himself a sensation of power and triumph which . . . invites him to stand up for himself as he is, to look upon his moral and intellectual endowment as excellent, complete." [6] As a consequence "mass-men" will be petulant and "incapable of submitting to direction of any kind . . . . They will wish to follow someone, and they will be unable. They will want to listen, and will discover they are deaf." [7] They are ignorant, volatile, incontinent, totalitarian, violent, devoid of morality and purpose. In other words, mass-men are barbarian and primitive. "We live at a time when man believes himself fabulously capable of creation, but does not know what to create. Lord of all things, he is not lord of himself. He feels lost amid his own abundance." [8] We are suffering a time afflicted by "nothing less than the political domination of the masses . . . . We are living, then, under the brutal empire of the masses"—a veritable "vertical invasion of the barbarians." [9] Fascism as a form of government exemplifies the traits of "mass-man." It is a form of government that is violent, irrational, ignorant, inconstant, and

----

[4] Ibid., pp. 107ff., 133.

[5] Ibid., p. 63.

[6] Ibid., p. 107.

[7] Ibid., p. 73.

[8] Ibid., p. 47.

[9] Ibid., pp. 17, 21, 57.

arbitrary as the masses are violent, irrational, ignorant, inconstant, and arbitrary.

The first thing that engages the reader's interest in such an account is the fact that it stands in manifest contradiction to the account that conceives Fascism to have been the product of a collective and pervasive sense of insecurity, powerlessness, and insignificance. Rather than a thirst for security, Fascism is, in this account, the product of an "inborn sense" of security and well-being. Rather than the product of an irrepressible sense of Oedipal guilt and a masochistic desire to be dominated, Fascism is the result of an ungovernable intemperance and a sense of dominance. Rather than the conservative product of a repressive family environment, Fascism is the nihilistic consequence of the family's failure to inculcate the values that hitherto informed social life. The "mass-man," in this account, rather than being obsessed by a reactive sense of duty and obligation, fails to possess "a sentiment of submission to something, a consciousness of service and obligation." [10] If Nathan, Reich, and Fromm conceive a collection of "authoritarian characters" produced by repression as the population base for Fascism—characters possessed of a need to be dominated—Ortega imagines Fascism to have been the consequence of a mass disposition to "absorb and annul the directing minorities and put themselves in their place . . . . In our time it is the mass-man who dominates, it is he who decides." [11]

Both interpretations, that of Nathan, et al., and that of Ortega, cannot be fully competent and both are probably, in large measure, in error. Ortega, for example, after insisting

---

[10] Ibid., p. 203.

[11] Ibid., pp. 21, 52.

that "mass-man" is "incapable of submitting to direction of any kind" and will "wish to follow someone," but be unable —tells us that "mass-man" has a "preference for living under an absolute authority . . . ." [12] With all his sense of power and intolerance, such a "spoiled" and "primitive" child, convinced of the truth of his every opinion, cannot live under a liberal regime of free discussion and "prefers" absolute authority. For a creature who wishes to listen, but cannot hear—for one who would follow,but cannot—"mass-man" listens, follows and submits to absolute authority.

The difficulty with all this is not that it all sounds hopelessly paradoxical. The personality traits of "mass-man" may, in fact, constitute a complex of contradictory elements. The difficulty, it would seem, lies in Ortega's evident readiness (shared with Le Bon) to make wholesale and unqualified ascriptions of personality traits to entire populations— the nationalities, classes, and categories of an entire continent—if not the entire globe. It would be difficult to imagine the kind of evidence to which Ortega might make recourse in attempting to warrant such ascriptions. Whatever evidence he does cite in the course of his discursive exposition is fragmentary, intuitionistic, and uncontrolled. Ortega seems to argue that the rapid expansion of population erodes small primary communities and releases "atomized" individuals. These individuals—shorn of a sense of community and confraternity—produce mobilizable masses. All of this seems plausible enough, but to insist upon making unrestricted ascriptions of complex psychological traits to entire populations as a consequence of such an analysis seems more the product of pique than research. The best Ortega can do is catalog those features of the Fascist regime of which he disapproved—its activism, its "irrationality," its "barbar-

---

[12] Ibid., p. 110.

ism" and cruelty—and insist that these are the reflection of character traits possessed by the vast multitudes of our times. Not only is such an account ad hoc and unsupported by independent evidence, but such an account makes Fascism "hyperdemocratic." Fascism is seen as the *direct* and *immediate* expression of the dispositions of the "masses." On such an account, Fascism would not govern the "masses," it would be their embodiment. As we shall suggest, there is far too much evidence available to make such an account anything but wildly implausible.

"The State of the Masses"

While such an interpretation was given a more substantial rendering in Emil Lederer's *The State of the Masses,* the central theses remained, nonetheless, remarkably similar. Lederer maintained that the effort to explain Fascism as "the last ditch . . . in which capitalism [had] entrenched itself to postpone the day of its doom," or "the rule of a single man by violence," or "the revolt of the middle classes against their decline," does "not explain its sociological nature." [13] What *does* explain Fascism's sociological nature is, according to Lederer, an analysis predicated on the conviction that Fascism is "a modern political system which rests on the amorphous masses." [14] The putative psychological traits of the masses not only explain the overt features of Fascism— these traits when institutionalized, maintain the dictator in power. Since mass psychology provides at least the necessary condition for Fascist rule, Fascism must destroy the complex

----

[13] Emil Lederer, *The State of the Masses: The Threat of the Classless Society* (Norton, 1940), p. 17.

[14] Ibid., p. 18.

of relatively autonomous groups that make up society, and institutionalize atomized crowds. Only with the destruction of society can men be reduced to the masses necessary for Fascist survival.

Lederer, like Le Bon, suggested that the masses constitute a "psychological entity *sui generis.*" [15] The mass mind, according to his account is something quite unique. Like Le Bon, Lederer insisted that the "mass mind" is unsystematic, irrational, emotional; it "does not think or reason at all." It is the product of "individuals who cease to be isolated, who cease thinking." [16]

A *group* Lederer argued (in an argument anticipated by Le Bon) as distinct from a *mass,* is composed of individuals *united by some common purpose,* a reasonably specific and reasonably concrete goal. As a consequence the thinking of a group is, in substantial part, rational and corrigible, governed by evidence and contingencies. The mass, on the other hand, is amorphous. Its goals are diffused and remote, and its behavior governed by emotions. It only succeeds to unity under the influence of leaders who energize emotions. Mass action is more simple emotional response than it is rational. The mass lives in an artificial atmosphere of emphatic emotional tension. The leaders who mobilize masses, and who are sustained by them, are the heirs of circumstances that follow the disaggregation of society. Such leaders exploit "atomization"—the dissolution of group and class association, and the social stratification that make up the substance of society. As a consequence such leaders, and the movements they lead, must set themselves steadfastly against group life. They must bend every effort to reduce group living to an agglomeration of atomic individuals. A

---

[15] Ibid., p. 223.

[16] Ibid., pp. 219, 32.

mass movement arises out of the disaggregated collective life of the past and then becomes possessed of the dynamics of mass psychology. Fascism was "a mass movement to which the leaders had to conform once it was well under way." [17] As a consequence the masses "have become a new, permanent and decisive force, molding the social and mental nature of society . . . ." [18]

On occasion it sounds as though Lederer were suggesting that Fascism was a captive of the "mass-mind"—as though Mussolini and the Fascist hierarchy had to "conform" to the will of the masses and we would have, once again, a characterization of Fascism as a "hyperdemocracy" in which the irrational will of a curious modern collectivity, the "amorphous masses," found direct expression. Fascism requires, in this analysis, an "irrational permanent connection between the leader and the crowd that is indispensable . . . . If the party represents only a social group, or concentrates on a program, the masses will disappear . . . ." [19] Fascism was the consequence of the disintegration of group life and, once in power, Fascism represented no other social force but that of the masses. All institutional life was "melted down" to a crowd existence. Neither the intellectuals, the capitalists, the organized working class, the bureaucracy, the monarchy, nor the army could effectively resist. The political system that resulted was neither "socialist nor capitalist"—it was a "mass state." Workers, capitalists, bureaucrats, intellectuals, and the military were all captives of a state that was the product of a mass-

---

[17] Ibid., p. 85.

[18] Ibid., p. 97.

[19] Ibid., pp. 234, 233.

mind to which they had all directly and indirectly contributed.

The entire process is understood to have been the product of a number of intersecting social and economic forces. Industrialization had produced multitudes of displaced workers, detached from their primary communities and ensconced in urban centers. They were uncertain and isolated, threatened by economic forces over which they had no control.

Alongside them the "new middle classes," the white collar employees and civil servants, made their appearance. They were not firmly rooted in the economic system, they possessed no real property, and with every economic dislocation they felt themselves threatened by a loss of income and status. They had few well developed defensive institutions. Industrial unions were ill suited to serve as their peculiar defense agencies. Furthermore, the "new middle classes" resisted identification with the industrial proletariat. They sought a secure place, ideally in an expanding productive system, for only such a system promised status and upward mobility.

Such population elements, both proletarian and middle class, subjected to a "power and authority deflation" that resulted from the catastrophe of World War I, and the urgent economic problems that followed, produced the masses that were to be the support base of Fascism. Unemployment made the life circumstances of the newly urbanized workers precarious. Pervasive inflation destroyed the job and savings securities of the new middle classes. All this coupled with a pervasive fear of "Bolshevism," reduced men to an amorphous mass.

Such an account is given in terms of a statement of necessary and contingent factors that taken together produced

Fascism in Italy as a mass movement. Masses of men, stripped of their identification with specific economic groups and productive categories, shorn of their commitments to established loyalties, displaced by their involvement in urban industrial complexes, provided the masses upon which Fascism arose.[20] Such a discursive account is, at one and the same time, both plausible and vexatiously general. Little empirical evidence is advanced to support the very general (if plausible) claims. Such evidence could probably be collected. Some of the best confirmed sociological and political science generalizations are those that indicate that men behave in manifestly different ways when they are detached from established social roles. Young people have, for example and in general, not assumed social roles, the patterned expectations that structure social relations. As a consequence they will, under appropriate situational stimuli, behave in "deviant" fashion. They will riot and disport themselves in singular fashion. They display "mass-like" properties. Newly urbanized individuals, similarly, detached from their hitherto established social patterns, make up, in large part, the membership of religious cults and bizarre political groups. War, furthermore, always seems to accelerate such "displacements." The young are mobilized, separated from family and community roles. Workers are drawn into metropolitan areas. The new middle class expands and individuals find themselves thrust into new and demanding social circumstances. Statistics identifying an increase in the number of the young, as well as population displacements, could probably be obtained by systematic study of funded archival materials. The real problem with such an account is not its lack of confirming empirical evidence, it lies in the interpretation imposed on the material.

----

[20] Ibid., p. 65.

To suggest that the circumstances that preceded, characterized and followed World War I, produced mobilizable masses—and that the psychology peculiar to masses influenced the organizational and mobilizational strategy of Fascism—is not to say that the masses either "produced" or "dominated" Fascism. To say that the mass leader constitutes a "sudden crystallization around which" the movement develops[21] is not to say that the mass leader must "conform" to, or be "dominated" by, those masses. Lederer is careful, for example, to indicate that "if the government has a monopoly of propaganda, it can lead the masses." [22]

Sigmund Neumann provides an interpretation of Fascism that reiterates the central theses of Ortega and Lederer. The "revolt of the masses" is conceived to be the "core" of Fascism.[23] He also admits, however, that the "concept of the masses is . . . devoid of precise scientific content . . . ." [24] The best Neumann does is to allude to the displacement of newly urbanized workers and the new middle classes. He addresses himself to the "loneliness," the "insecurity" and the lack of identity that seems to characterize such masses. He talks of the "rootless radicalism" and the "explosive nihilism" that characterizes them. He identifies the youthfulness of such masses. He provides an empirical account of the age differentials that characterize the mass-mobilizing Fascist movement as distinct from the orthodox political parties. He identifies the presence of disillusioned workers and the members of the threatened middle classes

---

[21] Ibid., p. 231.

[22] Ibid., p. 239.

[23] Sigmund Neumann, *Permanent Revolution: The Total State in a World at War* (Harper & Row, 1965), p. 97.

[24] Ibid., p. 102.

within the ranks of the Fascist cohorts. But he also indicates that the mass leader and his party dominate, "control," and "educate" the masses.[25]

In effect, what such accounts reduce themselves to is a collection of plausible assertions that suggest that a mass movement requires the availability of mobilizable population elements. These elements arise from the dislocations that have become so common in the twentieth century. The available masses are disillusioned, threatened, irrational, and aggressive. A movement that addresses itself to their sentiments has great recruitment potential. But because the masses respond viscerally to diffuse rather than specific problems, the mass-mobilizing movement can manipulate them with choreographic and histrionic strategies that are significantly different from those employed by "orthodox" political parties. In effect, Ortega is wrong. Masses are mobilizable not because they are secure, possessed of an inborn sense of well-being and confidence, but rather because they are insecure, faced with status and unemployment threats of impressive magnitude; they are not confident and sublimely self-sufficient; they are powerless and lonely. Moreover, the masses neither stand astride our times like a colossus, nor do they dominate politics. Rather, they are the materials with which the mass leader must work. They are the raw materials he, and his party, mold. They constitute the "elemental" energies he harnesses for his own, and his party's, political purposes. All institutions, all categories and classes, all partial and episodic goals, profits, wages, the entire economic system, are marshalled to the totalitarian party's purposes.

The evident plausibility of such a construal generated a spate of efforts that sought to continue the analysis. Both

---

[25] Ibid., p. 126.

during and after World War II analysts returned again and again to the same themes. In 1942 Talcott Parsons delivered himself of a brief account that conveniently summarized the efforts made until that time.

Parsons alluded to the "situations involving a certain type of social disorganization" productive of "anomie"— which in turn "produces" large numbers of people "imbued with a highly emotional, indeed often fanatical zeal for a cause." [26] The "anomic" behavior of which he spoke has all the same aggressive, emotional, self-effacing diffuseness to which Le Bon, Ortega and Lederer referred. The "generalized insecurity" that results from the "change in the social situation which upsets previous established definitions of the situation, or routines of life, or symbolic associations," Parsons suggested, produces "high levels" of "free-floating anxiety and aggression." [27] Parsons admitted, significantly, that such an "analysis" was "in no sense complete." He suggested that the account he offered might be selectively used to "orientate" ourselves "to some of the larger aspects" of generic fascism.[28] Parsons was circumspect about the explanatory pretensions of such accounts. At best they provide broad and imprecise conceptual categories that perhaps assist us in identifying some of the necessary conditions for the advent of fascism.

----

[26] Talcott Parsons, "Some Sociological Aspects of the Fascist Movements," *Essays in Sociological Theory* (Rev. ed. Free Press, 1949), p. 125.

[27] Ibid., p. 126

[28] Ibid., p. 141.

Post World War II Theories and Theorists

Eric Hoffer

No more could be said of the discursive and literary accounts that followed the termination of World War II. One of the more popular accounts in this tradition is that provided in Eric Hoffer's *The True Believer*. Although Hoffer's account initially strikes the reader as being outside this tradition, the most elementary analysis reveals its critical similarities.

Hoffer seems to argue that the men who commit themselves to mass movements are those who suffer "flawed lives" —and one receives the immediate impression that his account shares kinship with those who interpret Fascism as the consequence of individual psychological impairments. The impression is rapidly dispelled when it becomes evident that the "true believers" who invest mass movements, those whose lives are "irremediably spoiled," are, at least in substantial part, the products of the "crumbling or weakening of tribal solidarity and communal life." The true believer is an individual who has lost the "sheltering and soothing anonymity of a communal existence." [29] "The milieu most favorable for the rise and propagation of mass movements," Hoffer tells us, "is one in which a once compact corporate structure is, for one reason or another, in a state of disintegration." "The general rule seems to be that as one pattern of corporate cohesion weakens, conditions become ripe for

----

[29] Eric Hoffer, *The True Believer: Thoughts on the Nature of Mass Movements* (Harper & Row, 1951), p. 37.

the rise of a mass movement and the eventual establishment of a new and more rigorous form of compact unity." [30]

While Hoffer speaks of the "disaffected" as the recruitment base of mass-mobilizing movements—the poor, the misfits, the outcasts, the minorities, the adolescent youth, the ambitious, those in the grip of some vice or obsession, the impotent (in body or mind), the inordinately selfish, the bored, and the sinners—it seems fairly obvious that such types become particularly abundant or important for some reason. The obvious implication is that some one or another, or some special combination of social circumstances, either produce such types or render them significant political or social forces. Hoffer seems to grant as much. He does indicate that some conditions or other must obtain that "make the rise of a movement possible." Mass movements cannot be "conjured up out of a void." [31] The only condition that Hoffer seems to identify as conducive to the production of large numbers of men that lead "flawed lives" is a "disaster" that shakes a country "to its foundation." Such a catastrophe makes "autonomous individual lives untenable and meaningless" [32] and renders "frustrated men" susceptible to mobilization.

This, conjoined with the "general rule" that when one corporate structure is in a "state of disintegration" another rises to discharge its psychologically gratifying function, suggests that Hoffer's interpretation of Fascism goes no farther than that of Lederer, which interpreted Fascism to be the consequence of the "breakdown" of social institutions

----

[30] Ibid., p. 41.

[31] Ibid., p. 109.

[32] Ibid., p. 110.

and the release of "amorphous masses" into the political arena. Such "amorphous" masses display all the properties that Hoffer attributes to his botched and bungled, "frustrated" and "disaffected." Le Bon's "crowd" and Lederer's "masses" are Hoffer's "misfits." Hoffer's analysis is not one whit more sophisticated than that of Le Bon, published over seven decades ago. It suffers all the same disabilities of over-generalization and lack of specificity. The conditions necessary or sufficient for the advent of mass-mobilizing movements are never characterized with any precision. We are only informed that mass movements arise when institutions are "disintegrating." How one might measure "disintegration" is never specified. Moreover, even if one could measure "disintegration," there is no suggestion as to how much "disintegration" is necessary to insure the success of mass mobilization. The best we are offered is a recitation of some of the circumstances that might lead to "disintegration": "chronic incompetence," "stagnation," [33] and/or "severe depression or defeat in war." [34]

Hoffer's account, then, reduces itself to a typology of personality and emotional character traits that pretends to identify the "true believer" who fills out the ranks of a mass movement—a mass movement of whatever sort. "True believers" have apparently been available in all societies at least since the commencement of recorded history, although they are more emphatically in evidence among certain "marginal" groups (the new poor, the new middle classes, the sinners, the minorities, the "noncreative" intellectuals, the adolescent young, and so forth)—those that are "atomized" and "anomic." What acts as a real and final catalyst in the

----

[33] Ibid., pp. 163ff.

[34] Ibid., p. 120.

production of a mass movement like Mussolini's Fascism is some collection of social, economic, and political circumstances to which Hoffer vaguely alludes as the "disintegration" of "communal" life.

One has a precarious foothold on an explanation in so far as one can find representatives of these susceptible population groups among the leaders and followers of the Italian Fascist movement. At best the account telescopes into a vaguely formulated statement of some of the perhaps necessary conditions for the success of mass-mobilizing movements. But since the "frustrated" who made up the ranks of the Fascist movement might have just as easily joined the Communists according to Hoffer,[35] one is at a loss to explain the *specific* historic success of Mussolini's efforts.

Hoffer, like Parsons, is admirably candid. His account was not advanced as "explanatory." He offers what he calls "suggestive insights" into a complex phenomenon. Hoffer insisted that his work was not to be conceived as an "authoritative textbook." It was offered rather, as a "book of thoughts" that did not "shy away from half-truths so long as they seem to hint at a new approach and help to formulate new questions." [36]

Unhappily, neither Hoffer's book nor the descriptive, classificatory, and heuristic efforts that became available after World War II were new, nor did they help to formulate new questions. In almost all cases such accounts came directly out of the antecedent tradition, as old at least as Le Bon, that conceived revolutions to have been the product of the "entrance of the masses onto the historical stage." There was some new suggestive "fill," but little of

---

[35] Ibid., p. 17.

[36] Ibid., pp. xiii, 59.

this material significantly enhanced our ability to explain the entire complex sequence of events we associate with Fascism.

Hannah Arendt

Hannah Arendt's *The Origins of Totalitarianism* contains an entire catalog of putative intellectual factors that "shaped" modern totalitarian mass movements, but a central thesis of her account turns on her explanation of the availability of mobilizable masses. Mass movements, according to her literary treatment, are characterized (as they are for Le Bon, Lederer, and Hoffer) by the lack of self-interest of the masses (a feature to which Parsons alludes as well). She attributes this lack of self-interest (as do Le Bon, Lederer, Parsons, and Hoffer) to the unavailability of "stable social bodies" that might provide "transmission belts" between the individual, the group, and their common proximate interests.[37] "The revolt of the masses . . . ," she informs us, "was the result of their atomization, of their loss of social status along with which they lost the whole sector of communal relationships in whose framework common sense makes sense." [38] The masses are in a state of "spiritual and social homelessness . . . ." They constitute "unintegrated and disintegrating masses." They are "uprooted." [39] "Atomized masses" are composed of "undefinable, unstable and futile individuals" seeking "definition and identification." [40]

----

[37] Hannah Arendt, *The Origins of Totalitarianism* (Harcourt, Brace, 1951), p. 338.

[38] Ibid., p. 342.

[39] Ibid., p. 343.

[40] Ibid., p. 346.

A considerable part of Arendt's effort is devoted to a discursive and general account of the rise of "atomized masses" on the European scene. She begins her discussion by referring to an aggregate that is to play a central role in her story—"the mob"—"the *déclassés* of all classes." [41] "The mob," Arendt maintained (echoing Le Bon), "is primarily a group in which the residue of all classes are represented." [42] Arendt, like Ortega, conceives the "masses" to have been the product of "nineteenth century economy." [43] That economy, according to Arendt's account, was characterized by unbridled competition and ultimately by a system in which "swindle was the only law." The state was fragmented into political factions each seeking to use the machinery of government to enhance its financial manipulations. Wholesale corruption characterized the economy of the disintegrating European nation states. In France, again according to Arendt's rendering, "high society and politicians of the Third Republic had produced the French mob in a series of scandals and public frauds." Because they had fathered the mob, the social elites "felt a tender sentiment of parental familiarity with their offspring, a feeling mixed with admiration and fear . . . . The upper classes knew that the mob was flesh of their flesh and blood of their blood." [44]

The elite, in all European society, according to her account, was moved to satisfy an insatiable desire to accumulate wealth and property. All this had its "origin in the realm of business speculation, where expansion meant the permanent broadening of industrial production and economic

---

[41] Ibid., p. 10.

[42] Ibid., p. 107.

[43] Ibid., p. 94.

[44] Ibid., p. 107.

transactions characteristic of the nineteenth century." The capitalist system was characterized by an "inherent law [of] constant economic growth." [45] Imperialism was its natural outcome. Imperialism was the result of the bourgeois disposition to conceive politics as the handmaiden of infinite economic expansion. Surpluses of capital and of commodities required that the bourgeoisie involve the state in its enterprises. In order to provide both investment and market supplements to the capitalist enterprise the bourgeoisie captured the machinery of the state. Power became the "only content of politics, and . . . expansion . . . its only aim . . . ." Such a construal of national politics "perfectly answered the hidden desires and secret convictions of the economically and socially dominant classes." [46]

Bourgeois society, with its infinite need to expand, was afflicted with recurrent crises that drove large numbers of men out of productive involvement to become "permanently idle." Some of these superfluous men were "exported" as colonists. Where such outlets did not obtain—in Central and Eastern Europe particularly—this human debris formed itself into the "mob" that sought to subvert national institutions and national parties.[47] Such a "mob" was "composed . . . of the refuse of all classes." They were the "by-product of bourgeois society . . . ." And, as we have seen, because such human refuse was its product, "high society" harbored a "growing admiration" for this underworld. Europe's "retreat from morality" was a consequence of this misalliance between the "elite" and the "mob."

The more insecure the bourgeoisie became, the more it

----

[45] Ibid., pp. 125, 126.

[46] Ibid., p. 138.

[47] Ibid., p. 153.

shed whatever moral scruples remained. It more and more directly allied itself with the mob it had itself produced. The alliance between the bourgeoisie and the mob, predicated on the now debased principles of unbridled competition, infinite expansion, and the infinite accumulation of political power, gave rise to a collective rage for conquest, political and economic domination, racism, and ultimately the extermination of the unfit and all those conceived to be irremediably inferior. All of this brutality was supported by political legends and social myths, which provided the rationale for colonialism, imperialism, and oppression.[48] In Central and Eastern Europe where colonialism and imperialism were foreclosed by a variety of circumstances, the legends and the myths became more perverse. Pan-Slavism and pan-Germanism arose as the thwarted analogues of British imperialism.

Men "in the midst of communal disintegration and social atomization wanted to belong at any price." In their passion to belong to competitive and infinitely expanding communities, they created for themselves a fantasy community in the form of "tribal nationalism." The mob dreamed of total domination based on "tribal" loyalties—the historical and dispositional foundation for the "world conquest programs of Nazism and Bolshevism." [49] "Tribal nationalism grew out of [the] atmosphere of rootlessness . . . . Rootlessness was the true source of that 'enlarged tribal consciousness' which actually meant that members of these peoples had no definite home but felt at home wherever other members of their 'tribe' happened to live." [50] Rootless, isolated, and atomized, the mob attempted to "assuage the

----

[48] Ibid., pp. 207–211.

[49] Ibid., pp. 225, 226.

[50] Ibid., p. 232.

rightful apprehension of modern man as to what might happen to them if, as isolated individuals in an atomized society, they were not protected by sheer numbers and enforced uniform coherence." [51] Tribal nationalism is "well suited to the needs of the shifting masses of modern cities and was therefore grasped at once by totalitarianism . . . ." [52] The "uprooted masses of the big cities," enflamed by tribal nationalism and its implicit racism, constituted the recruitment base of mass mobilizing, totalitarian movements.[53] Conjoined with all this, and in large part its cause, was the dissolution of the "class basis" of political life. The "mob" more and more insistently became "masses," the spin-off of the disintegration of classes. In a variety of European countries class was undermined by migrations and heterogeneity of populations, as well as inflation and unemployment—all of which engendered fear and insecurity. Party politics gave way to "movement" politics and mass-mobilizing movements began to more and more threaten what had hitherto been orthodox party politics.[54] Mass-mobilizing movements made fewer and fewer appeals to economically defined classes and turned their attention to the "mob." In the "general fear" all "class divisions disappeared." [55] Mass movements arose to "command and rest upon mass support." [56] Out of the enormous population growth that characterized the history of Europe over the last century and a half, out of mass unemployment, there arose "the mass-man's typical feeling of superfluous-

----

[51] Ibid., p. 235.

[52] Ibid., p. 236.

[53] Ibid., p. 240.

[54] Ibid., pp. 260ff.

[55] Ibid., p. 264.

[56] Ibid., p. 301.

ness," which lent itself to the characteristic and total "unselfishness" of the adherent of mass movements.[57]

> Totalitarian movements are possible wherever there are masses who for one reason or another have acquired the appetite for political organization. Masses are not held together by a consciousness of common interest and they lack that specific class articulateness which is expressed in determined, limited and obtainable goals. The term masses applies only where we deal with people who either because of sheer numbers, or indifference, or a combination of both, cannot be integrated into any organization based on common interest, into political parties or municipal governments or professional organizations or trade unions.[58]

Moreover, according to Arendt, "it will make little difference whether totalitarian movements adopt the pattern of Nazism or Bolshevism, organize the masses in the name of race or class, pretend to follow the laws of life and nature or of dialectics and economics." [59] This is true because the masses share with the mob the fact that they both stand

> outside of all social ramifications and normal political representations . . . . In other words, membership in a class, its limited group obligations and traditional attitudes toward government, prevented the growth of a citizenry that felt individually and personally responsible for the rule of the country. This apolitical character of the nation-states' populations came to light only when the class system broke down and carried with it the whole fabric of visible and invisible threats which bound the people to the body poli-

---

[57] Ibid., pp. 303–305.

[58] Ibid., p. 305.

[59] Ibid., p. 306.

tic . . . . The fall of protecting class walls transformed
the slumbering majorities behind all parties into one great
unorganized, structureless mass of furious individuals who
had nothing in common except their vague apprehension
that the hopes of party members were doomed, that, consequently, the most respected, articulate and representative
members of the community were fools that all the powers
that be were not so much evil as they were equally stupid
and fraudulent . . . . In this atmosphere of the breakdown of class society the psychology of the European mass
man developed.[60]

The monotonous uniformity of their fate produced among
the masses a "self-centered bitterness" that could not resolve
itself in any common interest, economic, social, or political.
The mass-man developed a sense "that oneself does not matter." He developed the "feeling of being dispensable." Mass
men lost any interest in their own well-being. "Compared
with their nonmaterialism, a Christian monk looks like a
man absorbed in worldly affairs." [61] "The truth is that the
masses grew out of the fragments of a highly atomized society whose competitive structure and concomitant loneliness
of the individual had been held in check only through membership in a class. The chief characteristic of the mass-man
is not brutality and backwardness, but his isolation and lack
of normal social relationships." [62]

  There are several things that are interesting about such
an account. Other than the fact that it provides a great deal
of literary and speculative fill, it is substantially an explanation of "totalitarian" mass-mobilizing movements in terms of
an account that conceives them to be "mass organizations of

[60] Ibid., pp. 308ff.

[61] Ibid., p. 309.

[62] Ibid., p. 310.

atomized, isolated individuals," [63] the consequence of the diffusion of "bourgeois" ideas of unlimited expansion and domination and the disintegration of institutionalized classes. The "elites" that mobilize masses are the defectors from "a decaying class society," who mobilize the "wreckage of classes" in the service of a mass movement.[64] The critical variable in the account is the "breakdown of classes and their transformation into masses." [65] The masses, shorn of the "multiplicity of interchangeable roles and functions which society had imposed," fully conscious of the hypocrisy of "bourgeois morality," led by a cynical and alienated intellectual elite, create mass movements with totalitarian aspirations. For Arendt, just as for Lederer, Parsons, and Hoffer, such movements reflect the diffuseness of mass interests, the total lack of self-interest and rationality that characterizes them. Such movements treat "programs and platforms as needless scraps of paper and embarrassing promises, inconsistent with the style and impetus of a movement . . . ." [66] For Arendt all this was true because the bourgeoisie "confounded all moral issues by parading publicly virtues which it not only did not possess in private and business life, but actually held in contempt, it seemed revolutionary to admit cruelty, disregard of human values and general amorality, because this at least destroyed the duplicity upon which the existing society seemed to rest." [67]

In the last analysis, Arendt's account represents a conjunction of the "influence of ideas" thesis and the conviction

----

[63] Ibid., p. 316.

[64] Ibid., p. 319.

[65] Ibid., p. 321.

[66] Ibid., p. 318.

[67] Ibid., p. 327.

that some special sets of ideas penetrate because the "structure" of society, for a variety of reasons, is "disintegrating" or "decaying." Without empirical research of any sort—other than a careful reading of history and some "representative" literature—she is prepared to identify *all* the bourgeois with a relatively specific collection of moral, personality, and behavioral traits. Having discovered that, she is further prepared to identify the collective traits of the "mob," the *"déclassés* of all classes," as a caricature of those uniform but "hidden" and "secret" bourgeois traits. The "masses," in turn, take on some of the properties of the "mob" because they are bereft of stable social relations that "define" them. The mass becomes "fanaticized" to the point where "neither experience nor argument can reach [them]"[68]; they are devoid of "individual identity," [69] and disposed toward "the radical destruction of every existing creed, value, and institution"[70]; they "do not believe in anything visible, in the reality of their own experience; they do not trust their eyes and ears but only their imaginations"[71]; they "believe everything and nothing, think that everything [is] possible and that nothing [is] true." [72] All this because they are the refuse of a "society wholly permeated with the ideological outlook and moral standards of the bourgeoisie." [73] All this "explains" why the "masses" give themselves over to totalitarian movements, whether fascist or "Marxist," whose intentions are totally destructive and irrepressibly inhuman.

----

[68] Ibid., p. 302.

[69] Ibid., p. 307.

[70] Ibid., p. 329.

[71] Ibid., p. 341.

[72] Ibid., p. 369.

[73] Ibid., pp. 320ff.

Arendt seems to be at least vaguely aware of how implausible her special version of this account is. She indicates that her interpretation labors under the "seemingly absurd disparities between cause and effect which have become the hallmark of modern history." [74] She suggests that her account may not, in fact, be accepted because historians might well try to "dismiss the disturbing fact that so many of the important events in modern history look as though molehills had labored and had brought forth mountains." [75] Arendt insists that one section of the bourgeoisie—that *part* of the bourgeoisie involved in rapidly expanding and "imperialistic" productive enterprises—could transmit its "personality traits" to the *entire* bourgeois class—those involved in local shopkeeping and commerce, extractive industries, domestic industries, and agriculture—and from them to the "mob." This psychological contagion somehow and ultimately effected massive alternations in the psyche of the "masses." All of which sounds very much like molehills had indeed brought forth mountains.

Whatever one conceives the "bourgeoisie" to be (and the general defining property has been held to be the "ownership of the means of production"), it is hardly plausible to argue that *all* the constituent members of such a broad class were characterized by the *same* moral and personality traits. Surely profit-making characterizes modern capitalists, just as it did the farmers in slave-holding societies, but it is hard to imagine that profit-making could lay the foundations for a maniacal desire for unlimited power and possession "only through destruction." To suggest that a system based on the possession of property leads to a desire to secure that prop-

---

[74] Ibid., p. 131.

[75] Ibid., p. 132.

erty makes some common sense. To suggest, however, that "property by itself . . . is subject to use and consumption and therefore diminishes constantly," and that "the most radical and the only secure form of possession is destruction, for only what we have destroyed is safely and forever ours," [76] sounds like simple nonsense—an effort to force the camel of the "profit motive" through the eye of totalitarian inhumanity and nihilism.

To say that men who are "rootless," "homeless," and "lonely" will be "frustrated" and "insecure," makes common sense. To insist that such men must be completely devoid of self-interest, unthinking, amoral, and violent would require a great deal of supplementary evidence to make a plausible case. What is most surprising about Arendt's account is her total neglect of any empirical evidence that might support her unqualified and universal generalizations. She has taken us no further than did Le Bon who told us, almost three-quarters of a century ago, that "crowds" are subject to "infinite credulity and exaggerated sensibility, . . . short-sightedness, and their incapacity to respond to the influences of reason . . . . Reality and experience have no effect upon them. The multitude will admit anything; nothing is impossible in the eyes of the crowd." [77] "A people," Le Bon reminded his readers in 1913, "differs from a crowd in that it is composed of a collection of groups, each having different interests and passions" [78]—and when the "social bonds that formerly contained the multitude were day by day dissolving . . . it conceived a notion of unlimited

----

[76] Ibid., p. 145.

[77] Gustave Le Bon, *The Psychology of Revolution* (Putnam, 1913), pp. 102ff.

[78] Ibid., p. 106.

power . . . ." [79] Le Bon insisted that the "people" never make revolutions, "crowds" do. It is not the "peasants, traders, and workers" who make revolution; revolutions are made by "subversive social residue" composed of the poor, the thieves, the beggars—the marginal (and to use the contemporary expression) "atomized" classless debris.[80]

William Kornhauser

Far more compelling than the accounts left to us by Lederer, Parsons, Hoffer, or Arendt are the more empirically oriented formulations provided by William Kornhauser. His *Politics of Mass Society* moves a considerable distance beyond the generalizations to be found in Le Bon, Lederer, Parsons, or Hoffer. While the main thrust of his argument is in the tradition that Fascism is the product of mass society, he attempts a more adequate characterization of the conditions governing the effective transformation of a "mass society" into a "totalitarian" one.

Like the theorists convinced that Fascism is a phenomenon of "atomized masses," Kornhauser maintains that Fascism is "fundamentally" a *mass,* rather than a *class* movement.[81] The critical issues in his analysis turn on the differences between a *mass,* as distinct from a *totalitarian,* society. The argument commences with the now familiar analysis. A society composed of masses is one in which large numbers of individuals are no longer insulated in "autonomous

---

[79] Ibid., p. 65.

[80] Ibid., p. 80.

[81] William Kornhauser, *The Politics of Mass Society* (Free Press, 1959), p. 14.

groups" and thus become "available" for "mass mobilization." In such an atomized society the threat of *mass movements* is emphatic. If such a society is threatened by protracted and insistent crises, and dominant elites lose their
exclusiveness and become "accessible," the threat of the development of "mass movements" becomes insistent. "Old,"
or "established" elites, confined by traditional interests or
values may not be in a position to resist the pressures of
masses because of their "vulnerability." Traditional elites
may not be capable of instituting the changes required by
changed socioeconomic or political crises. "New" or contending elites may make their appearance. They may be prepared, by virtue of their alienation from the old order, and
because of the availability of masses for mobilization, to undertake vast social, economic, and political change. In order
to effect such changes both the masses and the contending
elite must have broken out of established routines. "Activism entails a readiness to reject routine modes of activity,
and therefore tends to be eschewed by groups whose very
power is bound to established routines." [82]

As distinct from traditional elites, revolutionary elites
tend to insulate themselves from the "masses." The mass-
mobilizing elites use the masses as an *instrument* for revolution. Revolution requires effective centralized control over
vast human resources. As distinct from mass society, which
is characterized by the availability of masses and the accessibility of elites, an effective mass movement is characterized
by available masses but low accessibility and low vulnerability of elites. What may grow out of the totalitarian *mass
movement* (under suitable conditions) is a *totalitarian society*.

----

[82] Ibid., p. 35.

The masses that provide the recruitment base of mass movements arise out of the dissolution of autonomous group life. If individuals maintain strong ties with their family, business, hobbies, township or ward, class, church, trade union, or "any other social group of which he is an active member," their proximate interests are goal directed and relatively specific. Complex problems are perceived through "several intervening layers of social relations." [83] Once devoid of such relations individuals focus on obscure and remote goals. They are disposed to attempt to solve complex social issues through direct intervention and when they meet resistance, tend to employ violence and coercion. Out of such materials a "totalitarian cadre" creates a mass movement that becomes the instrument for fashioning a totalitarian society. "A totalitarian movement attracts socially isolated members of *all* classes. Furthermore, whenever totalitarian groups gain power, they seek to smash all class organizations and to suppress all class interests." [84]

The general conditions favoring the appearance of mass movements are those broadly characterized as "atomization," the disintegration of stable and autonomous group associations devoted to the attainment of proximate ends. Where atomization has taken place, there are available masses. Such masses, in times of relative stability will generally appear apathetic and passive. In "times of crisis," however, such apathy may be displaced by aggressive and frenetic activity.[85] People who lack "proximate relations" are most likely to engage in mass behavior—a disposition shared both by masses and potential elites. Disaffected intel-

---

[83] Ibid., pp. 43f.

[84] Ibid., p. 49.

[85] Ibid., p. 61.

lectuals provide the reservoir of talent for the creation of a "contending elite." It is clear in Kornhauser's version of this interpretation that the contending elite uses the masses for its revolutionary purpose.

Kornhauser carefully marshalls a considerable amount of empirical evidence to show that "non-joiners," those individuals who display a low incidence of institutional or group attachments, are not only generally more ignorant concerning social issues, they are more extreme in their views and more authoritarian in their dispositions.[86] ". . . Within all strata, people divorced from community, occupation, and association are first and foremost among the supporters of extremism. The decisive social process in mass society is the *atomization* of social relations; even though this process is accentuated in the lower strata, it operates throughout the society." [87] The structure of mass society is one in which there is a marked fragility with respect to intermediate relations, an isolation of primary or familial relations, and a direct relationship between the isolated individual and/or his family and the larger national community. As a consequence there is the opportunity, exploited by the contending elites, to relate the individual directly to the broad community: the nation. The elite can politicize and nationalize all interests. Their programs emphasize broad and vague social goals and their methods tend to be extreme, activist, and authoritarian.

The lack of intermediary structures strips the individual of any protection from the political mass movement. Everyone is made "political," and all interests are "integrated" in a broad and ill-defined revolutionary program.

----

[86] Ibid., pp. 61–73.

[87] Ibid., p. 73.

Integral and consensual commitments characterize the mass movement during its insurrectionary and finally in its institutionalization phase. The end product is a totalitarian society with institutionalized masses as its power base. Because of their totalistic and consensual character, mass-mobilizing movements with totalitarian aspirations take on a populist character.

Kornhauser not only provides empirical supports for his propositions, he also critically assesses the conditions governing atomization. He indicates, for example, that urbanization, in and of itself, is not sufficient to produce mass behavior. It is rather a question of how urbanization takes place.

> In general, the proportion of a population supporting [an] extremist movement like . . . Fascism does not increase with the proportion living in cities . . . . What appears to be more important as a source of mass tendencies than the *degree* of urbanization is the *process* of urbanization, especially rapid rates of change in the size and composition of the population residing in an area . . . . The rapid influx of large numbers of people into newly developing urban areas invites mass movements.[88]

Similarly, it is not the *degree* of industrialization that produces mobilizable masses, but the *process* that attends it. If industrialization produces sharp discontinuities in social organization, mass behavior is more likely to result than if industrial growth is even and/or gradual and is attended by the proliferation of intermediary organizations that are autonomous and whose goals are proximate.[89]

---

[88] Ibid., pp. 144ff.

[89] Ibid., pp. 150–158.

Finally Kornhauser attempts to unpack the omnibus notion of "times of crises" that catalyze masses. He identifies some of the general circumstances subsumed under the rubric "crisis." Among them he specifically mentions "depression" and "national defeat." Both tend to weaken social structures and release individuals for mass mobilization— both undermine authority, thus making established elites vulnerable and providing contending elites the opportunity of building an organization with a potential for success.

While rapid economic depression stimulates mass behaviors, a stable and steady state of poverty does not. The rank order correlation between per capita income and the existence of extremist movements is negative. In general, where per capita income is low there are fewer extremist movements. On the other hand where unstable and unsteady income characterize populations, particularly in severe economic depressions, one finds emphatic extremist response. Where economic crisis is less severe populations tend to be attracted by reformist and mildly socialist politics (the Labor government in Great Britain and the New Deal in the United States during the Great Depression). Where and when such depressions are most severe (in terms of the percentage of the total labor force unemployed and/or in terms of idle productive capacity and a declining standard of living) populations tends to commit themselves to extreme solutions. In Germany and Italy during the postwar depressions that followed World War I the Socialist, Communist, National Socialist, and Fascist parties increased their memberships in such measure as to make them serious contenders for power.

Severe military defeat, in its turn, can cause a "power deflation" and a loss of authority. Institutions that are implicated in the defeat lose all credibility and individuals shorn of their identification with such shattered institutions become available for mass mobilization. Prolonged unemployment and national defeat, both individually and collectively, cause a loss of status, a sense of alienation, a disassociation of group ties, mounting frustration and a search for a ready and immediate solution to complex social and economic issues. Mass movements with totalitarian aspirations offer continuous and aggressive activity to disaffected individuals—an activity that we know (on the basis of suggestive empirical evidence) reduces anxiety, helplessness, and frustration.

Comparing Theory and Fact—Mass Movements and Italian Fascism

The explanation of Fascism that grows out of Kornhauser's account is perhaps the best of those that could be characterized as based on the "theory of mass society." The general outline he has provided can be mapped over the Fascist sequence as we now understand it. Italy, during the years preceding World War I *was* undergoing irregular and stressful industrial development. Large numbers of rural inhabitants *were* being displaced, drawn out of their traditional loyalties, and thrust into rapidly expanding urban areas. Employment *was* insecure and precarious. The war accelerated the process and compounded the social discontinuities by taking young men out of their established communities and placing them in traumatizing military environments for three or four years. Young rural dwellers *were* drawn more rapidly into the cities. Women *were* called upon to labor under emergency conditions. The war itself taxed all Italian institutions in terms of population dislocation, resources, and mobilizable wealth. The war was fought in a desultory way against the resistance of much of the population. After the war the inflation, labor unrest and unemployment that plagued the economy threatened the status and livelihood of large sections of the population. The magnitude of the price fluctuations destroyed savings, security, and promise. Large numbers of intellectuals could find little opportunity for meaningful employment. In effect, there were masses to be mobilized, potential mass movement cadres available, established elites were vulnerable, economic dislocation, and the discontinuities produced by war threatened large segments of the population and weakened institutional ties.

While all this is true, and Kornhauser's account—based as it is on independent, suggestive, and supportive empirical evidence—is clearly superior to any of its antecedents in this intellectual tradition, it is evident that such treatment provides only the beginnings of an explanation for as complicated and protracted a historical and political sequence as Fascism. Kornhauser grants as much. He tells us that he has provided only a "tentative statement of a theory." [90] Since the theory is tentative, the explanation of any particular occurrence employing the theory can only be, at best, elliptical, provisional, and incomplete. It is elliptical, for instance, because there are no clear indices of "atomization." We simply do not know when group life is sufficiently "autonomous," "viable," or "psychologically integrative" to forestall mobilization. It is clear that in Italy prior to Fascism's ascent to power, large numbers of potentially active persons were ensconced in organizations of various sorts. Most Italians, for example, were at least nominally members of the Roman Catholic Church. Many, if not most, urban and rural workers were members of various labor and

----

[90] Ibid., p. 5.

social organizations. In retrospect, one can argue that the Church really did not "engage" the loyalties or the energy of its members and that labor organizations had become too bureaucratized to permit members to feel that they were "meaningfully" participating. But all these qualifications sound very much like ex post facto and ad hoc explanations. Whenever there is a high incidence of "mass behavior," institutions and autonomous group life *must* be "disintegrating." Often there is no *independent* index of the "disintegration"—there is only evidence of the "mass behavior" which is supposed to be its *consequence*. Much the same thing can be said for other putative causes of mass behavior. Rapid industrialization and urbanization might very well give rise to the availability of masses, but we have not specified the contingencies with sufficient precision to permit even low level prediction. Japan seems to be the case in point. Japan seems to have been singularly lacking in mass behavior although Japan has undergone rapid industrialization at essentially the same rate and over essentially the same time period as the Soviet Union—which experienced a mass-mobilizing and totalitarian movement.

In effect, we have a "tentative theory" that has not been "rigorously tested" largely because it requires "further research and theoretical analysis." [91] Empirical indices of "atomization" and its psychological concomitants have not been identified with testable precision independent of the behaviors that are supposed to be their consequence. The magnitudes that characterize catalyzing "crises" that foster the rise of mass movements have not been specified in terms of testable thresholds above which mass behaviors are predictable and below which apathy and indifference are to be

----

[91] Ibid.

expected. At best, such an account is provisional. If we would provide the exhaustive and mutually exclusive definitions required to characterize "autonomous," "viable," "engaging," and "stable" groups independent of those that lack autonomy, viability, engaging qualities and stability, we would be able to identify potential masses. It is not enough to indicate that "non-joiners" and "non-members" display mass qualities—one would have to recognize that movements like Fascism provoke intraorganizational defections, the collapse of old institutions, and the abandonment of old loyalties. Such movements themselves undermine and liquidate established patterns. They are not only the heirs of social disintegration.

Fascist Theories of the "Anonymous and Multitudinal Masses"

The interpretive strategy we have considered seems beset with at least some of the weaknesses we have suggested. Most of the authors in this tradition have recognized the partiality and inadequacies of their analysis. One of the sources of its strength, on the other hand, derives not only from its general plausibility, but from the fact that Fascists themselves have held the account to be largely correct. Benito Mussolini, for example, early argued that Fascism was a by-product of the most singular feature of the modern political world: the appearance in it of "anonymous and multitudinous masses." [92] Fascists subsequently never tired of characterizing their regime as a "regime of uniform

---

[92] Benito Mussolini, "I morti che vivono . . . ," *Opera omnia* (La Fenice, 1951), VII: 120.

masses." Pietro Chimienti, for example, insisted that "Fascism . . . is a phenomenon of the mass." [93] Gustavo Pesenti, in his panoramic anticipation of the "New World" that was in the process of formation, insisted that the spectacular increase in populations, the pervasive economic and socio-political threats that afflicted the modern world, had produced a disposition in the masses to seek out leaders, men who, like *condottieri* of old, could govern and guide them.[94] In guiding and governing them, such leaders dismantle the institutional structure of the old society and impose new hierarchically constituted and centrally controlled agencies. The masses are "organized," their energies directed, and their security assured.[95] The system that results is neither capitalist nor socialist, but rather a new state form. In this both Fascist and non-Fascist commentators agree. Lederer, for example, insisted that "modern dictatorship must rest on masses and . . . therefore it will be neither capitalism nor socialism." [96] Neumann, similarly, maintained that the "economics of the garrison state" is essentially noncapitalist in character.[97] The same theme, employing the same and similar locutions, was a commonplace in Fascist apologetics. All population constituents, economic groups, and professional categories, were "harmonized" in the service of the

---

[93] Pietro Chimienti, "L'individuo e la massa," *Gerarchia*, 1935, 13/6: 483; cf. Agostino Nasti, "Civiltà collettivistica," *Critica fascista*, 1933, 11/16: 302.

[94] Gustavo Pesenti, "Alcuni aspetti del mondo nuovo," *Gerarchia*, 1935, 13/5: 389–402.

[95] Guido Bortolotto, *Die Revolution der jungen Voelker* (Kittlers Verlag, 1934), pp. 20–25.

[96] Lederer, *State of the Masses*, p. 157.

[97] Neumann, *Permanent Revolution*, pp. 159–174.

Fascist state.[98] The difference that distinguished Fascist from anti-Fascist accounts, of course, turned on the *purposes* to which "masses" are presumably mobilized. For Fascists the purposes were "national goals," "social justice," the "rights" of a "proletarian" community—and for the anti-Fascists the purposes were "war," "oppression," and national "aggression." To support either contention requires a special argument and sustained historical interpretation. For our purposes the interesting feature of this argument is that, after the most minimal analysis, both Fascist and non-Fascist interpretations collapse into substantial agreement. Ortega, Lederer, Parsons, Arendt, and Kornhauser agree that Fascism was the consequence of the "intrusion" into political life of "amorphous masses." With the exception of Ortega, and perhaps Lederer, they all concur that mass leaders dominate the emotional and irrational life of the displaced masses that result from the decay of institutions, the advent of "mass democracy," and the protracted crisis that followed World War I. Many of them allude to the work of early analysts of the "mass mind"—Gustave Le Bon, Scipio Sighele, and Vilfredo Pareto, for example—analysts to whom Mussolini and every Fascist intellectual made regular recourse. Some of the principal ideologues of Fascism had, in fact, undertaken, while they were still revolutionary socialists and syndicalists, extended analyses of mass behavior. A. O. Olivetti and Paolo Orano, contemporaries of Mussolini and later intellectual spokesmen for the Fascist regime, both wrote books on the psychology of "atomic" and "rootless" masses. Olivetti's essay, *Il problema della folla,* was published in 1903 and Orano's book, *Psicologia sociale,* appeared in 1902. Mussolini himself regularly insisted on the

---

[98] Nazareno Mezzetti, *Mussolini e la questione sociale* (Pinciana, 1931).

influence of the work of Le Bon on his strategy and tactics of mass mobilization. Fascist literature was alive with references to the works of Gabriel Tarde, Ludwig Gumplowicz, Le Bon, Sorel, and Pareto. The interpretation of Fascism as the intrusion of masses into political life grants, it would seem, too much to Fascists. In fact, the interpretation grants the substantial adequacy of Fascist accounts.

Whatever the shortcomings of the general thesis, it seems perfectly plausible to argue that masses provide the materials out of which Fascism as a political movement was, in large part, fashioned, and that Fascists expertly utilized every strategy for mass mobilization that the social psychology of the period afforded. But it must also be said that we have considerable historic evidence that Fascism did not, and could not, totally "melt down" the institutional structure of pre-Fascist Italy in order to exploit "rootless" masses. We have, in fact, the testimony of Mussolini himself to that effect. In January 1944, Mussolini lamented that during the twenty years of Fascist rule in Italy, the Fascist state failed to act as a "mediator" of class interests in Italy because "the greater force the capitalist classes were capable of deploying rendered inoperative the juridical equality upon which parity [between classes] was predicated. This superior force . . . permitted the capitalist classes to dominate, and turn to their own advantage every action by the state . . . ." [99] What Mussolini was alluding to was the fact, now well documented, [100] that the capitalists of Italy, organized in business institutes of prewar origin, were fully capable of resisting most of the pressures directed against them by organized Fascism. Many pre-Fascist institutions were dismantled dur-

---

[99] Mussolini, *Opera omnia*, XXXII: 294.

[100] Roland Sarti, *Fascism and the Industrial Leadership in Italy* (University of California Press, 1971).

ing the Fascist period, particularly political and working class institutions, but many survived. As Mussolini indicated, in his *Storia di un anno,*[101] the monarchy and the military survived, virtually intact, throughout the Fascist period and became the rallying points for opponents of the regime. Clearly Fascism had totalitarian intentions, and its aspirations included a dissolution and subsequent restructuring of all intermediate institutions. But we know that there remained a considerable gap between intention and fulfillment.[102] It seems clear, in fact, that Fascism was confined by a variety of institutional constraints that survived the March on Rome. Some of the institutions that survived Mussolini's advent to power continued to enjoy a considerable degree of autonomy, vigor and consolidation. This is particularly true of the *Confindustria,* the General Confederation of Italian Industry, the organization that housed the principal industrial magnates of Italy. The armed forces and the Church, in turn, maintained a considerable degree of similar autonomy and viability. Moreover, the infrastructural bureaucracy developed a significant awareness of special interests and independence.[103] In effect, Mussolini and his party could operate with only limited freedom. Fascism did enjoy "mass" support, but policy was frequently the consequence of arbitration and an adjustment of the articulate claims of various interest groups. Because these negotiations were not conducted publicly is not an indication that such negotiations did not transpire. Mussolini was neither the tool of the masses, nor were they his instrument.

---

[101] Mussolini, *Opera omnia,* XXXIV: 406–416.

[102] Alberto Aquarone, *L'organizzazione dello stato totalitario* (Einaudi, 1965).

[103] Gaetano Salvemini, *Under the Axe of Fascism* (Gollancz, 1936), pp. 419–429.

The masses did apparently provide decisive weight in his struggle for power, but his accession could not have been *solely* and *simply* the consequence of his ability to address himself to the restiveness, the insecurity, and the irrationality of masses. There were clearly instances of negotiation between rational interest groups during Fascism's rise to power, and there were equally clear instances of serious negotiation after its accession. Neither the masses, nor Mussolini, *exclusively* "dominated" Italian political life for a quarter century. Mussolini operated within the confines and with the support of existing institutional and interest groups in his environment both during his rise to power, his ascendancy, and his decline. Sometimes he could effectively manipulate those forces to achieve his ends. Often, however, his purposes were faulted by the resistance of groups that had lodged in the system and who were fully apprised of their own special regional and parochial interests.

All this can be said with considerable confidence both with respect to the operation of the established regime, as well as the circumstances surrounding its advent to power. We have considerable evidence that indicates that nascent Fascism was assisted, to a significant degree, by financial contributions made by entrepreneurial and propertied interests that considered the movement a defense agency in the service of their real and rational interests. Such contributions constituted investments in group, rather than "mass," security—and afford evidence of rational calculation. This is not to say (as we shall indicate later) that Fascism was the instrument of capitalist interests. Whatever information we have from the period indicates that capitalist associations and individual representatives of propertied classes gave contributions to all non-Communist political groups in their efforts to hedge all bets.

Pursuing such an analysis one can discover at least discursive evidence that Fascism recruited support from a variety of organized groups—each disposed, for its own reasons, to actively or passively support the movement. As has already been suggested, demobilized war veterans had every calculated reason to enlist in the Fascist ranks. The socialists and the radical left, opposed as they were to any expression of nationalism, singled out returning war veterans for particular abuse. Soldiers, for example, were advised not to wear their uniforms or decorations in public—in order not to enflame the socialists. One does not have to conduct research to anticipate the effects of such circumstances. War veterans made up significant numbers of the action squads of revolutionary Fascism in order to defend their dignity and material claims. Their enlistment in Fascist ranks was a perfectly rational response to status and personal threat, rather than an instance of "mass" behavior. The established government seemed ill-disposed to intercede actively in defense of returning service men. Mussolini early espoused their cause.[104]

The "new middle classes" were particularly afflicted by a runaway inflation that threatened to destroy all semblance of security. Moreover, the organized working class had managed to negotiate wage increases that in many critical cases surpassed the income levels of intellectuals, civil servants, and white collar workers. The Fascists promised to control inflation, balance the government's books, and provide juridical representation for all productive categories on the basis of parity[105]—a goal-specific program that could only attract the poorly organized new middle classes. It is hard

---

[104] Renzo De Felice, *Mussolini il rivoluzionario* (Einaudi, 1965), pp. 426ff.

[105] Robert Michels, *Sozialismus und Faschismus in Italien* (Meyer & Jensen, 1925), II: 253–259.

to "interpret" the response of such population elements as "selfless," "nihilistic," and exclusively, or essentially, irrational.

In the rural areas of the north of Italy, there is some contemporary evidence to indicate that the large and small property holders were not only threatened by Communist demands for "land to the peasants," but that the established socialist organizations had long acted in an arbitrary and abrasive fashion. Individuals who resisted joining socialist "cooperatives," those who attempted to resist "collective contracts," those who refused to employ card-carrying members of the socialist associations, or hired men who were not card-carrying members, were subjected to "boycotts," violence, and personal threats that produced a reasonably specific and (at least in substantial part) rational search for an alternative. The Fascists were explicitly opposed to the socialist organizations. The development of Fascism in the Po Valley—the development that heralded Fascism's advent to national prominence—was in considerable part the consequence of its offer of a perfectly reasonable alternative to large and small landholders.[106] In effect, reasonably specific groups were responding to reasonably specific rational group needs. They did not constitute a "mass."

Similarly, the constabulary of pre-Fascist Italy had every reason to find the socialists objectionable. For years socialists had insisted that the police were venal servitors of the interests of the "bourgeoisie." For years the constabulary had been the butt of socialist jibes and socialist violence. When the Fascists began to use street violence against socialists the constabulary were understandably prepared to turn a blind eye to their infractions. Again, this was a per-

---

[106] Mario Missiroli, *Il fascismo e il colpo di stato dell'Ottobre, 1922* (Cappelli, 1966).

fectly comprehensible group, rather than a "mass," response to the objective situation. All the evidence we have indicates that the central government and the police administration attempted to make the constabulary "apolitical," an agency for controlling *all* "anti-social" behavior.[107] It is equally evident that many policemen felt that it was in their rational, if narrow, self-interest to permit the Fascists to make short shrift of those elements that had, for so long, made their lives, as an organized group, difficult.

A similar analysis would suggest that a variety of organized population elements might very well find the Fascist program attractive. There was a reasonably large minority among the working class that found radical programs unrealistic. The attempt, for example, to occupy the factories late in 1920 seemed to establish the bankruptcy of "maximalist socialist" strategy.[108] The orthodox parties seemed to offer little other than the nostrums of the prewar period. The Fascists, in turn, were advertising a "national syndicalism," a union of "all productive categories" in the service of the rationalization and expansion of national production that seemed eminently realistic. The Fascists argued that Italy did not need socialist redistribution of property, but rather an expansion of industrial productivity in which all population elements could expect to profit. The program was certainly no less rational than the "dictatorship of the proletariat," or the "Christian socialism" of the Popular Party.

In effect, it would seem that both the Fascist and the non-Fascist interpretation of Fascism, — predicated on the notion that irrational, volatile, and aggressive "masses," subject to the mimetic influence of "magnetic" and "charis-

---

[107] De Felice, *Mussolini il fascista: la conquista del potere, 1921–1925* (Einaudi, 1966), pp. 25–30.

[108] De Felice, *Mussolini il rivoluzionario,* pp. 425–429.

matic" leaders, "produced" Fascism—provides, at best, a plausible *partial* account. However aggressive, violent, and emotional the behavior of large numbers of political actors might have been in the circumstances that surrounded the Fascist accession to power—it could not be said, without significant qualification, that their behavior was the consequence of their "atomization." Many men, in organized groups and as individuals, were serving what they understood to be their proximate and real interests. It might well be said that it was not so much the "rootlessness" and "atomization" of the masses that gave Fascism the substance that brought it to, and sustained it in, power, but that Mussolini was a consummate politician who could manipulate groups with proximate class and category interests in the service of his own, and Fascism's, more remote political ends.

That institutional, organizational, or class interests persisted through the formative and tenure phases of Fascism is suggested by the fact that Fascism tended to recruit persons of different social provenience than did socialism or communism. It does not appear to have been the case that "mass men" simply opted for *any* mass-mobilizing movement—irrespective of what Le Bon, Lederer, Hoffer, or Arendt claim. While it is true that Fascist movements have recruited members from every class and category, Fascism did enjoy recruitment advantages in petty bourgeois environs, while communism recruited largely, though not exclusively, rural and urban proletarian members. Empirically oriented researchers such as Kornhauser are emphatic on this point.[109] It is not true that politically active men under such circumstances simply make transit from one mass-mobilizing movement to another, which suggests that some real group interests function as determinants in their decision.

----

[109] Kornhauser, *Politics of Mass Society,* pp. 14, 196, 202.

Whatever evidence we have suggests that Fascism came to power in Italy at least in substantial part because organized sections of the Italian population found something in its program that promised to satisfy some of their real and proximate interests. Among Fascists and Fascist sympathizers were many who were members of stable intermediary groups. Those that lent support to Fascism lent support because Fascism promised the satisfaction of material, confessional or doctrinal needs. The suggestion that "mass men" do not think, are simply visceral, are fickle and promiscuous in their loyalties (they can be either communists or fascists without preference), despairing, totally devoid of self-interest, capable of believing nothing and everything, may describe some, perhaps even the majority, of the men swept into the train of mass-mobilizing movements. But such an account leaves a great deal to be said.

It is probably true that Fascism attracted many "rootless" and displaced elements. How large a contingent they constituted is hard to say. But Fascism's spectacular growth between 1920 and 1921 was probably the result not of a sudden and inexplicable increase of "rootlessness," but of the failure of Italy's political system to satisfy the real, effective, and organized interests of large sections of the population. Fascism did, in historic fact, solve some of the problems to which such groups addressed themselves. Fascism did, in fact and for example, destroy the monopoly enjoyed by socialist agrarian organizations. Fascism did reduce strike activity. Fascism did control inflation (pursuing policies already laid down by preceding governments). In effect, there was far more rational calculation and political bargaining going on in the insurrectional phases of Fascism than the "theory" of mass society seems prepared to countenance. Mussolini very carefully calculated on organized and articulate interests and sought to contain them within the structure of his movement. How complicated a task this was is evidenced by the contemporary assessments that saw Fascism composed exclusively of a collection of special and specific interests. We know, now, that Fascism was more than that, but we also know that Mussolini could not have been successful unless he either neutralized, satisfied, or absorbed organized and viable interest groups. This means that such groups persisted during the mobilization phase of Fascism (and continued, in many cases, to persist throughout the regime). Mussolini always had to effect a delicate balance between those interest groups—and at every stage in the trajectory of Fascism the influence of those groups was evident. Some interest groups never succeeded in restabilizing themselves, but some, including the *Confindustria* (Italy's organization of major industries), the Church, the military, and the monarchy, remained viable and vital and significantly influenced the operations of the "totalitarian state."

In its most compelling form, the "theory" of mass society, as an explanation of Fascism, provides at best a partial explanatory sketch. In its less competent form, it offers the occasion for the issuance of broad and shapeless generalizations about man's bestiality to man, and an unrealistic and inadequate characterization of some of the principal mass movements of our time.

CHAPTER FIVE

Fascism as the Consequence of Class Struggle

If the effort to interpret the rise, trajectory, and fall of Fascism in terms of the "intrusion" into history of "amorphous masses" is flawed by its apparent indisposition to recognize the influence of relatively rational group and class calculation, this cannot be said of the account that conceives the entire complex sequence to be the product of "class struggle." While the general interpretation of Fascism as the consequence of class struggle does afford room for the irrational and brutal "mass behaviors" that constitute the core of the account provided by authors like Emil Lederer, Hannah Arendt, and William Kornhauser, the principal determinants of the entire interconnected series of events are identified as rational, if mutually exclusive, class interests. However much "mass behaviors" may have influenced the surface features of events, the historic sequence is understood to have been the consequence of the rational calculation of identifiable interest groups. At critical junctures in such an account, the "propertied classes," the "bourgeoisie," or the "big capitalists" are understood to have "invoked," "subventionized," "used," and "directed" Fascism in the service of their calculated self-interest. As early as 1923, for example, Julius Deutsch insisted that Fascism was a political movement that mobilized and "fanaticized" petty bourgeois and adolescent population elements (with the "dark mysticism" so compatible with "Latin psychology") in the service of "profit-mad capitalist reaction." [1] Whatever variations the next fifty years were to bring in their train, the cast of characters and the plot-line were to remain substantially the same.

All the variants of this interpretation hold class interests, conscious or unconscious, to be the principal explana-

----

[1] Julius Deutsch, *Die Faschistengefahr* (Wiener Volksbuchhandlung, 1923), p. 5.

tory variables. The interpretation is generally referred to in the literature as the "Marxist" interpretation of Fascism— but it is obvious that there is no single "Marxist" interpretation. They all differ in important and interesting ways. They all bear, nonetheless, a family resemblance in so far as the principal factors in the account have class interests as their reference. Of all of them there is one, the "orthodox Marxist-Leninist version" that is by far the most well-developed. It constitutes a strategy of interpretation that has enjoyed the "official" sanction of the spokesmen of the Soviet Union— and for years enjoyed the imprimatur of Josef Stalin. It is the Marxist-Leninist version of the generic Marxist interpretation that affords the most ready access to exposition and criticism. Whatever can be said for Marxist interpretations of Fascism can best be said using the official Soviet account as a point of departure.

Unhappily, the Marxist-Leninist account itself has undergone extensive revisions over the half-century it has enjoyed official support. As a consequence, it seems reasonable to review the interpretation by following its development in time. Alternative Marxist accounts will make their appearance as they lend themselves to the exposition or the critique.

The first attempt at a Marxist-Leninist interpretation of Fascism was bruited during the Fourth World Congress of the Third International, held immediately after Mussolini's accession to power. At that time Italian communist intellectuals advanced what they held to be an adequate interpretation of the Fascist phenomenon. On that occasion they identified Fascism as "a weapon in the hands of the large landholders"—as though the "agrarian Fascism" that had manifested itself primarily in the regions of Florence, Ferrara, Romagna, and Bologna revealed the "essential class character" of the entire complex political movement. Fascism, according to this first effort, was an "instrument" consciously employed by the "agrarian capitalists" to defeat the "working-class revolution."

Fascism as a "Victory for Industrial Capital"

Approximately a week later, the thesis was transformed into one which conceived Fascism to be not simply a tool in the service of agrarian capitalism, but rather a "political offensive of the [entire] bourgeoisie against the working-class." [2] At about the same time the first major work in this tradition was being prepared for the press. It would, once again, transform the thesis. In 1923 the Hungarian communist, Djula Sas, published (under the pseudonym Giulio Aquila) his *Der Faschismus in Italien*.[3]

Aquila prefaced his account with a long preamble entitled, "The Essence and Historic Significance of Fascism," in which he maintained that he would reveal, beneath the complex and contradictory surface features of political events in Italy, the "true essence of Italian Fascism." For Aquila, Fascism represented, in "essence" and "historically," neither an "instrument" of agrarian capitalists, nor of the entire bourgeoisie. Fascism was a "victory for *industrial capital*"—a victory of the "industrial bourgeoisie." [4]

Having affirmed his central thesis, Aquila proceeded to

----

[2] Cf. John M. Cammett, "Communist Theories of Fascism, 1920–1935." *Science and Society,* 1967, 31/2: 150ff.

[3] The original Italian text has been lost. The available translation, G. Aquila, "Il fascismo italiano." In R. De Felice, ed., *Il fascismo e i partiti politici Italiana* (Cappelli, 1966), is a translation of the German text. A revised and enlarged edition, *Fascistkoi Italia,* appeared in Moscow in 1929.

[4] Aquila, "Il fascismo italiano," p. 421 (emphasis supplied).

state in very general propositions the circumstances that constituted the necessary conditions for the advent of Fascism. Aquila maintained that the "imperialist war" of 1914–18 had so dislocated the economic foundations of capitalist society that it was no longer possible to restore productive activity of the capitalist system through the "normal" means of working class exploitation. The ruinous economic conditions generated by the war necessitated, for the restabilization of the capitalist economy, an increased measure of exploitation of the proletariat. At the same time Aquila argued, the war had permitted the working class to effectively organize to resist such efforts. Because of the organized resistance of the working class, the entrepreneurial bourgeoisie could not effect their purpose through the institutions of traditional "democratic" forms and were driven, consequently, to abandon even the semblance of political democracy.

The fact that organized labor, from its position of strength, could not resist the political pressures of a postwar "reaction" was, in turn, a consequence of the betrayal of the proletariat by "reformist Social Democracy." The conditions for socialist revolution were, in Aquila's judgment, "ripe" in post-World War I Italy. What was lacking was decisive and knowledgeable revolutionary leadership. The absence of an effective communist party, the passive and ineffectual Social Democratic leadership, dissipated the revolutionary energies of the working class. The result was the predictable victory of Fascism.[5]

While, according to Aquila, Fascism served the exclusive interests of "big business," the industrial capitalists, it constituted, at the same time, a political, ideological, and military victory over the working class. Fascism was not

----

[5] Ibid., pp. 423ff.

simply armed reaction. It managed to attract to its ranks, quite spontaneously, broad strata of the petty-bourgeoisie—many intellectuals, civil servants, the constabulary, professional and semiprofessional elements, small farmers and peasants, war veterans, university students, and the active military, as well as a significant minority of the working class itself. Fascism's political victory was the immediate consequence of its "social demagoguery"—its invocation of nationalist sentiments, its appeals to the "collective interests," the "liberty" and "grandeur" of the nation. But the appeal to diffuse sentiments was not sufficient to assure the recruitment successes of Fascism. The necessary preconditions involved systematic sabotage of proletarian interests by Social Democratic leaders.[6]

Social Democratic leadership, either having been suborned—or because of their analytical and theoretical impoverishment—failed to understand that resistance to Fascism would have only been effective on the basis of militant working class opposition. Because they failed to understand political reality, Social Democratic leadership attempted to invoke collaboration with the bourgeoisie as an effective strategy against the armed reaction of the bourgeoisie itself. It was a strategy calculated to fail. In the effort to resist Fascism, Social Democracy attempted to ally itself to the "liberal" and "democratic" bourgeoisie. In so doing it undermined the disposition of the working class to defend its interests with arms. It psychologically and morally impaired the proletarian will to resist. With its hopeless strategies, it dissipated revolutionary energies. It foreswore "extralegal" methods and appealed to "constitutional defenses" against Fascist violence. At the same time (and predictably, according to Aquila's account), the bourgeoisie facilitated Fascist

---

[6] Ibid., pp. 428, 429, 430, 444, 446, 469ff., 475ff., 494.

outrages and permitted the constabulary and the military to openly conspire with Fascist squads in their depredations against the organized working class. To complete the process, Giovanni Giolitti, the head of the bourgeois government, succeeded in "legalizing" the Fascists by recruiting them into a parliamentary "national bloc." [7]

It is clear, Aquila argued, that there are divergent interests among the bourgeoisie as a class, but that divergence ends at the point where the "sacred interests of capital" come into question. The working class cannot defend itself within the confines of bourgeois "democracy," since bourgeois "democracy" can only serve bourgeois interests, and cannot be an effective instrument in the hands of a class attempting to overthrow capitalism. What the working class requires to defeat Fascism is a unitary and armed revolutionary movement, committed to the capture of state power, which will disarm and extirpate not only the armed militia of the bourgeoisie—the Fascists—but the bourgeoisie itself. The proletariat cannot reasonably expect the bourgeoisie to aid in its own liquidation as a class.

More interesting than Aquila's account itself is the evidence he advances to support his inferences. He alludes, for example, to instances in which the constabulary and the military passively or actively supported the Fascist squads. He refers to the subventions received by the Fascist movement from agrarian associations composed of large and small landholders in the regions of Ferrara, Florence, and Bologna, as well as support received from industrialists, both as individuals and associations. He also insists that "bourgeois" statesmen, like Giovanni Giolitti and Luigi Facta significantly aided Fascism during its insurrectional phase. This is enough, apparently, to warrant the judgment that Fascism

----

[7] Ibid., pp. 446ff., 453, 494ff.

was a bourgeois "instrument," and Mussolini a "conscious agent of the bourgeoisie." [8]

Six months after Fascism's accession to power (at the time Aquila was writing his account), the fact that Fascism had effectively destroyed the institutional infrastructure of working class organizations, that it had, in some cases, significantly reduced wages, that it had abolished the extraordinary taxes imposed on inheritance and "war profits," was enough to characterize its operation as serving the *exclusive* interests of "industrial capitalism." Fascism's programmatic intention, emphatic since at least 1918, to "maximize national production" was construed as evidence that it sought to restore the integrity of the capitalist enterprise at the expense of labor.

That Aquila's judgments are inferential is self-evident. He offers no direct evidence that Mussolini, or Fascism in general, were the "*conscious* instruments" of the policies of "industrial capitalism." His inferences are as defensible as the indirect evidence in their support is subject to only one interpretation. Moreover, the inferences rest on several unexamined premises that provide much of their plausibility. Those premises include at least the following:

1. That capitalism in Italy after World War I, could *in no way* restabilize without the suppression of "democratic" forms;
2. That there are *objective limits* beyond which the entire "bourgeoisie" will not go to defend "democratic" forms;
3. And, probably, that some of the protagonists in the entire drama were *consciously* aware of what the defense of "bourgeois" interests objectively required.

---

[8] Ibid., pp. 482, 494.

Clearly, Aquila believed that Mussolini *consciously* served the interests of the "industrial bourgeoisie." In Aquila's judgment, in fact, the "Fascist state" *consistently* and *exclusively* served the interests of the "big bourgeoisie," the "industrial capitalists."

Taken together all these propositions—some broad and "axiomatic," others less general and derivative—constitute a general and discursive "theory" of Fascism. How lacking in rigor the entire structure of the theory remains, in Aquila's account, is evident in the fact that he is prepared to admit that the "bourgeoisie" of Italy was afflicted by many contrasting interests all of which Fascism could not conceivably serve. Only "heavy industry," in his judgment, provided the unqualified support base of Fascism.[9] Nonetheless, in Aquila's judgment, even though Fascist economic policy, tailored exclusively to the interests of heavy industry threatened Italy with economic ruin, the "objective limits" of the class interests of the "bourgeoisie" could be defined with sufficient specificity to make the argument plausible. The conviction, however, was not argued. It was simply pronounced. There are "class limits" outside of which the "bourgeoisie" in its entirety will not transgress even though Fascism's service to the industrial capitalists threatened the entire bourgeoisie with ruin.

Most of the weight of the "theory" rests on the major empirical premises at its base. Should those premises be false, the entire "theory" would dissolve into fragmentary data, unsupported generalizations, and instantial descriptive reports. The inferential judgments Aquila entertained were as good as the "theory" of which they were derivative products.

Much the same must be said for the formulations de-

---

[9] Ibid., pp. 477ff.

livered by Clara Zetkin at the executive meeting of the Communist International held in Moscow in June 1923. Zetkin was seriously ill at the time and this fact perhaps explains why her communication, *Der Kampf gegen den Faschismus*,[10] is little more than a synopsis of Aquila's essay. If Aquila did not himself author entire sections of her exposition, Zetkin cribbed them from his manuscript. Not only does she, echoing Aquila, claim to reveal the "historic essence" of the Fascist phenomenon as a "tool" of industrial capital, she advanced as true all of the explicit and implicit premises of Aquila's account.

Not only are the general theses of Zetkin's account identical with those of Aquila, but whole phrases from Aquila's essay resurface in Zetkin's prose. For Aquila, for example, Fascism was not "a simple victory of arms, but an ideological and political victory" over the working class movement. For Zetkin, Fascism was not a "military phenomenon," it was an "ideological and political victory over the working class movement." [11] Moreover, in producing the data she advanced as evidence of Fascism's "bourgeois" essence, Zetkin simply repeated, with only the slightest modification, an account of the legislation bearing on political, social, fiscal, and military affairs forthcoming under the Fascist regime to be found in Aquila's earlier exposition.[12] When Aquila mentions working-class wage reductions of "20, 30 and even 50 percent," Zetkin goes him somewhat better by making it reductions of "20–30 percent, with

----

[10] Clara Zetkin, "Der Kampf gegen den Faschismus." In Ernst Nolte, ed., *Theorien ueber den Faschismus* (Kiepenheuer & Witsch, 1967), pp. 88–111.

[11] Aquila, "Il fascismo italiano," p. 469; Zetkin, "Der Kampf gegen den Faschismus," p. 99.

[12] Compare Aquila, "Il fascismo italiano," pp. 458–467, and Zetkin, "Der Kampf gegen den Faschismus," pp. 99–105.

many workers suffering a reduction of even 50 percent and in some cases even 60 percent." [13] When Aquila mentions the resistance to Fascism that had mounted in "Naples, Turin, Trieste, and Venice," Zetkin makes this "Turin, Naples, Trieste and Venice." [14] Aquila mentions the resistance of workers at Monfalcone in Trieste; Zetkin makes the same reference. Aquila mentions 24,000 workers dismissed from their places of employment in the offices of the military bureaucracy; Zetkin makes the same reference. Aquila mentions the workers' resistance in Boscoreale in Naples; Zetkin makes the same reference. There is, in fact, not a single factual reference made in Zetkin's communication that is not to be found in Aquila's earlier essay. There are two or three pages in Zetkin's exposition that refer specifically to the German situation, which appear to have been specially written for the Moscow delivery, but they do not materially alter the substance of the presentation. In sum therefore, Zetkin's account, sometimes conceived as a "more comprehensive and intelligent interpretation" of Fascism than any hitherto available,[15] is little more than a synopsis of Aquila's essay of the preceding year.

Fascism as the Product of the "Big Bourgeoisie"

For all the consistency evidenced in the joint account of Aquila and Zetkin, the fact remained that the "theory" re-

---

[13] Aquila, "Il fascismo italiano," p. 462; Zetkin, "Der Kampf gegen den Faschismus," p. 100.

[14] Aquila, "Il fascismo italiano," p. 472 and Zetkin, "Der Kampf gegen den Faschismus," p. 105.

[15] Cammett, "Communist Theories of Fascism," p. 151.

mained informal and porous. The thesis central to the "official" version remained essentially unaltered in the formal communication approved by the Third Congress of the Italian Communist Party of 1926.[16] The "inherent weaknesses of capitalism" remained the critical necessary conditions for the appearance and success of Fascism. The immediate contingent condition of its victory was the "betrayal" of the proletariat by the "reformist Social Democratic leadership" of pre-Fascist Italy. The "social basis" of Fascism remained the "petty bourgeoisie" of the urban areas and the "new petty bourgeoisie" of the rural areas. Fascism was, however, conceived *not* as the "instrument" of the "industrial bourgeoisie," as it was for Aquila and Zetkin, but of "an *industrial and agrarian* oligarchy." [17] Fascism, in the account of 1926, was an "industrial-agrarian reaction"—and produced an "industrial-agrarian dictatorship." [18] While for Aquila, Fascism had a "progressive function" in dismantling the old political system that served "financial and agrarian" interests in order to meet the growth needs of "heavy industry"—and for Zetkin the Fascists responded to the objective needs of the "North Italian industrial bourgeoisie" against those of the "agrarian and finance capitalists"—for the Communist theoreticians in 1926, Fascism was a *joint* dictatorship of both *industrial* and *agrarian* capitalists.

Similarly, in 1928 the Communist International continued to identify Fascism loosely with "the terroristic dictatorship of big capital . . . . Fascism [is the political expression of the] . . . undivided, open and consistent dictatorship [of] *bankers,* the *big industrialists* and the *agrar-*

----

[16] "La lotta di classe e il fascismo." In C. Casucci, ed., *Il fascismo* (Mulino, 1961), pp. 265–278.

[17] Ibid., p. 271.

[18] Ibid., pp. 275, 276.

ians." [19] Fascism was not conceived to be exclusively or essentially the "tool" of the industrial bourgeoisie—it was a sort of "joint dictatorship" of a collegium of "big capital." Thus in 1928 Palmiro Togliatti, in his *A proposito del fascismo*[20] repeated most of the central theses of the account provided by Aquila and Zetkin, but insisted that Fascism was a product of the "big bourgeoisie," *la grossa borghesia,*[21] rather than the industrial bourgeoisie alone.

In Togliatti's judgment the Fascist movement did not initially intend to serve as a "dictatorship of industrial and finance capital," but since the interstitial bourgeoisie, which made up its social base, did not possess a "political consciousness" of its own, it inevitably lapsed into the service of the "great bourgeoisie and the agrarians." Ultimately, Fascism lost whatever autonomy it had and was compelled to effect "brutally and without reserve" the political purposes of "finance capital," the purposes of "big industry and the bankers." It became a "dictatorship of finance capital and heavy industry [*la grande industria*]."

By 1928 Fascism was no longer conceived to be the "dictatorship of heavy industry," nor was it the "dictatorship of heavy industry and agrarian capitalists"—it was the "dictatorship of financial, industrial and agrarian capital." [22] Needless to say, such a generous reformulation indicates the porosity of the original "theory." More than that such a reformulation generated some real theoretical tensions.

Any dictatorship that attempted to satisfy *all* the de-

----

[19] As cited, R. Palme Dutt, *Fascism and Social Revolution* (International, 1934), pp. 88ff. (emphasis supplied).

[20] Palmiro Togliatti, "A proposito del fascismo." In C. Casucci, ed., *Il Fascismo,* pp. 279–301.

[21] Ibid., p, 291.

[22] Ibid., pp. 292, 298; cf. p. 294.

mands of financial, industrial, and agrarian interest groups would find itself beset with problems. It is sometimes considered an economic commonplace that agrarian groups tend to pursue free trade policies, while the representatives of nascent or destabilized national industries tend to favor protectionist policies. Similarly, it is generally argued that among industrial capitalists well-entrenched industries with a heavy volume of export trade (like Italy's textile industries of the period) tend to favor free trade to reduce the threat of reactive restrictive trade policies on the part of their trade partners. Noncompetitive industries (like Italy's maritime industry), in turn, tend to favor protection. On the other hand, some agrarian interests (like Italy's beet sugar industry and sugar refineries) tend to favor protection, while those industries which, even if marginally established, depend on the importation of essential raw materials (like the steel industry of Italy) tend to favor free trade. Some financial groups tend to favor inflationary fiscal policy; some oppose them. Any dictatorship "subservient" to all these interests would not enjoy a long half-life—or it would regularly fail to serve its patrons.

Nonetheless, it could be said that such problems could be resolved through negotiation among the constituent elements of the "dictatorship"—and the capitalists might prefer some such arrangement to one in which the representatives of organized labor or the public at large might intrude themselves. They might prefer, in effect, a Fascist dictatorship to any "liberal bourgeois" government.

For all that, the "Marxist-Leninist" accounts available in 1928 were far from compelling. It was never quite clear to whom Fascism was "subservient": the bankers, the industrialists, the landowners, or all of them together. The fragmentary evidence in support of their thesis that "Marxist-Leninist" theorists made available were laced together by a thread of suppositions and prejudgments that involved un-supported convictions concerning elaborate conspiracies and inexplicable and wholesale betrayals.

Fascism as a Conspiracy of "Finance Capitalists"

The official "Marxist-Leninist" interpretation of Fascism re-mained in this parlous and elliptical state up to and through the early thirties when the leadership of the Third Interna-tional officially decided that there was only one competent interpretation of fascism. Although there were any number of alternative non-Soviet "Marxist" interpretations, and con-siderable variations among spokesmen for the Third Inter-national, Stalinists settled on a formulation that construed Italian Fascism in particular, and generic fascism in general, to be nothing more than the "open and terroristic dictator-ship of the most reactionary, most chauvinistic and most im-perialistic elements of *finance capital*." [23] Fascism was no longer the "instrument" of the magnates of heavy industry, or the agent of a combination of industrial and agrarian capitalists, or even a "tool" of the "big bourgeoisie." It was the simple instrument of a conspiracy on the part of "finance capitalists."

The appearance of R. Palme Dutt's *Fascism and Social Revolution* in 1934 provided a reasonably competent ex-position of what Soviet "Marxist-Leninists" were to take to be a comprehensive interpretation of generic fascism. Dutt's account was the first in this intellectual tradition that at-

---

[23] "Resolution of the VII Congress of the Communist International," in T. Pirker, ed., *Utopie und Mythos der Weltrevolution* (DTV, 1964), pp. 226–229.

tempted to disinter the critical premises that sustained the general interpretation. Not only was it intended to be a theoretically sound interpretation of Italian Fascism, but it pretended to explain the advent, and the historical and political trajectory, of generic fascism as well.

Palme Dutt's volume of 1934 was written with the express intention of providing an intellectually satisfying account of the "true character of Fascism." [24] His effort, for our purposes, was an attempt to provide a sustained and compelling argument in support of the then standard Soviet interpretation. Critical to this effort are his exposition and support of the three central propositions of the "Marxist-Leninist" account:

1. Fascism is a necessary and inevitable product of the laws governing the capitalist economic system, which make it impossible for capitalism to survive within traditional political forms;
2. The limits of "bourgeois" defense of traditional "liberal" and "democratic" political forms can be specified with objective precision;
3. Fascism is the contrived product of the *conscious* intentions and overt *conspiratorial* policy of identifiable historic agents.

The first two chapters of Dutt's major work are devoted to a stenographic account of the inevitable historic trends that characterize the capitalist productive system. Capitalism, according to Dutt's account, entered into a fatal and irreversible decline sometime during the first two decades of the twentieth century. Since at least 1914, capitalism has collapsed into an irremediable and final "general crisis." Because capitalism had entered into its *inherent* and *in-*

---

[24] Dutt, *Fascism and Social Revolution,* p. viii.

evitable declining phase, any restoration of capitalism of the prewar type was no longer possible. The final general crisis of capitalism, according to Dutt's view, was the consequence of the "conflict between the ever-growing productive forces and the limits of existing property society." "The development of the productive forces has rendered the old class society obsolete." The "realities of capitalism . . . both in fact and in iron necessity" require that capitalists reduce productive costs regularly by increasing the measure and rate of exploitation of the work force. This takes place at a time when capitalism finds itself afflicted with a constantly dwindling foreign market for its products. The real and/or relative decline in effective consumer demand in the home market, which is the necessary and ultimate consequence of the exploitation of the working class, conjoined with the erosion of foreign markets and the increasing competition among advanced industrial states, produces insoluble contradictions for contemporary capitalism. The "gigantic" productive capacity of contemporary capitalism cannot find an equally "gigantic" outlet for the effective realization of profit. If the market cannot expand commensurately with increased productivity, capitalism finds itself embroiled in a fatal impasse.[25]

Pioneer capitalist systems such as England's, which enjoyed privileged access to an insulated colonial market and a partial monopoly of manufacture, could utilize the "superprofits" these privileges provided in order to create an "aristocracy of labor," a small subset of the working class that battened on a "bourgeois" standard of living. Utilizing this "bribed" strata of the working class, the capitalist system could thwart the effective organization of the revolutionary working class. But as those "superprofits" diminish

-----

[25] Ibid., pp. 9, 10, 11, 15, 20ff., 26, 27, 31, 32, 42, 60.

in quantity, capitalism can no longer depend on its working-class auxiliaries. The working-class movement becomes better organized and more insistent in its demands. The capitalist system goes into a protracted final crisis. With "increasing clearness and consciousness," the "leaders of capitalism" recognize the circumstances of their situation. They "clearly and consciously" recognize that the prewar strategies for maintaining their system must be abandoned. Their subsequent policies are "completely rational and calculated." ". . . the demand becomes increasingly strong from the representatives of capitalism for the throwing aside or modification of the old parliamentary democratic forms, which no longer serve their purpose, and the establishment of open and strengthened forms of repression and dictatorship." [26]

Because of the general crisis that has settled upon capitalism—in which it can no longer profitably empty its inventories—there is a necessary demand for *restriction of production,* a curtailment of *technological innovation,* and a *systematic destruction of wealth.* The demand is for "controlled" production within the confines of a restricted consumer market. The circumstances require an artificially reduced and stabilized rate of consumption. Completely cartelized or monopolized production is distributed only in quantities fixed at levels that maximize profit in an industrial system in which labor costs are one of the principal cost factors. Workers' wages must be kept low in order to insure low productive costs, but wages provide a major source of effective demand. Given the decline in foreign markets and reduced effective demand produced by low wages, capitalism must control both production and consumption within strictly prescribed limits in order to maximize profit. In do-

----

[26] Ibid., pp. 41, 57, 60ff., 68.

ing so, both production and consumption must be reduced to low levels. The entire system is characterized by a "suppression" and a "restriction" of the forces of production, "throttling down production to fixed limits suitable to monopolist capital" and "preventing new development." Capitalism is "stabilized" on "a basis approximating to simply reproduction of capital . . . this would mean a static nonprogressive tendency, with regulated quotas of production, prices, levels of wages and profits." [27]

In order to accomplish all this, capitalists must effectively destroy the resistance of the organized working class. They also must have the support of a mass base in order to effect the transition from the old "bourgeois liberal" form of capitalist rule to the new, retrogressive dictatorship. The passage from the one to the other can most effectively take place on the crest of "popular" demand. Masses must be mobilized to this purpose. Mobilizable elements are to be found among the large numbers of "non-productive" petty bourgeoisie available in abundance in the contemporary capitalist system. These "intermediate strata" are "parasitic" in character, being "tied up with the processes of exploitation" and are, consequently, "easily controlled" by their capitalist masters. The "mixed intermediate strata or so-called middle classes . . . can play no independent political role . . . ." They are either mobilized to the political purposes of the revolutionary working class movement or pass, by default, into the service of "finance capital." [28]

During the period of the final and general crisis of capitalism, therefore, the limits of bourgeois support for democratic political forms are determined by the vital in-

---

[27] Ibid., pp. 225, 226.
[28] Ibid., pp. 237, 273.

terests of the "cool," "calculating" and "completely rational" "finance capitalists." The vital interests of "finance capital," in turn, are functions of the "inherent laws" of capitalist production. Dutt has provided an explicit account of some of the central premises on which the standard version implicitly rested. How confident Dutt was in the empirical substance of those premises and the impeccability of his (informal) logic, is revealed in his disposition to talk of "inevitabilities" and "inescapable" consequences. Dutt felt that he could insist that

> *only two paths* are therefore open before present society . . . the alternative of Fascism or Communism . . . . [The] dream of a third alternative is in fact illusory. . . . present society is ripe, is rotten ripe for the social revolution . . . . But if the social revolution is delayed, then *Fascism becomes inevitable* . . . because Fascism is only a form, a means of capitalist class rule in conditions of extreme decay.

Since the "development of the productive forces has rendered the old class-society obsolete" there are "two alternatives, *and only two,* [confronting] existing society . . . . One is to throttle the development of the productive forces in order to save class society . . . . This is the path which finds its most complete and organized expression in Fascism. The other is to organize the productive forces for the whole society by abolishing the class ownership of the means of production, and building up the classless communist society . . . ." The "only alternative" to Fascism is the "socialist revolution." "Those who hesitate at the issue of the socialist revolution," Dutt ominously reminded us, "will do well to ponder closely this *inevitable final alterna-*

tive . . . ." "Fascism . . . becomes *inevitable* if the working class follows the line of reformism . . . ." [29]

Dutt produced, in effect, a partially formalized social science theory calculated to explain the "essence" of Fascism. As such it contained unrestricted generalizations that could be deployed over an entire universe of phenomena: the capitalist productive system. These generalizations were linked through partial axiomatization and informal logic to generate explanations of historic phenomena and provide low level predictions, hedged by vague time qualifiers, about the future. The advent and successes of fascism in Italy and Germany were explained, and predictions were tendered about the development of fascism in England, France, and the United States where, unless there was a "communist social revolution," the descent into fascism was, at some time or another, "inevitable."

With this kind of theoretical and conceptual machinery at his disposal, Dutt proceeded to explain Italian Fascism —his paradigmatic instantial case. Italy, according to Dutt, because it was afflicted with only an inadequately developed industrial system, suffered the mortal contradictions of capitalism in exaggerated form. Without the supplements provided by the superprofits available to privileged capitalist states, Italian capitalism was forced to seek recourse to Fascism before any other community.

Italy, according to Dutt, was "ripe" for the communist revolution in 1918–1920. "The communist revolution was fully possible in Italy in September 1920" and was only prevented by "the reformist leadership." The bourgeoisie "calculated on the reformist socialist leadership to break the revolutionary offensive" while at the same time "the big

------

[29] Ibid., pp. viii, ix, x, xi, 15, 24ff., 86, 228ff., 286 (emphasis supplied).

landlords, the big industrialists and the big financiers . . .
maintained [Fascism] in funds and finally placed it in
power." ". . . [The] so-called Fascist 'revolution' . . . was
in fact carried through from start to finish by the bourgeois
dictatorship from above." Fascism, and Mussolini himself,
were the simple and pliant "instruments" of "finance capital." [30] Fascism was the

> weapon of finance-capital, utilising the support of the mid-
> dle-class, of the slum proletariat and of demoralized
> working-class elements against the organized working-
> class, but throughout acting as the instrument and effective
> representative of the interests of finance-capital . . . .
> Fascism, in short, is a movement of mixed elements, domi-
> nantly petit-bourgeois, but also slum proletarian and de-
> moralized working class, financed and directed by finance-
> capital, by the big industrialists, landlords and financiers
> to defeat the working-class revolution and smash the work-
> ing-class organizations . . . . [Fascism, thus,] discloses it-
> self as a terrorist dictatorship of big capital.[31]

Once ensconced, Fascism creates a social system that
services the needs of declining capitalism: overall production declines, industrial production languishes, the growth of
fixed capital assets is restricted, the national income is
eroded, unemployment becomes pandemic, social services
are reduced. The entire system winds down to a "lower technical and economic level" to satisfy the requirements of
retrogressive capitalism. The forces of production are fet-
tered by productive relations that have become obsolete.[32]
This is the simple and predictive consequence of Fascism's

---

[30] Ibid., pp. 79ff., 99, 101, 106, 189n.; cf. p. 95.

[31] Ibid., pp. 77, 82, 89.

[32] Ibid., pp. 193, 206ff.

obligation to the "heads of finance-capital" who are its "actual paymasters and controllers." For "Fascism is solely a tactical method of finance capital." [33]

The "big capitalists" had suborned the reformist labor leaders, they had given Giovanni Giolitti, the prime minister of Italy, the "task" of demoralizing the working class, and had "directed" the constabulary, the magistracy, and the military to aid and abet Fascist organization, mobilization, and violence. All this was done with the "calculated" and "fully rational" intention of reducing Italy to a "barbarous state" in order to defend their class privileges. Finance-capitalists gave "orders" that were abjectly obeyed; leaders of governments became their "puppets." Since the interstitial classes have "no independent role," they were (since they were not captured by the organized working class movement) "sharply affected . . . by all the operations of finance-capital . . . . They [became] easy prey for the demagogic propaganda of finance-capital." [34]

Since the thesis, at critical junctures, is informal at best, it is often difficult to state explicitly what specific claims Dutt is actually making. For example, Dutt moves artlessly from talking about the "big bourgeoisie," "the leaders of capitalism," "the big landholders, big industrialists and financiers," to "monopoly capitalists," and then to "finance-capital" as though the reference class to which all these expressions referred was substantially the same, if not denotatively identical. We are told that the "leaders of capitalism" govern political developments. Then we are told that the "big landholders, big industrialists and financiers . . . place Fascism in power." Then we are told that Fascism is

---

[33] Ibid., p. 178.

[34] Ibid., pp. 254, 255, 273.

the "terrorist dictatorship of big capital." Alternatively, it is the "instrument" or the "weapon" of "finance capital." [35]

It seems relatively clear that for Dutt, the "middle" and "petty" bourgeoisie have no independent political role to play. What is not immediately clear is whether the "big industrialists," the "big landholders," or the "monopoly capitalists" have any degree of autonomy. There seems to be an assumption buried in Dutt's prose that "finance capital" is, in some unspecified sense, the *ultimate arbiter* in all the political maneuverings of the entire "bourgeoisie." This assumption seems to be borrowed uncritically from Lenin's "Imperialism" in which we are informed that in the circumstances of "monopoly capitalism," banking institutions no longer serve as "modest middlemen," but become powerful combines that have "at their command almost the whole of the money capital of *all* the capitalists . . . ." As a consequence, "scattered capitalists are transformed into *a single collective capitalist*" and the banks "*subordinate to their will* all the operations . . . of the *whole capitalist society*." [36] Whatever else can be said for this notion, it is obviously the missing premise in Dutt's argument.

Society is faced with only two alternatives: Fascism or Communism. This is because—given the contemporary decay of capitalism—there are only two significant social and political forces: finance capital on the one hand, and the organized working class under the direction of the Communist party on the other. The Communist party leadership is the cool, calculating, and eminently rational agent in mobilizing society for the Communist revolution and the mo-

----

[35] Cf. for example, ibid., pp. 75, 77, 79ff., 80, 81, 82, 84, 85, 86.

[36] V. I. Lenin, "Imperialism: The Highest Stage of Capitalism." In James Conner, ed., *Lenin: On Politics and Revolution* (Pegasus, 1968), pp. 121, 123 (emphasis supplied).

guls of finance capital are the cool, calculating, and eminently rational protagonists in mobilizing Fascism.

Nowhere in his book does Dutt attempt an analysis that might provide empirical support for the claim that "finance capital" dominated Italian industry, trade, or agriculture during the period prior to, during or after World War I. As a matter of fact, Italian banking institutions were understood to have so little influence over Italian economic life that the first theoreticians with whom we have been concerned—Aquila and Zetkin—construed Fascism to have been a victory of "industrial capital" *over* "agrarian and finance capital." Dutt, without having inspected the Italian economic system, simply uncritically accepted what had by that time become an article of "Marxist-Leninist" faith: *finance capital* dominates contemporary capitalism.

The fact is that banking institutions in Italy during the first decades of the twentieth century were, in and of themselves, in no position to significantly influence either the Italian economy or Italian political life. With the advent of World War I, it was *heavy industry* that enjoyed an impressive rate of growth, which in turn permitted industrialists to buy into the public stock of financial establishments and thereby acquire a decisive influence over the operations of the major banking institutions of the peninsula.[37] Italian industrialists had organized into an effective confederation as early as 1906, and by 1910 the Italian Confederation of Industry (*Confindustria*) was the best organized capitalist interest group in the country. Between 1918 and 1919 the industrialists of *Confindustria* attempted to bring together, under one organizational structure, all the major capitalist interest groups—agriculture, banking, commerce and indus-

----

[37] Cf. L. Salvatorelli and G. Mira, *Storia d'Italia nel periodo fascista* (Einaudi, 1964), p. 40.

try—but the project foundered on mutual rivalries and antagonisms.[38] Banking interests organized themselves separately and throughout the Fascist period remained peripheral to the main currents in Italian economic and political life.

We have, in effect, considerable empirical evidence that indicates that "finance capital" could not have conceivably served as the *principal* conspirator in Dutt's scenario. Moreover the same evidence suggests that the "capitalist class" was, in no sense, homogeneous in its interests, its loyalties, or its political preferences.

In point of fact, Dutt's entire interpretive effort was largely unsuccessful. His central thesis concerning the "inherent fatal contradiction" in capitalism between the forces of production and productive relations—that is to say, capitalism's inability after 1914 to further develop productive capabilities because it could no longer profitably distribute its commodities—has shown itself to be hopelessly wide of the mark. The spectacular economic development that has characterized the capitalist countries since World War II indicates that whatever capitalism was suffering after 1914, it was not its *final* crisis. But more than that, Dutt's predictions concerning the "winding down" of Fascist Italy's productive plant and its predictable pandemic unemployment were disconfirmed early and significantly. By the mid-thirties, it was evident that Fascist Italy had enjoyed a steady rate of economic growth, and in some sectors had made quite spectacular gains. The total volume of agricultural production, for example, rose during the Fascist period from the base index of 100 in 1922 to 147.8 in 1937, while population growth was indexed at 100 in 1922 and rose to only

----

[38] Cf. R. Sarti, *Fascism and the Industrial Leadership in Italy: 1919–1940* (University of California Press, 1971), pp. 11ff.

111.1 in 1937. Quite spectacular gains were made in the production of wheat. By 1937, Italy was producing 15.5 quintals of wheat per hectare while it had produced 9.5 quintals per hectare in 1922. For the first time in its modern history, Italy was producing enough wheat for its domestic population. Again using 1922 as a base index of 100, the aggregate indices of industrial production in Italy show almost universal advances. There was improvement in every major industry with the general index rising to 182.2 in 1934. The metallurgical, building, automotive, aircraft, textile, and hydroelectrical generating industries all showed marked advances. "As these figures indicate, Italy . . . made considerable progress in the expansion of some of her industries during [the Fascist period]." [39]

The standardized figures that became available after World War II indicate that Fascist Italy more than kept pace with the economic rates of growth of more resource-favored capitalist countries, and in some areas showed quite significant superiority. By 1938 (Fascism's last full peacetime year), using 1913 as a benchmark, the index of aggregate volume of output for Fascist Italy was 153.8. This compared more than favorably with that of France, which stood at 109.4, and with Germany, whose index stood at 149.9. By 1938, the aggregate index for output per man stood at 145.2 for Fascist Italy and 136.5 for France, 122.4 for Germany, 143.6 for the United Kingdom, and 136.0 for the United States. The aggregate index for output per man hour stood at 191.1 for Fascist Italy in 1938 and at 178.5 for France, 137.1 for Germany, and 167.9 for the United Kingdom.

Clearly, Fascist Italy did not "suppress" or "restrict" the forces of production, nor did it "stabilize" at the level of

----

[39] W. Welk, *Fascist Economic Policy* (Harvard, 1938), p. 200; cf. pp. 191–205.

"simple reproduction of capital." By 1938, in Fascist Italy, 15.9 percent of the gross national product was employed in fixed asset formation as compared to the 11.5 percent of the United Kingdom, and the 14 percent of the United States. Nor could Fascist Italy be adequately characterized as a country in which unemployment was pandemic. Throughout the Fascist period unemployment never exceeded 5.9 percent of the total work force, while the corresponding figures for the same year (1932) were 14.8 percent in Germany, 11.7 percent in the United Kingdom, and 24.7 percent in the United States.[40]

Given Italy's total lack of essential resources, the absence of fossil fuels, iron ore, and critical minerals, the Fascist performance could hardly be characterized as a "winding down" to a "lower technical and productive level." Nor could the system be characterized as one of "pandemic unemployment." If the "calculating" capitalist conspirators who "controlled and directed" Fascism were compelled by the inherent laws of capitalism to "wind down" the economic system, they seem to have failed. If "decaying" capitalism requires a "suppression" of the productive forces, and the magnates of "finance capital" engineer a system to effect that "suppression," they seem to have been singularly unsuccessful in Fascist Italy.

But more than that, Dutt's entire account of the advent of Fascism is at best a caricature of the actual political and historical sequence. To suggest that Fascism was "financed, controlled and directed" by "big capitalists," the "big landlords," the "big industrialists," or "finance capital" is a simplism that hardly merits analysis. We know that Mussolini received subventions from agrarian and industrial interests in their efforts to contain and neutralize the revolutionary

----

[40] Angus Maddison, *Economic Growth in the West* (Twentieth Century Fund, 1964), Appendices A, E, H, I.

socialist movement. But we also know that Mussolini assidu-
ously maintained his political independence. While he cul-
tivated support from a variety of entrenched interests, he
maintained an independent political posture. That Fascism
received the passive or active support of the constabulary,
the magistrature, and the military was a consequence, as we
have seen, not of a "capitalist conspiracy," but of the fact
that the socialists had succeeded in alienating almost everyone by 1920. They had defamed the military, attacked and
abused war veterans. They had stigmatized the constabulary
as the "venal agents of the bourgeoisie." They had made a
public display of their contempt for the "petty bourgeoisie"
—the professionals, the intellectuals, small landholders,
shopkeepers, artisans—all the "parasitic and nonproductive
interstitial" strata. Moreover, large sections of the working
class itself were disillusioned by socialist strategies. It is not
necessary to invoke obscure notions about a "conspiracy"
and a "finance capitalist" high command to explain the
passive or active support Fascist squads received after the
high wave of "proletarian" revolutionary activity had crested
in 1920.[41]

Flaws in the "Finance Capitalist" Theory

Even if one were to grant a more generous interpretation of
Dutt's account and substitute the "big industrialists" for his
"finance capitalists" his candidate explanation remains un-

---

[41] In this regard cf. Angelo Tasca, *Nascita e avento del fascismo* (La
Nuova Italia, 1950), pp. 513–525; De Felice, *Mussolini il rivoluzionario*,
chap. 14, *Mussolini il fascista: la conquista del potere*, chaps. 1–4; M.
Missiroli, *Il fascismo e il colpo di stato dell' Ottobre 1922* (Cappelli,
1966); R. Michels, "Elemente zur Entstehungsgeschichte des italienischen
Faschismus (1922)," *Sozialismus und Faschismus in Italien* (Meyer &
Jensen, 1925).

convincing. We know that Italian industrialists interacted with Fascism from a position of strength, and we also know that their interests and the interests of the Fascists coincided at critical and broad junctures. But all the evidence we now have at our disposal indicates that the industrialists were never able to "control" much less "direct" Fascism. Fascism frequently, if not regularly, compensated the organized industrialists of Italy for their submission to Fascist control, but the evidence clearly indicates that business interests were tied and subordinate to Fascist political priorities. Fascism's political priorities often prevailed over capitalist interest when a choice had to be made.[42] Not only did Mussolini sometimes sacrifice business and financial interests when it served Fascism's political purpose, but he did not hesitate to dismiss, and in significant instances exile, influential business leaders in whom he had no confidence. Mussolini's alliance with business, agrarian or financial interests seems to have been based on political considerations.[43] This was particularly true with respect to foreign policy where Mussolini operated with almost absolute independence.[44]

---

[42] The thesis that Fascism was a "tool" of the industrial capitalists is one that was, as we have seen, advanced by Aquila and Zetkin. In the thirties it was similarly argued by some "Trotskyists"; cf. D. Guerin, *Fascism and Big Business* (Pioneer, 1939). Sarti's book provides a good counterweight to this form of "Marxist" interpretation. Much of the material in the detailed historical accounts provided by Renzo De Felice perform the same service.

[43] The best evidence for this kind of behavior is afforded by a careful scrutiny of Fascist practice in cases directly involving issues like the "pegging" of the Italian lira at an artificially high international rate—in defense of Italian "prestige" and at considerable disadvantage to very specific "capitalist" interests. Cf. De Felice, *Mussolini il fascista: l'organizzazione dello stato fascista* (Finaudi, 1968), chap. 3.

[44] Cf. G. Ciano, *Ciano's Hidden Diary: 1937–1938* (Dutton, 1953), *The Ciano Diaries: 1939–1943* (Doubleday, 1946); cf. also G. Rumi, *Alle origini della politica estera fascista* (Laterza, 1968); L. Villari, *Italian Foreign Policy Under Mussolini* (Devin-Adair, 1956).

Mussolini was prepared to grant that if Italy were to be a "great nation" it must *maximize production*. This was a political and economic reality recognized by Mussolini as early as 1918.[45] When the socialists gave ample evidence of not being able to continue production in the occupied factories at the end of 1920, Mussolini was clearly prepared to admit that his political goals could only be served by allying himself with the "entrepreneurial" or "productive" bourgeoisie.

Given his productivist bias, and the failure of the socialist occupation of productive plant, Mussolini was prepared to ally himself with those agrarian and industrial interests that could defend and "maximize production." [46] From that point on there was an alliance of convenience between Fascism and the heterogeneous interests that Marxists identify loosely with "capitalism." In the course of the relationship, the "bourgeoisie" was forced to submit to Fascist political domination—for which they were compensated by a neutralization of "revolutionary" threats from below and impressive profit rates that they were, in turn, compelled to reinvest in enterprises calculated to serve Fascism's developmental and political purposes. Fascism's adventures in Ethiopia, the Balkans, and Spain, and finally the catastrophic involvement in World War II, were only part of the price paid for partnership in the alliance. These adventures often were undertaken over the express objections of significant sections of the "possessing classes." In each instance, Mussolini's will prevailed and the "economic elites" had to

----

[45] Cf. Gregor, *The Ideology of Fascism* (Free Press, 1969), pp. 147–149, 161–163, 180.

[46] Cf. Mussolini, "Atto di nascita del fascismo," *Opera omnia* (La Fenice, 1953), 12: 327; "Per una economia di massimo produzione," Postulati del programma fascista (May, 1920). In De Felice, *Mussolini il rivoluzionario,* p. 747.

content themselves with whatever compensations were forth-coming.

Revising the "Standard Version"

All this was not completely lost on postwar Marxist-Leninist theoreticians. By the end of World War II, it was all but universally recognized that the official Soviet version of Fascism was hopelessly impaired. Marxist-Leninists began discretely to jettison whole segments of the account and extensively to modify the remainder, until by the end of the sixties a far different version began to gain currency. By 1970 we were provided a significantly different "Revised Standard Version."

Throughout the three decades that stretched from the mid-thirties to the mid-sixties, few serious Marxist scholars were content with the official Marxist-Leninist standard version of Fascism. Through the thirties a number of reasonably independent Marxist scholars attempted to formulate interpretations of Fascism that bore more relationship to political reality. August Thalheimer, an "opposition" member of the Communist party of Germany, insisted as early as 1930 that Fascism could be most coherently construed as an *autonomous* mass-mobilizing political movement that arose in social and economic circumstances that found the "bour-geoisie" incapable of ruling effectively. The Fascist movement protected the *economic* and *social* position of the bour-geoisie, but it arrogated to itself *political* power.[47] Arthur Rosenberg, in turn, accepted the principal outlines of the standard version, but insisted that the "task" of Fascism

---

[47] August Thalheimer, "Ueber den Faschismus." In W. Abendroth, ed., *Faschismus und Kapitalismus* (Europaeische Verlagsanstalt, 1967), pp. 19–38.

(naturally at the behest of industrial and finance capital) was to "further develop the productive forces of Italy." He insisted that the clear evidence was that Fascism had "systematically spurred" development in heavy industry, in chemicals, automotive and aircraft industries, and the maritime trade.[48] Rather than "winding down" productive enterprise, *Fascism had created conditions for its acceleration.*

Otto Bauer, in 1936, insisted that Fascism constituted too strong a force to be contained by the established elites. It could not, in effect, be employed as "a simple tool of the bourgeoisie." "Fascism," he argued "grew over the heads of the capitalist classes." The bourgeoisie imagined that they could domesticate Fascism, but Fascism extended its power over all classes on the peninsula. Bauer did insist that, ultimately, Fascism came to terms with the capitalist elites, but he also indicated that the confluence of interest between Fascism and its non-Fascist allies was at best temporary and partial. The foreign policy of Fascism, for example, must necessarily work against the vested interests of broad segments of the capitalist class. It is clear that for Bauer, the relationship between Fascism and the possessing classes was far more complex than anything suggested in the standard version.[49]

Perhaps the most significant variation in this general tradition was expressed in the essay by Franz Borkenau in 1933.[50] Borkenau denied that conditions in Italy in 1920 were "ripe" for socialist revolution. He insisted that in an

---

[48] Arthur Rosenberg, "Der Faschismus als Massenbewegung." In Abendroth, ed., *Faschismus und Kapitalismus,* p. 114.

[49] Otto Bauer, "Der Faschismus," in Abendroth, ed., *Faschismus und Kapitalismus,* pp. 143–167, particularly 151, 153, 156, 162.

[50] Franz Borkenau, "Zur Soziologie des Faschismus." In Nolte, ed., *Theorien ueber den Faschismus,* pp. 156–181.

"objective sense" the demands raised by the maximalists and the Leninists in the Italian situation were "reactionary." What Italy required after the termination of World War I was not proletarian revolution, but a rapid increase in over-all productivity. The wage demands and the ill-conceived political innovations demanded by the working class augured ill for the weakened economy of postwar Italy. What Italy required was a control on nonproductive consumption so that available assets could be devoted to basic industrial growth and agricultural modernization—a transfer from nonproductive consumption to productive fixed assets. Italy required an increased "tempo of accumulation," a period of intensive "primitive accumulation," that was the precondi-tion of a drive to industrial and agricultural maturity. Fas-cism, Borkenau insisted, was alive with a modernizing fervor typified by the presence in its ranks of the Futurists, who were machine fetishists, and the technical bourgeoisie who advocated a rapid growth in the industrial potential of the peninsula. Fascism was not the tool of industrial or finance capital. *Fascism created the preconditions for, and fostered, the development of industry.* The industrial and finance cap-italists were, in fact, Fascism's *creatures* rather than its *crea-tors.* Fascism performed its "historic function": *it multiplied industrial production.* Electrification was undertaken and rapidly expanded. The automotive and textile industry flour-ished. The communications system was expanded and ra-tionalized. The banking system was centralized and rendered efficient. The independence of the traditionalist agrarian financial interests of the south was compromised. Agricul-ture was modernized and extensive road-building and land-reclamation undertaken. To accomplish all that, the defense capabilities of organized labor had to be broken, wages kept at a minimum to permit the rapid accumulation of in-vestment capital, and collective enthusiasm kept at a high salience to sustain the intensive labor output required by modernization.[51] Fascism, in Borkenau's judgment, was *a mass-mobilizing developmental dictatorship under one party auspices*. It was a "transitional" form of rule developed in an environment suffering thwarted industrial development and agricultural stagnation.

After World War II works emanating from the Soviet Union continued to talk of Fascism as the "tool" of "capitalism," and the postwar *Brief Philosophical Dictionary* continued to speak of Fascism as the "open terroristic dictatorship of finance capital," [52] but it became quite clear that the insistence was more feigned than convinced.

The "Revised Standard Version"

By 1965 Soviet commentators could lament that the negative influence of the Stalin "cult of personality" had forced the discussion of Fascism to assume a contentious and abstract character with efforts to "schematize reality" and "replace concrete study" with the "repetition of this or that general resolution of the Communist International . . . ." [53]

----

[51] Cf. ibid., particularly pp. 164, 165, 178.

[52] M. Rosenthal and P. Yudin, eds., *A Dictionary of Philosophy* (Progress Publishers, 1967), p. 158; cf. also G. Klaus and M. Buhr, eds., *Philosophisches Woerterbuch* (VEB, 1966), p. 191. For treatments by Soviet theoreticians immediately after World War II, cf. S. M. Slobodskoi, *Storia del fascismo* (Riuniti, 1962) originally published in Moscow in 1945. A German edition appeared as *Der italienische Faschismus und sein Zusammenbruch* in 1948; also I. Fetscher, "Faschismus und Nationalsozialismus." *Politische Vierteljahresschrift,* 1962, 3/1: 43, n. 2.

[53] Boris Lopukhov, "Il problema del fascismo italiano negli scritti di autori sovietici." *Studi storici,* 1965, 6/2: 255.

Finally, in 1970 Alexander Galkin published an account of Fascism that now constitutes an official Soviet "Revised Standard Version." [54] In the newly revised version we find that Fascism arose, not as a consequence of the *final or general* crisis of capitalism, but rather as a consequence of only "*one* of its severest crises." Fascism is no longer conceived of as the swan song of "decaying capitalism"—it is the product of capitalism in but one of its crises. Under crisis conditions the standard methods of bourgeois rule lose "their former efficiency." In the crisis that followed World War I, capitalism required more modern techniques to husband its growth to a "new level": that of "state monopoly capitalism." The Fascists had to neutralize the working class opposition and mobilize energies to "carry out changes meeting the interests of the ruling class."

For Galkin there is no intrinsic reason why capitalism must traverse Fascism in order to attain this new socioeconomic and political level. In fact, the "ruling classes" of many nations have found ways of making the transit without abandoning "one or another form of bourgeois democracy." It is not, Galkin insisted, a question of "a fatal inevitability, but a variant of the way of development." Fascism was, in effect, one form of modernizing movement, and it succeeded in carrying Italy from one economic stage to the next. Moreover, in the revised version, Fascism arose as an autonomous movement, in circumstances of special crisis, and only subsequently did the "ruling circles" recognize that it might serve their interests. The fact that Fascism had an independent origin did pose problems for the "ruling class" because while Fascism "met the interests of the ruling class and its upper crust as a whole," it "inevitably entailed the

----

[54] A. Galkin, "Capitalist Society and Fascism." *Social Sciences: USSR Academy of Sciences*, 1970, 2.

infringement of the concrete interests of its separate representatives and entire factions." Not only that, but as Fascism extended its bureaucratic controls over the economic
system, "the settlement of questions which for centuries were
the prerogative of the big capitalists, in some measure was
becoming the function of the state bureaucratic agencies."
Power was concentrated in the hands of the Fascist leadership and consequently "the handing over of power [by the
monopolies] to the Fascists implied at the same time subor-
dination to the regime . . . ." Furthermore, "since the
transfer of leadership implied a change in the form of power
it inevitably led to a reconstruction and, in a number of
cases, to a break-up of the old party political mechanism.
This ran counter to the intrinsic conservatism of the bourgeoisie and dictated renunciation of its former political sym-
pathies and ties." All this meant that the "bourgeoisie," composed as it was of heterogeneous interests, frequently found
itself suffering "inconveniences and at times tangible losses."
Given these conflicts, the ruling class afforded Fascism no
more, at times, than "friendly neutrality."

The movement that was for Palme Dutt retrogressive in
essence—devoted to "winding down" the productive processes in Italy, paid for, controlled, directed, and placed into
power by "finance-capital"—has become, for contemporary
Soviet Marxist-Leninists, a modernizing movement that
arose spontaneously, and which enjoyed considerable political autonomy. The movement that in the standard version
had been the simple lackey of finance-capital is now conceived capable of violating the interests and outraging the
conservatism of the "ruling class." The "finance-capitalists,"
which the standard version considered to be the prime mov-
ers of the Fascist drama, have disappeared into a vague and
omnibus "ruling class" that does not dominate, but insures
Fascism a "friendly neutrality."

Years ago Paolo Alatri, an Italian Marxist-Leninist, warned that one must abandon the "mechanical" and "rigid" interpretation of Fascism. Moreover, he insisted that it was absurd to suggest that the world faced only two alternatives, either the "proletarian revolution" or "Fascism." Fascism was only *one* form of "antiproletarian reaction." Moreover, Alatri insisted, "no one could dream of thinking that Mussolini was purely and simply the executor of the directives of Italian industrialists." Mussolini was, in fact, "the absolute master of Italy." [55] In his anticipation of the now standard revised version, the "finance capitalists" made only a fleeting appearance. It was the omnibus "ruling classes," not the "finance capitalists," that conspired with Fascism, and even they were "deluded" into believing that Fascism could be domesticated. Moreover, Fascism operated from a position of strength in Italy, because "in reality the objective conditions for the [proletarian] revolution had not yet been realized." [56]

In 1971, much of this came together in Reinhard Kuehnl's faithful German rendering of the revised standard Soviet interpretation of generic fascism.[57] Kuehnl does not seem disposed to go quite as far as Galkin on some issues, but he does grant that fascism did create a "qualitatively new" form of political structure, one of whose functions was to maintain a high profit rate for industrial and agricultural enterprise[58] a guarded and elliptic way of saying that the fascist state provided an attractive environment for investment opportunities that resulted in considerable industrial

----

[55] Alatri, *Le origini del fascismo* (Riuniti, 1963), pp. xv, xxi, 264.

[56] Ibid., pp. 24, 108.

[57] R. Kuehnl, *Formen buergerlicher Herrschaft: Liberalismus-Faschismus* (Rowohlt, 1971).

[58] Ibid., pp. 123ff.

expansion and agricultural modernization. Capitalists did not, after all, squirrel away profits in their mattresses. Kuehnl grants that the fascists did set the "economy once more in motion"—by maintaining an attractive investment climate, but also through large-scale public enterprises—a weak echo, perhaps, of what Galkin calls Fascism's "social philanthropy." [59]

Kuehnl's account is largely a reaffirmation of Galkin's. For our purposes the latest version that has come out of the Soviet bloc environment is more interesting. In the summer of 1972, *Telos* published a chapter of an as yet unpublished manuscript by Mihaly Vajda, a Researcher for the Hungarian Academy of Science in Budapest. [60]

While Palme Dutt remains unnamed in Vajda's account, it is clear that in inveighing against the "Stalinist" interpretation of Fascism, he is indicting its principal theoretician. Vajda argues, as a case in point, that any suggestion that there is a "typical trend in the history of bourgeois society which leads from democracy to [Fascist] dictatorship . . ." is mistaken. Vajda insists that bourgeois democracy can effectively negotiate the transition to a qualitatively new "regulated economy" without fascism in whatever form. For Vajda, as for Galkin, Fascism constituted a singular effort to resolve the *developmental* problems of capitalism under special crisis conditions. Vajda states that Fascism was possible in Italy not because capitalism was strong, but rather because it was weak. Italy had, in fact, only begun its modernization. Given Italy's retarded economic development, the demands of the Italian labor movement were, in Vajda's judgment, "overtly reactionary"—they "hindered

---

[59] Ibid.

[60] M. Vajda, "The Rise of Fascism in Italy and Germany." *Telos,* 1972, 12: 3026.

the development of the [Italian] economy." Fascism, with its clearly industrial biases, offered the weak industrial bourgeois a powerful political ally that might accomplish their ends: *the rapid industrialization of the peninsula.* Italian Fascism, in Vajda's account, "remained the only progressive solution" to the crisis of Italy's underdevelopment. "The progressive function of Italian Fascism," Vajda maintained, "consisted in the capitalization of the economy . . . . In Italy the defense of democracy against Fascism from the position of proletarian democracy was reactionary since the alternative between bourgeois democracy and Fascism was one between economic stagnation and economic development." [61]

In effect Vajda's account, coupled with those of Galkin and Kuehnl, provides a revised standard version that is critically different from the standard version of the ,Stalinist period. Vajda has, in effect, completely rehabilitated the version provided by the "unorthodox" Franz Borkenau in the early thirties.[62] While Fascism still, somehow, serves the "historic interests of capitalism"—its overt features are clearly "progressive" and, in a critical sense, "revolutionary." What is most interesting about this revised standard version is the effort made by its protagonists to force this modified version into a more "orthodox" "Marxist" framework.

Galkin, Kuehnl, and Vajda admit that generic fascism was very threatening to traditional capitalist elites, wresting from their hands the "settlement of questions that for centuries" had been their prerogative. They all grant, explicitly or implicitly, that the "bourgeoisie," in "handing over . . . power to the fascists" had, at the same time, "subordinated"

---

[61] Ibid., pp. 5ff., 11ff., 13.

[62] See Vajda's direct references, "The Rise of Fascism," pp. 10, 12.

itself to the regime.[63] But irrespective of the fact that the "bourgeoisie" no longer can exercise its prerogatives in decision making and must subordinate itself to the Fascist regime, the regime remains for Galkin, Kuehnl, and Vajda a "form of bourgeois rule"! Even though generic fascism "ran counter to the intrinsic conservativism of the bourgeoisie," [64] fascism was, nonetheless, "bourgeois." Even though Italian Fascism had so much "autonomy" that Mussolini was "absolute master" of the peninsula, there remains the insistence that Fascism somehow served the interests of the "big bourgeoisie." Even though there is a careful documentation of the use of political coercion and ultimately the use of terror against individuals and whole segments of the "big bourgeoisie," we are still expected to accept the judgment that Fascism, nonetheless, served their "collective interests." With friends like the Fascists, it would seem that capitalism would have little use for enemies.

The contemporary interpretation of Fascism emanating from official Soviet Marxist-Leninist sources is a curious product indeed. Generic fascism no longer appears as the unqualifiedly "reactionary" or "conservative" movement that official Soviet Marxism-Leninism regularly identified as such in the prewar literature. Fascism now has clearly "progressive" features and, in some critical respects, "revolutionary" functions. That it is still somehow identified with the "interests" of the "ruling class" is an unpersuasive effort to maintain the semblance of continuity between the first and the revised standard versions.

Moreover, in Vajda's account the "historic functions" of Italian Fascism and National Socialism are rather emphatically distinguished. Neither Galkin nor Kuehnl draw

---

[63] Galkin, "Capitalist Society and Fascism," p. 130.

[64] Ibid.

the distinction, but in Vajda's exposition the "progressive function of Italian Fascism consisted in the capitalization of the economy—something that German Fascism could not have done since between the two wars Germany was already the third strongest capitalist power in the world." [65]

The interpretation of Fascism as a consequence of class struggle has had a long and checkered career. As an interpretation it never attained the level of reasonably rigorous "theory"—as "theory" is understood in contemporary social science. The closest it ever came to being a "theory" was in the partially formalized and articulated account provided by Palme Dutt in his effort to lend substance to the Stalinist characterization of fascism as the "terroristic tool of finance-capital." In this form the "theory" was transparently incompetent. Since World War II, Soviet theoreticians have been trying to come to grips with some of the political and economic realities of the interwar period. What has resulted has been a searching reappraisal of their own views—and while they seem to remain constrained by a collection of apparently irrepressible preconceptions, they have displayed a quite remarkable degree of flexibility. Recognizing the disabilities under which theory construction labors in highly ideologized environments, it is gratifying to recognize the gradual convergence of views represented in such works as Vajda's and that of non-Marxist theoreticians in the West.

In the immediate past any number of Western scholars have suggested that Italian Fascism might well be understood in the context of the national problems generated by thwarted or delayed industrialization. [66] Contemporary dis-

---

[65] Vajda, "The Rise of Fascism in Italy and Germany," p. 13.

[66] In this regard cf. A. F. K. Organski, *The Stages of Political Development* (Knopf, 1965), "Fascism and Modernization." In S. J. Woolf, ed., *The Nature of Fascism* (Random House, 1969); M. Matossian

cussants who suggest that "Marxist" notions concerning fascism have little to contribute to the interpretation of fascism, particularly Italian Fascism, as an episode in contemporary modernization and industrialization[67] are in error. In Vajda's judgment,

> Under Fascist rule, Italy underwent rapid capitalist development with the electrification of the whole country, the blossoming of automobile and silk industries, the creation of an up-to-date banking system, the prospering of agriculture, the reclaiming of substantial agricultural areas through the draining of marshlands, the construction of a considerable network of highways, etc. Italy's rapid progress after WWII and the fact that today it is already moving toward intensive capitalist development would have been unimaginable without the social processes begun during the Fascist period.[68]

Such judgments are all but indistinguishable from similar ones advanced by Ludovico Garruccio who conceives Italian Fascism to have been an exemplar of the class of developmental dictatorships under single party auspices.[69] In the case of the reinterpretation of Italian Fascism, what we may be witnessing is another instance of "convergence" between Soviet and Western thought. It may even mean that scholars in both East and West are prepared to embark upon a serious study of the entire fascist phenomenon. It is to some of those interpretations we can now turn.

"Ideologies of Delayed Industrialization." In J. H. Kautsky, ed., *Political Change in Underdeveloped Countries* (Wiley, 1962).

[67] H. A. Turner, "Fascism and Modernization." *World Politics,* 1972, 24: 549.

[68] Vajda, "The Rise of Fascism in Italy and Germany," pp. 12ff.

[69] Cf. L. Garruccio, *L'industrializzazione tra nazionalismo e rivoluzione* (Mulino, 1969).

CHAPTER SIX

Fascism as a Function of a Particular Stage of Economic Development

One of the most interesting, original, complex and confusing interpretations of Fascism that made its appearance after World War II is identified with the general notion of "stages of economic growth" or "development." Although there were clear intimations of this kind of analysis of Fascism during the interwar years, particularly in the work of men like Otto Bauer and Franz Borkenau, the conception of re-lating Fascism to a particular stage of economic, particu-larly industrial, growth matured only in the postwar period. That such an interpretation should have developed at this relatively late date is difficult to explain, particularly since Fascists consistently had identified the problem of modern-ization and industrialization as central to their social and political program. As early as 1919, Mussolini made the problem of production the sustaining "common interest which cancels and suppresses the class struggle." [1] One month before the founding of the *Fasci di Combattimento,* Mussolini outlined the tentative program of his "productive socialism" and insisted the program was "calculated to in-sure the progressive development of the nation." [2] In March 1919, at the founding meeting of the Fascist movement, he insisted that a revolutionary movement must bear in mind two irrepressible realities: "the reality of production and the reality of the nation." [3] The productivist theme became a predictable constant in all subsequent Fascist apologetics. As early as 1924, Sergio Panunzio insisted that Fascism was a "means" to the enhancement of national production. In 1930 Aldo Bertele argued that Fascist organization and

---

[1] Benito Mussolini, "Nel mondo sindacale Italiano," *Opera omnia* (La Fenice, 1953), XII: 250.

[2] "Conquiste e programmi," ibid., 245.

[3] "Atto di nascita del fascismo," ibid., p. 325.

strategy were calculated to produce "more intensive productive levels" in Italy, in order to insure "national strength." [4] In 1931 Nazareno Mezzetti asserted that "Italy's most urgent problem is one of production, rather than distribution . . . ." [5] Fascist insistence on the primacy of production was constant throughout the Fascist period. Fascists regularly characterized themselves as modernizers—as industrializers of a retarded economic system.

The general indisposition on the part of foreign commentators to take Fascist pronouncements seriously, the prevalence of more "popular" interpretations of Fascism, and the significant lack of concern with macroeconomic theories of growth (although some essentially "static" theories were available[6]), all probably contributed to the failure between the wars to attempt to grapple with the possibility that Fascism represented an attempt at the industrialization of a backward economy. It was only with the appearance of many new nations that followed the dissolution of the old colonial system that the problem of modernization and industrialization began to come into focus. The urgency of serious contemporary problems, the evident erosion of the credibility of prewar interpretations of Fascism, mutually influenced the development of an alternative candidate account.

----

[4] Aldo Bertele, *Aspetti ideologici del fascismo* (Druetto, 1930), p. 57.

[5] Nazareno Mezzetti, *Mussolini e la questione sociale* (Pinciana, 1931), p. 212.

[6] Cf. Y. S. Brenner, *Theories of Economic Development and Growth* (George Allen and Unwin, 1966), chap. 5.

Rostow and the Five Stages of Economic Growth

In 1952 W. W. Rostow published the first edition of his book, *The Process of Economic Growth*. Between 1953 and 1959 he enhanced his analysis with an outline of definable and general stages of growth.[7] In 1960 Rostow published a brief volume entitled *The Stages of Economic Growth*. His work, while clearly not immune to criticism,[8] did provide the schematic "working hypotheses" for several critically important works devoted to the interpretation of Fascism.

Rostow characterized his efforts as attempting "a theory of economic growth and a more general, if still highly partial, theory about modern history as a whole." [9] In his treatment he proceeded to offer "an impressionistic definition" of five major stages of growth that mark the transition from a traditional society, characterized by limited production functions, through successive stages until the stage is reached that is identified with the diffusion, on a mass basis, of durable consumer goods and consumer services. The five stages of growth that Rostow provides are given as:

1. Traditional society
2. A society in which the preconditions for economic "take-off" manifest themselves

----

[7] W. W. Rostow, *The Process of Economic Growth* (2nd ed., Norton, 1962), chap. 13.

[8] Pierre Bilar, "Développment historique et progrès social: les étapes et les critères." In *Crecimiento y desarollo* (Ariel, 1964).

[9] W. W. Rostow, *The Stages of Economic Growth* (Cambridge University Press, 1960), p. 1.

3. The "take-off" itself
4. Society in which there is a sustained drive toward maturity
5. A society that enjoys high mass consumption.

Each of these five stages is characterized by relatively specific, if dynamic and changing, traits. These traits concern themselves with demand, production and supply functions of economic systems at various levels of "maturity."

What Rostow attempted was a "dynamic theory of production . . . which focuses directly and in some detail on the composition of investment and on developments within particular sectors of the economy . . . ." Rostow proposed "a flexible, disaggregated theory of production," that would "isolate empirically" the stages of growth of specific economic systems.[10] He conceived the rate of expansion of such sectors of an economic system as having a direct and indirect influence in shaping and imparting overall momentum to the economy. The fact that, in each circumstance, some sectors of the economy are developing more rapidly than others provides the basis for characterizing economic development in terms of stages rather than in terms of a simple continuum. Given these considerations there is a recognition that differential sectoral development requires differential distribution of incomes, changes in the character of demand, and variability in disposable investment capital. Alterations in such allocations, income flow, demands, and rates of investment require, at least in part, *political decisions* that transcend traditional market processes. In surveying the broad and "impressionistic" stages of growth one is not examining only the subsectoral and sectoral development of different socioeconomic systems, but one catalogs a succession of strategic

---

[10] Rostow, *Process of Economic Growth*, pp. 397ff.

political decisions concerning how societies choose to allocate their resources. "While it is true that economic change has political and social consequence, economic change is, itself, viewed here as the consequence of political and social as well as narrowly economic forces. And in terms of human motivation, many of the most profound economic changes are viewed as the consequence of noneconomic human motives and aspirations." [11]

The First Stage

A traditional society, according to Rostow's schema (irrespective of changes in scale and patterns of trade, the level and fluctuations of agricultural output, population density, manufactures, and income) is one in which there exists a "productivity ceiling" that requires approximately seventy-five percent of the effective work force be occupied in *agrarian* pursuits. Whatever surplus such systems produced was devoted to nonproductive or low-productivity outlays: monuments, wars, the maintenance of decorative harems or liveried personnel. In general, such economic systems are devoid of any special understanding or control of their physical environment, and consequently are incapable of making technological invention a more or less regular and cumulative occurrence. The corresponding social and political structures of such traditional systems tended to be absolutistic, authoritarian, and hierarchical. For a variety of historical and social reasons such systems can, and do, enter into phased change. In the Western world the introduction of science, the age of maritime exploration and interdynastic competition threw traditional systems into crisis

----

[11] Rostow, *Stages of Economic Growth,* p. 2; *Process of Economic Growth,* p. 311.

and provoked sectoral and subsectoral differential development. Obviously, the conditions that generate systematic crisis vary from one historic and geographic circumstance to another. In the modern world traditional societies are severely shaken by the intrusion of more advanced economic systems. Central to the pervasive changes wrought by such factors is the reorganization of the productive community into a national state that provides not only for the effective accumulation of capital in the service of social overhead—provision for *general defense* and *public security,* the construction of *transportation* and *educational* systems, and so forth—but the consequent expansion of internal and external market.

The Second Stage

Once the preconditions for economic take-off have been met, the forces making for cumulative economic progress, which hitherto produced only limited and episodic yield, expand and begin to characterize the major part of society. Economic growth becomes a natural and self-sustaining process. One of the cardinal features of the take-off stage is a high rate of effective savings and investment. During this period *new industries* are generated and expand, yielding high profit rates which are, by and large, reinvested in new facilities. These new industries stimulate increased demands from urban workers and a subsequent proliferation of secondary industries. The entire process of expansion in the "modern sector" produces a self-sustaining rate of income in the hands of those "who not only save at high rates but place their savings at the disposal of those engaged in modern sector [i.e., industrial] activities." [12]

---

[12] Rostow, *Stages of Economic Growth,* p. 8.

The Third and Fourth Stages

An economy at the stage of take-off develops around a relatively narrow complex of industry and technology. As an economy develops industrial processes expand vertically and laterally—vertically to involve the entire processes of agricultural production and the extraction of natural resources—and laterally to incorporate all the processes of commodity production, their marketing and servicing. When this process is as complete as circumstances allow, a society has reached the stage of *economic maturity*. The process commences with an economic system that is characteristically agrarian and nonindustrial and ends with one that is fully industrialized. Rostow estimates that the time period between the commencement and terminus of this process is approximately sixty years. At the stage of economic maturity the society gives evidence of having the productive capacity, the technological and entrepreneurial skills, as well as the institutional structure, that permits it to produce anything it chooses or, within its resource limitations, it can produce. Society has effectively applied the range of available technology to the bulk of its resources.

The Fifth Stage

The final stage, the stage of high mass consumption, is that stage in which per capita income reaches a level which makes mass consumption of durable commodities a reality. It is a period characterized by a high rate of urbanization, an increased number of "nonproductive" workers in offices, schools and distributive industries. The society allocates an increased measure of social capital to welfare programs servicing dense urban populations and to efforts designed to maintain full employment.

The Political Consequences of Economic Growth

For our purposes it is important to note that each stage in the sequence of stages is marked by momentous political choices. Take-off, for example, is that period in the productive life of society during which there is approximately a ten percent annual rate of net investment. In order to sustain such a rate of investment a full range of transformations of social and political institutions is required. The relationship between the modern and traditional sectors of the economy have to be redefined. The income, traditionally in the hands of those members of traditional or agrarian sectors, must be shifted to those who will spend it on developing the communications and educational infrastructure and, ultimately, manufacturing plant. Only massive shifts in income distribution can effect a rise in the rate of investment in the modern sectors that regularly, substantially and perceptibly outstrips population growth and generates a self-sustaining process that marks the drive toward economic maturity. "In a generalized sense modernization takes a lot of working capital . . . . It is, therefore, an essential condition for a successful transition [to maturity] that investment be increased . . . ." [13]

A successful transition from a traditional society to one that enjoys industrial maturity is characterized by political developments that manifest themselves in a substitution of

----

[13] Ibid., pp. 21, 22.

political elites—a modernizing for a traditional elite. A modernizing elite can, in general, be characterized as a strategic and functional group of political actors who not only desire to achieve economic maturity, but who wish to "assert national independence . . . and are prepared to create an urban-based society." Such an elite has major technical tasks to perform.

> [It] must be capable of organizing the nation so that unified commercial markets develop; it must create and maintain a tax and fiscal system which diverts resources into modern uses, if necessary at the expense of the old rent-collectors; and it must lead the way through the whole spectrum of national policy—from tariffs to education and public health—toward the modernization of the economy and the society of which it is part . . . . [It] is the inescapable responsibility of the state to make sure the stock of social overhead capital required for take-off is built; and it is likely as well that only vigorous leadership from the central government can bring about those radical changes in the productivity of agriculture and the use of other natural resources whose quick achievement may also constitute a precondition for take-off.

After the initial phases of take-off have transpired, the modernizing elite must insure a fiscal and tax structure which "permits a high marginal rate of savings." Economic development is the result of shifting income from those who will spend less productively to those who will spend productively. The take-off stage is, in fact, characterized by shifting society's resources "away from consumption to profits." [14] Should the capital resources of society be so distributed as to achieve an improvement in the effective purchasing power of the general population in a relatively un-

---

[14] Ibid., pp. 30f., 39, 48.

derdeveloped economy, there is a disposition for these resources to dissipate themselves "nonproductively," by fostering the purchase of cheaper imported goods from more advanced economies. Foreigners would enjoy increased profit margins and the effective demand of the underdeveloped economy would serve to enhance the capabilities of the competitors of native industry.[15]

Fascism as an "Ideology of Delayed Industrialization"

The features that characterize the stages of self-sustaining industrial growth and the drive to economic maturity are of particular significance for the interpretation of Fascism, since political analysts have subsequently used them to explain some of the species properties of Mussolini's regime. Mary Matossian was among the first to explicitly identify Fascism as an "ideology of delayed industrialization." The qualifier "delayed" is important because Matossian indicates that economic systems that have developed during the twentieth century have had to face pervasive threats, imposing competition and frequent humiliation at the hands of more advanced economies.[16] An ideology of delayed industrialization is in large part the product of real and imagined threat, and a real sense of status deprivation. As a consequence such ideologies tend to be nationalistic, assertive, and revolutionary. They attempt to provide the motive energy, in highly charged emotional environments, for mass mobilization in the service of a revolutionary program of

----

[15] Brenner, *Theories of Economic Development,* p. 171.

[16] Mary Matossian, "Ideologies of Delayed Industrialization: Some Tensions and Ambiguities." In John Kautsky, ed., *Political Change in Underdeveloped Countries* (Wiley, 1962), pp. 252ff.

industrialization. In this general sense "Marxism-Leninism, Shintoism, Italian Fascism, Kemalism, Gandhism, the current Egyptian Philosophy of the Revolution, Sun Yat-sen's Three Principles of the People, the Indonesian Pantjasila, and many others" are members of the class of "ideologies of delayed industrialization." Whatever specific differences there are between and among them, they remain, nonetheless, members of the same political genus.

Matossian is aware that her effort at providing a "morphology" of such ideologies is "premature" and remains, at best, only an "indication" of where further probing might be productive.[17] The account provided by A. F. K. Organski in 1965 proceeds to attempt a "first approximation" of a "new theoretical framework for the study of comparative politics." His work begins, and remains based throughout, on the antecedent work by Rostow. He adapts Rostow's schematization to a four stage sequence of political development that includes:

1. The politics of primitive unification
2. The politics of industrialization
3. The politics of national welfare
4. The politics of abundance.

Organski clearly identifies the first stage, "the politics of primitive unification," with that stage of economic growth that Rostow calls "the preconditions for take-off." It is the stage in which the nation-state is created. The stage comes to a close when the nation begins to industrialize in earnest —when, thanks to internally generated growth, the society begins take-off. Until such time the principal political problem that weighs on the political elite is national unification —one of the preconditions, in itself, of economic self-

---

[17] Ibid., p. 254.

sustaining growth. At the close of the first phase in political development the nation "may be viable but still is far from full-grown . . . . The fabric of political and economic unity is thin and torn. A vast chasm separates the rulers from the ruled, for though the common people are politically subject they participate little in the life of the nation. The national government offers them little or nothing in services, and they for their part cannot be mobilized to contribute wealth, time, effort or concern to national purposes." [18] What Organski might have been describing, stenographically, was Italy toward the close of the nineteenth century. Italy had been unified by an exiguous elite, under a constitutional monarch. Political participation by the Italian people was extremely limited. Not only were there restrictive suffrage regulations, but Italian life was largely agrarian, illiteracy rates were extremely high, and a modern communications system all but nonexistent. Italian political life was fragmentary and factional, loyalties were mostly regional, personal, and parochial. The "government" was something alien and impersonal to most of the people. In 1890 the per capita income of Italy was forty dollars. The corresponding figures for Great Britain and France were one hundred and fifty-five dollars and one hundred and thirty dollars respectively. In 1882 only seven percent of the population had access to the ballot box. By the turn of the century a special modern sector of the economy had matured. Milan displaced Lyons as the textile center of Europe. Conjointly, Genoa overtook Marseilles as the principal port of the Mediterranean. By the year 1900 Italy had begun the late, but fateful progression from take-off to economic maturity.

----

[18] A. F. K. Organski, *Stages of Political Development* (Knopf, 1965), pp. vii, 8, 9.

It is during this phase, which is identified by Organski as the stage involving the "politics of industrialization," that Fascism manifested itself. It is during this stage that "a new class takes power, a new economy is built, and the mass of the citizenry is finally incorporated into the nation." The "primary function of government in this second stage of political development," we are informed, "is to permit and aid economic modernization . . . . First they make possible a shift of political power from the hands of the traditional elite to the industrial managers who wish to modernize the economy . . . . Second, [the government] . . . permits and assists the accumulation of capital, so essential for industrial development. This is done primarily by holding down mass consumption while permitting capital to accumulate in the hands of those who will reinvest at least a portion of it in capital goods." [19]

These are the tasks of all modernizing movements—and they are the tasks assumed by the Fascism of Mussolini. What is at once interesting and curious about this kind of account is the fact that such general tasks are the tasks of *all* governments that guide their societies through the processes of take-off and the drive to maturity. Organski admits as much:

> This, then is the course of nations: a struggle for unity; the steep, hard climb of industrialization; a turn to common welfare and, for some, democracy; and finally automation and the battle to make it a blessing instead of a curse.
>
> No nation can skip these stages, leap straight from stage one, for example, into stage three, or skip two and three altogether, for the national government has important

---

[19] Ibid., pp. 9, 10.

work to do at each stage and by executing its function at one stage lays the necessary groundwork for the next.[20]

He goes on to affirm that "to date, industrial nations have achieved their status through three quite different systems: bourgeois politics, stalinist politics, and fascist politics." [21] We have, then, a typology that is presumably composed of three mutually exclusive and exhaustive categories covering the politics of industrialization.

Organski goes on to add that all the nations that industrialized in the nineteenth century uniformly chose the "bourgeois" pattern, while those that have industrialized in the twentieth have, by and large, all suffered "a protracted period of totalitarian rule at crucial points in their modernization." [22] The proposed three-part typology, according to his schema, is unevenly segmented in time. Industrialization in the nineteenth century took place under the auspices of the bourgeoisie, and industrialization in the twentieth was undertaken, at least in large part, under totalitarian auspices. There are two major forms of totalitarianism, stalinism and *fascism*. "Totalitarianisms" would seem to be ideologies of "delayed industrialization." Organski seems to conceive them to be ideologies functionally employed to shepherd political communities through take-off and the drive to economic maturity in the twentieth century.

----

[20] Ibid., p. 212.

[21] Ibid., p. 57.

[22] Ibid., p. 214.

Problems of the Theory Linking Industrialization and Totalitarianisms

Telescoping "ideologies of delayed industrialization" into "totalitarianism" presents us with some serious problems. Not all of the ideologies alluded to by Matossian could be identified as totalitarian. While many authors have identified Marxism-Leninism (in its Stalinist and Maoist variants), Italian Fascism, and even Shintoism as totalitarian, hardly any would so characterize Kemalism, "the current Egyptian Philosophy of the Revolution or Sun Yat-sen's Three Principles of the People," and still less, "Gandhism." It would seem that there is a class of ideologies called the "ideologies of delayed industrialization" that includes all those belief systems that aspire to unify, industrialize, and modernize their nations. Some seem to be clearly nontotalitarian—at least to our intuitive judgment. But Organski claims that "all the *major* countries that *have* industrialized in the twentieth century" [23] have suffered totalitarian rule. This can be taken to mean that those ideologies of delayed industrialization that *have succeeded* in industrializing a *major* country in the twentieth century have been "totalitarian." This seems to identify the ideologies of Fascist Italy, Stalinist Russia, Shintoist Japan, and, perhaps, Maoist China (should its industrialization be successful) as both "ideologies of delayed industrialization" and "totalitarian." We are —given the restriction that the effort to industrialize must be successful and must have transpired in a "major" economy—not in any position to make a determination of the "totalitarian" or "nontotalitarian" character of "ideologies

---

[23] Ibid., emphasis supplied.

of delayed industrialization" such as Nkrumah's Ghana, Castro's Cuba, Nasser's Egypt, North Viet Nam, North Korea, or Tito's Yugoslavia—not to mention a veritable host of others. Such a disability should not be, in view of our basic interests, of particular concern. More relevant is the apparent confusion that seems to afflict some of Organski's discussion about "totalitarianism"—not so much because we are particularly occupied, at this point, with "totalitarian-isms" other than Fascism, but because the presence of confusion in such an account renders one suspicious about the remainder of the analysis.

Organski does not seem to have anything like a plausible definition of "totalitarian rule," but he did suggest that all the major countries that have industrialized in the twentieth century "have had at least a protracted period of totalitarian rule at crucial points in their modernization." After having made the claim, he proceeded to indicate that Japan succeeded in successfully industrializing by pursuing "roughly the bourgeois pattern." [24] Now Organski is either wrong in asserting that *all* major countries that have industrialized in the twentieth century have suffered "totalitarian rule," or it is possible to have "totalitarian rule" of a "bourgeois" sort. It is not at all clear what option we should take, but it is reasonably clear that Organski's notion of "totalitarianism" is at least very vague and ambiguous. But for all that Organski does proceed to make a distinction between Japan's "bourgeois" process of industrialization and that pursued by Italy under the Fascist regime. Industrialization in Fascist Italy took place under "syncratic" auspices.

Organski attempts to map his three categories—"bourgeois" "stalinist" and "fascist political systems"—over a three-part continuum, "primitive unification," "the politics

----

[24] Ibid., p. 82.

of industrialization," and the "politics of national welfare." The politics of industrialization can be characterized as "bourgeois" if the process was undertaken (largely) during the eighteenth or nineteenth centuries. If the politics of industrialization are undertaken during the twentieth century, Organski seems to argue, the strategies invoked are "totalitarian." Of the totalitarian strategies "stalinism" is a "revolution from below," involving the "masses" in a drive to economic maturity. The old propertied elites are eliminated or neutralized. If a "fascist" strategy is employed, it is largely the consequence of a balance between the "traditional" and the "new" industrializing elite. The industrializing elite cannot eliminate or neutralize the traditional elites. Consequently "fascist" strategies are compromisory. The political system is a "syncratic" one—a system that attempts industrialization without infringing upon the interests of the established traditional elites. Organski argues that generic fascism, and Italian Fascism in particular, appears as a point in the continuum of economic development within which neither the forces representing the modern or industrial sectors, nor those representing the traditional or agrarian sectors, can fully dominate the government.[25] Syncratic governments are "dual governments" attempting to represent the interests of *both* the industrial and the agrarian elites. If such systems develop under circumstances in which there are restive masses that are upwardly aspirant, the entrenched industrial and agrarian elites may enter into a coalition to suppress the "revolutionary" forces that threaten them. Under these circumstances a movement may appear that is prepared to *socially* demobilize the upwardly aspirant masses by destroying the institutions the masses have cre-

----

[25] A. F. K. Organski, "Fascism and Modernization." In S. J. Woolf, ed., *The Nature of Fascism* (Random House, 1969), p. 22.

ated to serve their ends. Such a movement could easily win the support of the threatened elites. If such a movement were to attempt to seriously neutralize the threat of revolution from below, however, they could not rest content with social demobilization. They must also *politically* mobilize the masses in order to bring them under the movement's control, so that the masses could not regroup to once again threaten the entrenched elites. Fascism was just a movement. It socially demobilized the masses while politically mobilizing them to undertake "symbolic" and "empty" political acts—the chanting of slogans, the wearing of uniforms, and the involvement in foolish pageantry.[26]

Thus, while it is true that Fascism was "manned by the lower petty bourgeoisie . . . there is no doubt that the movement is subservient to elitist needs regardless of the social background of the adherents and the leadership." "The fascist movements operated within the framework established by the interests of the elites and supported those interests as effectively as if the elites had ruled directly." The immediate effect of Fascist syncratic rule is that *both* modern (industrial) and traditional (agrarian) elites are protected and permitted to maintain their systems of social, economic, and political privilege. The necessary consequence of class privilege is that whatever investment capital is required in the interests of the modern sectors must be tapped neither from the traditional sector, which is equally protected by Fascism, nor from the modern sector itself, but exclusively from the industrial working class strata. The Fascist government thus assists the modern sector by direct loans and financial subventions, by extensive "salvaging" operations of unprofitable but necessary enterprises, and by extensive government purchases of armaments. However,

----

[26] Organski, *Stages of Political Development,* pp. 125–138, 142f.

since both the traditional and modern sector insulate themselves from the growth demands of the economy, investment capital can only come from the defenseless industrial working class. As a consequence, there is a reduction in the rate of capital accumulation available for industry. Thus, "it seems likely . . . although it is difficult to prove, that syncratic politics slows the pace of industrialization, for it slows down the rate of capital accumulation, the key to industrialization." [27]

In the few years that transpired between the publication of Organski's book in 1965 and his return to the problem in 1969, his judgment concerning this last issue became more pronounced. In 1969 he could insist that syncratic or Fascist politics, was not only "likely" to slow down the pace of industrialization, it did in fact *all but terminate industrialization*. He insists that "the rate of economic growth [in Fascist Italy] slowed down between World War I and 1929" and "virtually came to a halt in the thirties." [28] We are provided, in effect, with a dismal picture of an essentially reactionary political system that all but succeeded in halting the process of industrialization—in order to please the elites to which it was "subservient."

Such a picture is not only implausible, it seems to be disconfirmed by whatever evidence we have from the actual Fascist experiment. If the modern sector, in the service of its own interests, pursues a program of industrial expansion and the traditional sector, in the service of its own interests, pursues a program of resisting industrial expansion, the syncratic system is so beset with contradictions that no political leader, no matter how subservient, could serve both masters.

---

[27] Organski, "Fascism and Modernization," p. 29, *Stages of Political Development*, pp. 137, 140, 144.

[28] Organski, "Fascism and Modernization," pp. 34, 38.

Mussolini would be compelled by the system itself to violate the interests of one or the other or both. Organski is well aware of the intrinsic instability of the system he pictures, and yet seems unaware of how implausible his characterization of Fascism as a system "subservient" to *both* elites necessarily becomes as a consequence. To escape this obvious implausibility, he seems to attempt a resolution by arguing that the Fascists *primarily* served the interests of the *traditional* sector. The modern sector had to be content not only with a decline in the rate of industrialization during the twenties, but with a dead stop in the thirties. We are asked, as a necessary consequence, to believe that Mussolini, driven by some kind of irrepressible impulse "to get into wars," was prepared to sacrifice industrial development, *the necessary material base for waging wars,* in order to serve the interests of the traditional sectors. Surely Mussolini, under those conditions was not only a tool of the elites, he was a fool as well. The explanation for the Fascist phenomenon is to be sought not as an "episode in the modernization of the country," but in terms of Mussolini's psychological disabilities.[29]

Data on the Italian Economy under Fascism

As a matter of fact, Organski offers no evidence whatsoever to establish that the Italian economy under the Fascists suffered a decline in the rate of industrialization during the first decade of Fascist rule and ceased entirely during the second. And that is unfortunate because his case hangs largely on such data. Whatever evidence we have seems to indicate that the rate of industrial expansion during the first

----

[29] Ibid., pp. 38 and 19.

decade of Fascist rule was reasonably impressive. Given the indices of overall industrial production, and using 1913 as the base, Fascist industrial production rose from 81 in 1922, to 127 in 1926, when Italy began to feel the first impact of the end of the postwar boom. By 1927 the overall index had declined to 114. Even under the adverse world economic conditions of the period, Fascist Italy had generated a 41 percent increment in overall industrial production exceeding French production, which had grown 40 percent; German production, which had grown 31 percent; American production, which had grown 26 percent; and England's production, which had grown 16.5 percent. If one considers the standardized statistics of the volume of total output, using 1913 as a benchmark, output volume of Italy in 1922 was 113.4. By 1928, before the full impact of the Great Depression, the index rose to 130.4. In the interim France's index had achieved 118.8, the United Kingdom had reached 126.5 and Germany languished with 106.7. Fascist Italy's rate of increased total output, relative to its position in 1913, had surpassed those of its major European competitors. Only the Scandinavian countries, favored by a variety of factors, exceeded Fascist Italy's rate of growth. By 1938 the index for Fascist Italy was 153.8, which evidences a rapid recovery from the impact of the Depression. Germany's index, under the impact of National Socialist development was 149.9. France's index lagged at 109.4, and only the United Kingdom made a relatively better showing with an index of 158.3. In terms of output per man, again using 1913 as a benchmark, Fascist Italy had achieved a productivity per man index of 126.3 by 1929 and a level of 145.2 by 1938. In France, productivity per man had declined from 136.5 in 1929 to 125.7 in 1938. Germany's index had risen from 96.5 in 1929 to 122.4 in 1938. The productivity per man in the United Kingdom had risen from

121.6 in 1929 to 143.6. Fascist Italy's productivity per man had exceeded even that of the United States, which relative to 1913, had achieved an index of 136 compared to Italy's 145.2. In terms of the gross domestic investment as a proportion of the gross national product, Italy was investing 13.4 percent in 1922 and 17.2 percent in 1929. Even in 1938 Fascist Italy was still investing 15.9 percent of its gross national product as fixed asset formation, surpassing all the major European countries (with the possible exception of National Socialist Germany) and the United States.[30]

Recognizing that we are dealing with economies at different levels of industrial maturity and, in the case of Italy, with a much narrower industrial base, William Welk nonetheless characterized the period between 1922 and 1926, for example, as one in which "Italy experienced a period of continuous industrial growth and prosperity." If the aggregate statistics are disaggregated, we find that production in the leading modern sectors, iron and steel rose from one million tons in 1922 to almost two million tons in 1926. By 1929 iron and steel production had increased to two and a quarter million tons, an overall increment in production of 225 percent since 1922. In 1925 Fascist Italy produced 6.9 billions KWH of hydroelectric power. In 1937 it produced 14.4 billions, an overall increment of over 200 percent. The metallurgical, hydroelectric, and textile industries, the backbone of the Italian economy, showed "surprising elements of strength" in the face of world depression. The chemical industry expanded. Thus the largest and most significant elements in the modern sector were apparently

----

[30] Cf. Antonio Stefano Benni, "Lo sviluppo industriale dell'Italia fascista." In T. Sillani, ed., *Lo Stato Mussoliniano* (La Rassegna Italiana, 1930) and Angus Maddison, *Economic Growth in the West: Comparative Experience in Europe and North America* (Twentieth Century Fund, 1964), Appendices.

directly and indirectly supported by the regime. The communications system was expanded. An extensive road system was constructed under the aegis of the *Azienda Autonoma Statale della Strada*. The railroad system was rapidly electrified. There was a 280 percent increment in the growth of electrified railway lines between 1923 and 1934. Moreover, there was a relatively rapid expansion of the automobile, aircraft, and shipping industries.[31]

The capital for industrial expansion was provided primarily through controlled consumption, which permitted a high profit rate. From 1922 through 1926 savings represented 12 percent of the national income, a percentage only surpassed in the "economic miracle" of rapid postwar expansion. The high rate of savings, and the attendant high investment rates, apparently derived via the maintenance of high profit structures, supplied the capital for productive expansion. Not only was consumption controlled but there were taxes on wages and agricultural income.[32] In fact, the agricultural sector was *forced* to invest in government bonds in order to provide additional working capital—some of which clearly went for the expansion and maintenance of the economic infrastructure necessary to modernization, and the salvaging of threatened, but necessary, industries.[33]

Given these considerations, and recalling the fact that Italy was almost totally devoid of the natural resources necessary to heavy industry such as iron ore and fossil fuels, the performance of the regime could hardly be adequately de-

----

[31] William Welk, *Fascist Economic Policy* (Harvard University, 1938), pp. 161, 198–200, 201, 203.

[32] S. Lombardini, "Italian Fascism and the Economy." In S. J. Woolf, ed., *The Nature of Fascism,* p. 157.

[33] Ludovico Garruccio, *L'industrializzazione tra nazionalismo e rivoluzione* (Mulino, 1969), p. 140.

scribed as "retarding" the rate of industrial growth. We have no way of judging what the rate might have been if the Fascist government had not pursued a policy of developing the industrial system largely without recourse to foreign investment capital (as occurred after World War II). But the decision to expand the industrial sectors out of Italy's autonomous capital resources was largely a *political* decision and was based on Fascist doctrinal dispositions. Nonetheless, granting the dearth of Italian material and financial resources, and a worldwide depression of unprecedented magnitude, Fascist Italy by 1937 "effected the passage from an agrarian to an industrial society." After twenty years of Fascist rule, in circumstances almost entirely devoid of the resources necessary for industrialization, having been involved in a worldwide depression, several military adventures, and a disastrous war, postwar Italy inherited an "unexpectedly sound economic base." In less than a decade after World War II, Italy enjoyed its "little economic miracle" and made the transit to a society of high mass consumption.[34]

Traditionalist and Non-Traditionalist Aspects of Fascist Economy

Not only does Organski's account of industrialization in Fascist Italy seem to be at considerable variance with whatever evidence we have, but his interpretation of the relationship between the entrenched elites and Fascism leaves a great deal to be desired. The fact seems to be that the "tra-

----

[34] Cf. Emilio Radius, *Usi e costumi dell'uomo fascista* (Rizzoli, 1964), p. 354; Mihaly Vajda, "The Rise of Fascism in Italy and Germany," *Telos,* 1972, 12: 12ff.

ditional sector," that is to say Italy's agricultural economy, could hardly be conceived to be peripheral to any serious program of integral modernization. Whatever "modernization" can be taken to mean, it cannot be understood to mean that agriculture should languish—particularly in a country which, at the point of commencing its drive to maturity, is densely populated and is compelled to import foodstuffs (with a consequent loss of capital resources) to sustain its population. If economic maturity implies, as it seems to, that under conditions of maturity a society is capable of effectively applying all the modern technology available to the *entire* range of its productive enterprises, then one could hardly expect a modernizing movement to neglect the "traditional" or agricultural sectors. Some modernizing movements, of course, have done precisely that and suffered grievously as a consequence. As Organski indicates, the Stalinists forced the vast bulk of their capital potential into select sectors of basic industry to the serious neglect of agriculture. That, together with a range of subsequent political decisions, created an agrarian problem in the Soviet Union that has not yet been resolved.

Fascists did show considerable favor to the established "traditional" sectors of Italian society. But that fact need not necessarily be construed as evidence that Fascism was "subservient" to the traditional elite, or that Fascism was "the last victory for the landed aristocracy." [35]

In 1924 Fascists indicated that agricultural production in Italy was "incapable of adequately keeping step with the growth of the population," and that the problems that faced the regime involved "maintaining the balance between agriculture and other industries in relation to the rapidly ex-

----

[35] Organski, *Stages of Political Development*, p. 155.

panding population." [36] (One might add that this seems to be the problem Maoists are now facing when they speak of moving into the future on "two legs" [industry *and* agriculture] rather than on "one" [industry alone]). The Fascist agricultural program of *bonifica integrale* (integral improvement rather than narrowly agricultural improvement) has been characterized by specialists, after the war, as "the most successful and positive" accomplishment of Fascism.[37] By 1934 the "battle for grain" had been, in effect, won. In that year Italy, as we have noted earlier, produced for the first time in its modern history, all the grain needed for internal consumption. In 1922 Italy produced 9.5 quintals of wheat per hectare and in 1933, 15.9 quintals per hectare. The success was purchased, of course, by enormous sacrifices (including higher bread prices), but the technical achievement was the consequence of the application of scientific agricultural techniques to agricultural sectors—a process that is characteristically "modern." Under the Fascist regime three times as much was expended on land reclamation than that allocated by all previous administrations since 1870. A "vast program of agricultural education and instruction" was also undertaken. "Agricultural schools and colleges, scientific and research stations, and an extensive system of agrarian credit [were] instituted. Vast propaganda campaigns for the preservation of national forests and for increases in the leading types of agricultural production were put into effect." It is hard to read that kind of a program, however bungled and however much it profited large

----

[36] Fulvio Zugaro, "La produzione del suolo Italiano." *Annali di economia,* 1924, 1: 283.

[37] Luigi Salvatorelli and Giovanni Mira, *Storia d'Italia nel periodo fascista* (Einaudi, 1964), p. 561.

landholders, as *simply* the result of "subservience" to the "traditional" sectors.[38]

A plausible case can be made for the thesis that Fascism was a mass-mobilizing developmental dictatorship committed to the modernization of Italy's economy. Given the devastating decline in productivity, both industrial and agricultural, that marked the first ten years of Bolshevik rule in the Soviet Union, there is no reason to imagine that Fascists should have been disposed to try similar experiments in Italy even if they could have done so. Mussolini insisted that while a "political revolution" could be made overnight, "surgical methods" were dangerously inappropriate for a relatively complex economy. He argued that "revolution" in the "Bolshevik style" would only produce a collapse in industrial and agricultural production. He maintained that Fascists were neither prejudiced in favor of private ownership nor tendentiously opposed to it. The strategy to be used, he insisted, would be pragmatic. *Whatever* increased national production would be Fascist policy.[39] Fascist policies frequently changed (sometimes with alarming rapidity); there was much waste and corruption; for a long period there was little that could pass as central planning; but the overall features of Fascist policy appear clear enough. Fascist economic policy was calculated, within confines drawn in part by natural resource limitation, by international economic dislocations and in part by the interests of non-Fascist allies, to develop Italy's industrial potential to the level where it could support defense and aggressive capabilities. Italy was to be a "Great Nation." As has been

---

[38] Welk, *Fascist Economic Policy,* p. 193; cf. Carl Schmidt, *The Plough and the Sword* (Columbia University Press, 1938).

[39] Mussolini, "I diritti della vittoria," 14: 53; "Alla moda Russa?" 15: 178–181; "Discorso di Cremona," 15: 182–189.

suggested by most serious commentators on the Fascist experiment, Fascism was not a "tool" of any one, or any two, "elites." Fascism ultimately came to dominate Italian society in the service of what it conceived to be "the national interest."

That Fascism was "accommodating" with respect to entrenched economic elites cannot be gainsaid. That economic maturity was purchased by a policy of severely controlled mass consumption has been admitted frankly and openly by Fascist apologists.[40] The members of the industrial and agrarian working class *were* socially demobilized so that they could not resist wage reductions and consumption controls, while they were at the same time politically mobilized in order to provide them with what Drucker has aptly called "non-economic social benefits."[41] The marching, pageantry, and ritual were explicitly conceived by Fascists as providing the working classes with a sense of community identity, of purpose and status by involvement in a collective enterprise of "world historical" moment. How successful this effort was is hard to document, but enough authors have alluded to the mass support Fascism enjoyed until World War II to suggest that such activities provided more than some gratification to participants. In effect, such activities could hardly be characterized as "empty." They apparently provided some considerable measure of non-economic satisfactions essential to the maintenance of collective morale during the protracted period of economic austerity required for rapid capital accumulation, industrial development, and modernization.

----

[40] Harold E. Goad, *What is Fascism?* (Italian Mail & Tribune, 1929), p. 21.

[41] Peter Drucker, *End of Economic Man*, chap. 6.

If such an account seems plausible, it suggests that Fascism was a mass-mobilizing development dictatorship negotiating Italy through the drive to economic maturity. Fascism arose in Milan, the center of Italy's modern industrial sector. As early as 1923, Giovanni Ansaldo, in response to Luigi Salvatorelli's suggestion that Fascism was the product of the "humanistic petty bourgeoisie," argued that Fascism, rather than originating in and reflecting "humanistic" concerns, was animated by "the apotheosis of the industrial development of the nation" [42]—a concern of the "technical" rather than the "humanistic" petty bourgeoisie. Initially, Fascists apparently were prepared to countenance the possibility that their developmental program could be undertaken by the working class under the Fascist leadership—almost all petty bourgeois in origin. With the failure to mobilize any substantial number of workers, conjoined with the anti-Fascist intransigence of the official socialist parties, and the subsequent failure of the "workers' revolution"—Fascism found itself in singular historic and political circumstances. The propertied elites were badly frightened and disposed to support any aggressive "antisocialist" movement. Fascism profited from that support and rapidly expanded—quite spontaneously in the agrarian regions, primarily in the north. For some considerable time it appeared that Fascism was to be nothing more than the violence of agrarian reaction against the socialist leagues and cooperatives. (Lenin seems to have so conceived Fascism.) But it would appear that the "agrarian Fascists," men of the prominence of Roberto Farinacci, Italo Balbo, and Dino Grandi were compelled, ultimately, to "adapt themselves to the

---

[42] Giovanni Ansaldo, "Il fascismo e la piccola borghesia technica." In C. Casucci, ed., *Il fascismo* (Mulino, 1961), p. 208; cf. Luigi Salvatorelli, *Nazionalfascismo* (Gobetti, 1923).

dynamism of Milanese Fascism . . . ," the Fascism of a "developmental bourgeoisie." [43] One need but read the Futurist manifestoes of the period to get the feel of the sentiments that animated the most aggressive leadership elements of Milanese Fascism.[44] All their literature was shot through with allusions to "production," to mechanical and electrical "dynamism," to "progress," "development," and "modernity." The students who provided much of the cadre of Fascism were, to a substantial degree, "machine fetishists." [45] Fascism, the argument proceeds, was a union of the "technical petty bourgeoisie" and students, supported (in the service of their own interests) by elements of the industrial and agrarian capitalist class. Fascism was a revolutionary and developmental mass-mobilizing movement. Any leadership that derived from the "traditional sectors" was quickly domesticated or "purged." [46] Almost all contemporary commentators, even the most convinced Marxists, will concede that the Italian "working class [was] unable to bring about the socialist revolution" and that "the objective conditions for [socialist] revolution were not ripe." [47] Under the circumstances the Fascists made their own revolution— and they made revolution with the active and passive support of vast strata of the nonelite population. The membership in the Fascist ranks represented all segments of the population, including the working classes. As far as we can

----

[43] Garruccio, *L'industrializzione,* pp. 104ff.

[44] F. T. Marinetti, *Teoria e invezione futurista* (Mondadori, 1968).

[45] Luigi Scrivo, *Sintesi del futurismo* (Bulzoni, 1968).

[46] Garruccio, *L'industrializzione,* pp. 105ff.

[47] J. Solé-Tura, "The Political 'Instrumentality' of Fascism." In Woolf, ed., *Nature of Fascism,* p. 42; Paolo Alatri, *Le origini del fascismo* (Riuniti, 1963), p. 108.

determine agrarian and industrial workers composed about forty percent of the Fascist membership.

Fascism as a Developmental Regime

The Fascist revolution, both political and economic, carried Italy from the beginnings to the conclusion of the drive to economic maturity. There was apparently considerable upward mobility for segments of the petty bourgeoisie that provided the cadre of the movement.[48] In a substantial sense Barrington Moore's account of Fascism, framed in the concepts of economic development, is correct. Fascism produced a "revolution from above," a process that modernizes and industrializes an economic system while at the same time keeping the "social structure" or "class system" essentially intact.[49] But Moore seems too much wedded to Organski's notion of syncratic government—he seems to conceive Fascism to have been nothing more than a coalition of industrial and agrarian elites that *dominated* the government of Italy. The counterargument, of course, is that Fascism used the possessing class as *repositories of investment capital.* Once credit and banking controls passed into Fascist hands, Fascists gained important leverage on the system. In the end, Fascists came to control Italy's economy more extensively than could any "liberal" or "capitalist" government.[50] And, in the last analysis, it was Fascism and

----

[48] Renzo Sereno, "The Fascists: The Changing Elite." In Harold D. Lasswell and Daniel Lerner, eds., *The World Revolutionary Elites* (M.I.T. Press, 1965).

[49] Barrington Moore, Jr., *Social Origins of Dictatorship and Democracy* (Beacon, 1966).

[50] Roland Sarti, *Fascism and the Industrial Leadership in Italy: 1919–1940* (University of California Press, 1971), p. 124.

not the coalition of propertied elites that came to control the political and economic system.

This is, in substantial part, the interpretation given by Ludovico Garruccio and suggested by others.[51] Such a candidate interpretation has considerable cognitive merit. First, it seems to fit the available historic and economic evidence. That is, it exploits the available funded data more effectively than the psychoanalytic or the empirically oriented sociological interpretations. Secondly, it permits whatever survives of alternate interpretations to find a place in the account. For example, Garruccio insists that the drive to economic maturity involves social tensions of considerable magnitude. Old institutions are destroyed or reshaped. There are large-scale population movements. Such circumstances, exacerbated by protracted crisis, might well produce the high incidence of violence and considerable free-floating hostility that savaged Italy from 1919 to 1925. The mass behaviors and the emphasis on violence would be predictable consequences of such circumstances.[52] The employment of inflated and symbolic speech, the free exercise of violence and the posturings of force, are explained not in terms of "biological rigidity," "sexual repression," the psychology of the "mob" or the prevalence of "authoritarian characters," but rather as a predictable consequence of the tensions involved in vast economic and social change under crisis conditions. Such predictions are the lower-order, quasi-deductive consequence of the set of propositions that characterize the process of development.

The interpretation of Fascism as a developmental regime would provide, furthermore, some understanding of

----

[51] Garruccio, *L'industrializzione*; A. J. Gregor, *The Ideology of Fascism* (Free Press, 1969), pp. xiiff.

[52] Garruccio, *L'industrializzione,* pp. 32–46.

the features regularly alluded to in Marxist accounts. The Fascists *did* stabilize the class system, and the various propertied elements *were* compensated for their involvement in the system, but Fascism did, with some regularity, violate their "concrete and real" interests, and did impose itself upon Italy as a new "political ruling class" that exercised considerable autonomy in the determination of policy.[53] Finally, this interpretation takes into consideration the fact which almost all non-Marxist, and sometimes Marxists of various persuasions, have as we have seen insisted upon: there is a substantial and sustained similarity between Fascism and "Stalinism." Even Daniel Guerin, as a "left-wing" intellectual, in writing a new introduction to his prewar volume on Fascism, has argued that both Fascism and Stalinism shared impressive affinities.[54] N. Kogan, in responding to Organski's analysis, granted that Fascism had destroyed the independent labor movement in Italy "making the workers and peasants pay the bill for economic development . . . ," but he went on to indicate that "these characteristics could be described in Soviet Russia: there was no independent labor movement, as it had been destroyed; the labor unions had become an instrument of the party; and savings to build up development in Russia came from the workers and peasants, as they did under fascist regimes. These particular characteristics did not distinguish fascism from communism . . . ."[55] Moreover, the studies conducted by Harold Lasswell and David Lerner, indicate that the leadership of both the communist movements and the

---

[53] Ibid., p. 106.

[54] Daniel Guerin, *Fascismo e gran capitale* (Schwarz, 1956), pp. 12–14.

[55] N. Kogan, "Discussion—Fascism and the Polity." In Woolf, ed., *Nature of Fascism,* pp. 58f.

fascist movements come uniformly, and almost exclusively, from the declassed petty bourgeoisie.[56] Furthermore, the rank and file membership of various communist movements, does not generally come from the industrial proletariat.

Mussolini early indicated that the Fascist movement in Italy could boast more *bona fide* proletarian members than could the Bolshevik party in the Soviet Union in 1920.[57] Both movements were led by petty bourgeois elements, their recruitment base was not essentially among the urban proletariat, their intentions were clearly developmental, and they both proceeded to force draught their countries to the stage of economic maturity. All such mass-mobilizing, developmental movements seem to recruit *where they can,* and compensate whatever strata of the population they must in order to keep the process going. Conceiving Fascism as a developmental dictatorship, one could argue that the Fascists compensated the propertied elements because they did not wish to alienate enterprisory and entrepreneurial skills or indulge in "revolutionary" experiments that had given every indication of drastically reducing industrial and agricultural productive yield. The Soviets, in their turn, introduced significant wage differentials to maintain and attract such skills. Various classes in the Soviet Union enjoyed, and still enjoy, differential wage and welfare benefits and access to power. Both Fascism and various communist movements employ pageantry, ritual, ceremony, and parades to provide the noneconomic supplements necessary to mobilize the whole population behind their program which will be, of necessity, long, austere, and demanding. All such systems talk of "moral" rather than "material" incentives. All ex-

----

[56] Lasswell and Lerner, *The World Revolutionary Elites.*

[57] Mussolini, "Alla moda Russa?" 15: 180.

ploit the working classes in order to accumulate the necessary investment capital to realize their programs of industrial development.

Garruccio documents all these features with impressive insistence. All modernizing movements share significant structural and political similarities and display similar modal behavioral properties. Garruccio speaks of Fascism and the various forms of Stalinism as "brothers under the skin." In one place he even speaks of "national-fascist movements," which include not only Fascism, but Castroism, Peronism, Nasserism, "and so forth." He speaks of Fascist Italy offering a "paradigm" for the general interpretation of developmental systems. It is clear that he does not wish to assimilate *all* modernizing movements under such a paradigm. Some modernizing movements are not mass-mobilizing; some might proceed not under "hegemonic" parties, but under modernizing traditional elites or under military auspices—and some are not "totalitarian," and others not dictatorial. They are all, however, "ideologies of delayed industrialization," and consequently share some critical features in common. All can, however, under vaguely specified conditions "develop" or "devolve" (as one chooses) into some form of fascism. It would seem that the most explicit Fascist form is "totalitarianism." Fascism was the first mass-mobilizing development dictatorship that provided a frank, complete, and relatively coherent rationale for totalitarianism. Marxism—with its original emphasis on distributionism, on the "voluntary association of productive communes," on a political system called the "dictatorship of the proletariat" that involves universal suffrage, referendum and recall and abjures "hierarchical investitude"—really has very little to say to contemporary developmental political systems. Garruccio speaks of the behavioral modalities of some of the most important developmental systems, their "rage for unity," their emphasis on "dynamic youth," their insistence on the "leadership principle," their mass-mobilizing strategies, their emphatic nationalism, their pragmatic and tactical ideological postures, their bureaucratic disposition, their adoption of policies calculated to isolate the national community from "corrupting external influences," and their subsequent autarchic and xenophobic character, their hyperbolic style, and their emphasis on violence, voluntarism and activism. Fascism was the first and most transparent exemplar of the class. The demands of the take-off stage, when national unity and collective mobilization become the preconditions for, and become involved in, the successful drive to maturity—the straining of traditional institutions; the attendant changes in, and the wrenching of, established loyalties; the necessity of severely controlled and restricted consumption and the "primitive accumulation" of investment capital—all are, according to this account, productive of the dispositions that find expression in these behavior modalities.[58]

Towards a Classificational Schema of Developmental Systems

The simple trichotomy of the "bourgeois," "stalinist," and "fascist" patterns of development, as entertained in Organski's "framework," gives way to a comparative classificational schema that is *very* complex. Any proposed schema that would accommodate all the distinctions to which Garruccio alludes would be very intricate. Some very subtle distinctions would have to be drawn—and yet each variant of the "genus" of the developmental systems would have to

----

[58] Garruccio, *L'industrializzione,* pp. 131, 118, 50, chap. 3.

share some common attributes with the others. Neither Garruccio, nor anyone else to date, has attempted to formulate such complex and discriminating sorting criteria for identifying the subspecies and the species types of the genus "ideologies of delayed industrialization." The universe of such developmental systems remains uncharted. A great deal of logical and analytic work would have to be done before social scientists would have anything like a collection of mutually exclusive categories that might exhaust the universe of such economic and political systems.

That having been said, the interpretation of Fascism as one of the principal variants in the class of developmental systems, has a great deal to recommend it. It is a generally plausible preliminary account that seems to accord reasonably well with whatever historical and economic evidence we have. Such an account seems capable of assimilating whatever survives from antecedent interpretations without inheriting at the same time their major defects. On the other hand, there are critical immediate problems that turn on typological and analytic issues of no small magnitude. Finally, the entire account rests on the competence of a particular interpretation of macroeconomic dynamics that is, by no means, universally accepted.

For the purposes of our exposition there is one persistent anomaly that attends such accounts. If Fascism was indeed one of the forms that developmental systems might take on, and such systems characteristically appear between the stages of take-off and economic maturity, one has prima facie difficulty understanding what National Socialism might have been. All analysts in this particular tradition, Matossian, Organski, Garruccio, and Barrington Moore (if he can be identified with this persuasion), are compelled to recognize that National Socialism, in industrially mature Germany, shared many, if not all the principal species traits of Fascism. If Fascism is to be understood as a developmental, mass-mobilizing, and totalitarian dictatorship—and if Fascism was a function of late industrial development— one seems at a loss to explain the appearance of National Socialism in industrially mature Germany. National Socialism as a totalitarian, mass-mobilizing dictatorship can hardly be understood to have been *essentially* a "modernizing" or "industrializing" movement. Matossian is obviously embarrassed by the necessity of identifying National Socialism as a member of the class of "ideologies of delayed industrialization." [59] Organski attempts the seemingly desperate strategy of: 1. Denying explicitly that National Socialism was a "fascism," and 2. Insisting that National Socialism was a system involved in "the politics of national welfare." National Socialism, for Organski, was "a welfare state that brought to the surface the irrational drives of man." [60] National Socialism, in this view, was a system appropriate to an economy of mass consumption, but one that has apparently inexplicable pathological features. National Socialism was a "lunatic" movement that had many, if not all the behavioral modal traits of developmental Fascism, but it was not a fascism because it manifested itself in a society at the stage of industrial maturity.

While Organski's effort to produce a viable typology of political systems seems singularly unpersuasive with respect to his analysis of National Socialism, our interest here is focused, rather, on the specific analysis of Fascism. Organski's efforts at conceptual formation draws attention, however, to a central and critical typological or classificational problem. Organski insists that there is some sort of political system, never adequately characterized, that is "to-

----

[59] Matossian, "Ideologies of Delayed Industrialization," p. 253, n. 2.
[60] Organski, *Stages of Political Development,* pp. 123, 170–177.

talitarian," and which can make its appearance at *any* stage of economic growth and political development. He talks about "totalitarian repression" at the very "beginning of industrialization," at the stage of rapid industrialization, and under conditions of high mass consumption as well.[61] While Fascism is a political system that characteristically develops under conditions of the drive for industrial maturity, it is, at the same time, a political system that is a member of an apparently broader class of systems called "totalitarian"— a more inclusive class that includes political systems to be found at *every* stage of economic development. Garruccio is less specific on this account, but it is clear that in his volume of 1969 he was prepared to argue that Fascism, Stalinism, and National Socialism were, in a broad and substantial sense, fundamentally similar political systems. In a long essay published in 1971 Garruccio has spoken of the "three ages of Fascism" and has suggested that *fascism* can be found at all levels of industrial development, immediately prior to and during industrial take-off, during the drive to maturity, and in an economy of high mass consumption as well. Under such circumstances all the distinctions between Fascism, totalitarianism, and the stages of economic development seem to have become insubstantial and vague.

The attempt on the part of contemporary analysts to provide an account of Fascism in terms of the stages of industrial growth has provided us with a reasonably plausible preliminary interpretation of Fascism that might be completely filled in with more archival data after some of its theoretical substructure has been scrutinized with more critical attention, after some of its assumptions have been explicated with more precision, and after some empirical indices have been generated to help plot aspects of the regime

---

[61] Ibid., pp. 218, 142ff., 182.

that have remained obscure. But this admirable *tour de force* has been accomplished at the price of confusing whatever commonplace and familiar typologies we might have inherited from our intellectual past. We must face once again the problem of "totalitarianism," the recognition that a number of seemingly disparate political systems display common species properties yet appear at different stages of economic growth. Peter Drucker, Sigmund Neumann, Peter Nathan, Wilhelm Reich, Franz Borkenau, Hannah Arendt, Daniel Guerin, not to mention a host of others, have all insisted that there are fundamental similarities that unite Fascism, Stalinism, and National Socialism (not to speak of more modern versions of the same genus or family). The difficulty is that such "totalitarianisms" can occupy space anywhere on the continuum from post-traditional economic systems through economies of high mass consumption. This suggests a number of possibilities, among them are that "totalitarianism" is a genus designation and "fascism" is a specific member of the genus, or conceivably that all "totalitarianisms" are "fascisms," or that there are "fascisms" at all stages of economic growth with some "fascisms" being "fascisms" at the "dualistic or syncratic phase of modernization," and some "fascisms" being "fascisms of economies of mass consumption." [62] Outside of such "fascisms" there might be "non-fascist" "totalitarian" systems that occupy space along the continuum that marks the stages of economic growth. In many cases it is all but impossible to decide what analytic and descriptive strategy to use. There is more than a suggestion that Garruccio has begun to identify all "totalitarianisms" as variants of Fascism. He talks not only of a "Stalinism" that is a "fascism," but of a "Castro-

---

[62] Ludovico Garruccio, "Le tre età del fascismo." *Il Mulino,* 1971, 213: 55.

ism" that is a "fascism." "Fascism," we are told, "can be defined as the dictatorship of the developmental bourgeoisie in the name of national unity." [63] It seems fairly obvious that, given such an interpretation, not only Stalinism, National Socialism, Peronism, Nasserism, Shintoism, and Castroism become both "fascisms" and perhaps "totalitarianisms" as well, but we seem driven to include Maoism, Nkrumahism, the political systems of North Korea and North Viet Nam, as well as any number of African Socialist one-party states and developmental military dictatorships (staffed by members of the "developmental bourgeoisie") in the all-inclusive class as well. In effect, we seem to be embarrassed by abundance. While such an account seems very suggestive, it would seem to lack the power of discrimination necessary to make the distinctions that comparative analysis requires.

At the moment social scientists seem to have one immediate recourse in the literature: the analysis of the concept "totalitarianism." During the period immediately following World War II a great deal of literature had collected around the concept. It is to that literature we can now turn for assistance.

----

[63] Ibid., pp. 69, 70, 68ff.

CHAPTER SEVEN
Fascism as Totalitarianism

Of all the literature that collected around the interpretation of Fascism after World War II none is perhaps as interesting and sophisticated as that devoted to the analysis of Fascism as "totalitarian." The literature is interesting and sophisticated because much of it is devoted to very serious methodological issues that are central to social science. The discussion that has grown up around the concept "totalitarianism" provides some measure of the increased methodological maturity that has come to characterize postwar social science.

Towards a Taxonomy of Totalitarianism

Critical to this discussion has been the work of Carl Friedrich and Zbigniew K. Brzezinski. In *Totalitarian Dictatorship and Autocracy,* Friedrich and Brzezinski offered what they took to be a catalog of defining traits that would identify a class of political systems they referred to as "totalitarianisms." Fascist Italy was included in the class so characterized. They spoke of a set of "basic features or traits" that are "generally recognized to be common to totalitarian dictatorships." "The 'syndrome,' or pattern of interrelated traits, of the totalitarian dictatorship," they went on to indicate, "consists of an ideology, a single party typically led by one man, a terroristic policy, a communications monopoly, a weapons monopoly, and a centrally directed economy." It was equally clear to them that the political systems explicitly or implicitly included in the set were not "identical" (whatever that might be taken to mean), and that the syndrome of traits conceived as defining the class could not be considered definitive in any sense. What was offered, according to the authors, was "a general, descriptive theory of a novel form of government," a "general model of totalitarian dictatorship and of the society which it has created," which could "fit into the general framework of our knowledge of government and politics." [1]

What such a "descriptive theory" or "model" seems to involve, essentially, is *pretheoretical conceptualizing,* an attempt to provide a loose (and consequently general) *criterial definition* of a critical concept, conjoined with an indeterminate number of attendant propositions that might afford social science practitioners the occasion conveniently to store, retrieve, and employ a large body of information that might otherwise not be cataloged or might be cataloged differently and, consequently, retrieved only with considerably more effort. [2] The authors clearly imagined that the provision of a *preliminary conceptual schema* constructed around the concept "totalitarianism" would provide a convenient storage bin for a wide range of "reasonably well-established matters of fact," as well as serve as a pedagogical aid of some consequence. (They hoped to "provide a basis . . . for more effective teaching . . . .") What such a "descriptive theory" or "model" was clearly not intended to achieve was *explanation.* While there is, as we shall suggest, considerable confusion on this count, it seems that the authors were consciously aware that they could not "explain why this dictatorship came into being . . . ," since they were convinced that "such an explanation is not feasible at the present time, though some of the essential conditions can be described." ". . . At the present time," they continued, "we cannot fully explain the rise of totalitarian

---

[1] Carl Friedrich and Zbigniew K. Brzezinski, *Totalitarian Dictatorship and Autocracy* (Praeger, 1956), pp. 3, 9; cf. pp. 8, 10.

[2] Cf. A. J. Gregor, *An Introduction to Metapolitics* (Free Press, 1971), pp. 131–135. A criterial definition is understood to provide a list of observable traits, some or all of which serve to identify instances of a class; it provides a set of traits that serve as admission criteria into a class.

dictatorship. All we can do is to explain it partially by identifying some of the antecedent and concomitant conditions." [3]

Logically (but not necessarily chronologically) speak-
ing, what we have is a pretheoretical effort at typologizing
or categorizing. We have an incomplete set of attributes that
provide prima facie, nonrigorous, but plausible, criteria for
admission into the class "totalitarian," and a first, and ad-
mittedly modest, attempt to generate a taxonomic schema.
"Totalitarianisms" are, for example, a subset, or a "species,"
of the "genus" "autocracies." The "logical opposite" of "autocracy" is, apparently, another "genus," i.e., "responsible
or constitutional government." We have, then, a primitive
taxonomy: *two* genera, "heterocracies" and "autocracies,"
one species, "totalitarianism," subsumed under one genus,
"autocracy," and *several* subspecies lodged under the species "totalitarian." [4]

Clearly, Robert Burrowes' basic judgments concerning
Friedrich and Brzezinski's *Totalitarian Dictatorship and
Autocracy* are well taken. The book is not the product of a
"rigorous typological approach" that "would facilitate comparison," nor does it contain "a solid core of theory." [5] The
work contains a nonrigorous, essentially pretheoretical preliminary conceptual schema calculated to serve, primarily,
as a device that assists in fostering ready recall, a pedagogical aid, and a storage convenience. Such schemata (and
there are many in the informal social sciences) also serve to
provide suggestions for further research. The fact that some
discrete collection of entities displays certain overt proper-

---

[3] Friedrich and Brzezinski, *Totalitarian Dictatorship*, pp. vii, 7.

[4] Ibid., pp. 3ff.

[5] Robert Burrowes, "Totalitarianism: The Revised Standard Version."
World Politics, 1969, 21/2: 281, 282.

ties *may* imply the presence of antecedent common causes. For example, Friedrich and Brzezinski insist, in a number of places, that they are "primarily" concerned with "the fact" of one or another attribute, rather than "its explanation." This is not to say that they do not, on occasion, attempt "partial explanations" of the attributes to which they allude. "Expansionism," or "the struggle for world conquest," for instance, is spoken of as "the outward thrust of the 'passion for unanimity' " that is supposed to be characteristic of totalitarian systems. The "passion for unanimity," on the other hand is "at least partially" explained by the "totalitarian belief in the big lie as a propaganda technique," but in "the last analysis, the passion for unanimity seems to spring from the pseudoreligious fervor of the totalitarian ideology." Clearly such "explanations" are at their very best, "partial." Most are offered as "suggestions": "The history of the Communist Party of the USSR *suggests* that the leadership of the party, operating in context devoid of democratic devices for assuring efficiency . . . is faced with the dilemma of resolving the problem . . . while maintaining the elite status of the party" and so forth, or, "The purge accordingly *appears* to be inherent in modern totalitarianism. It is produced both by the existential conditions of the system and by the subjective motivations of its leadership." [6] These kinds of schematic explanations are at best suggestive of vaguely characterized causal factors and their interconnection. Their merit could only be heuristic— serving to orient researchers.

It is unfortunate that contemporary social scientists should continue to use terms like "theory," "model," and "explanation" as cavalierly as they do. Most of the objec-

----

[6] Friedrich and Brzezinski, *Totalitarian Dictatorship,* pp. 28, 63, 134, 135, 152 (emphasis supplied), 154 (emphasis supplied).

tions directed against the work produced by Friedrich and Brzezinski are the consequence of having misinterpreted the major thrust of their effort. Alexander Groth's interesting article devoted to the issue of "totalitarianism" focuses on what seem to be the *predictive pretensions* assumed by Friedrich and Brzezinski. Groth seems to conceive the principal, or at least one of the major, thrusts of Friedrich and Brzezinski's work as an attempt to enable social scientists to "be able to predict the future course of [totalitarianism] from the common model." [7] It seems reasonably clear that whatever "predictions" Friedrich and Brzezinski permit to escape are of an extremely modest variety—"there is no present reason to conclude that . . . though this possibility cannot be excluded," and so forth.[8] Again, the efforts are heuristic, not theoretical. A *theoretical proposition* is one that can be, in principle, confirmed or disconfirmed by some determinate public procedure. A *theory* is a collection of systematically related theoretical propositions, containing one or more lawlike assertions, capable of affording explanations and making time-conditioned predictions or retrodictions. At best, Friedrich and Brzezinski offer "partial explanations," that is to say they present a partial catalog of seemingly necessary or contingent conditions for the occurrence of any specific event or collection of events, but they do not undertake systematic predictive or explanatory efforts. Thus William Ebenstein is wrong when he maintains that the authors sought to "develop a general theory . . . of totalitarian dictatorship." [9] The same kind

---

[7] Alexander Groth, "The 'isms' in Totalitarianism." *American Political Science Review,* 1964, 58/4: 888.

[8] Friedrich and Brzezinski, *Totalitarian Dictatorship,* p. 6.

[9] William Ebenstein, "The Study of Totalitarianism," *World Politics,* 1958, 10/2: 274–288.

of mistake has become a commonplace in the literature. Otto Stammer, Peter Christian Ludz, and Oskar Anweiler, among many others, continue to talk about "a general theory of totalitarianism" when the very best that Friedrich and Brzezinski offered was a partial and primitive taxonomic scheme and some schematic accounts of some of the seemingly necessary and contingent conditions for the manifestations of some of the species, or subspecific, properties with which they were concerned.[10] It makes very little sense, for example, to charge them, as Ebenstein does, with the error of failing to explain why it is that if "modern technology" is the "key characteristic of totalitarianism," the most "technologically advanced" political systems are not totalitarian, when the best Friedrich and Brzezinski claimed was some of the manifest traits of totalitarianism were "technologically *conditioned.*" ". . . Modern technology," they insisted cannot be understood to have "caused" totalitarianism, but rather to have "made it possible." [11] Since they do not specify whether technology is a contingent and substitutable condition of totalitarianism, it is hard to challenge their claim. There is no *serious* theoretical claim imbedded in such a discursive and descriptive account. One simply does not know how to conduct a verification study of such general claims. Such claims are neither true nor false—they are vague and general—and perhaps theoretically suggestive. Hopefully research might grow out of them. But a great deal of preliminary work would have to be done first.

----

[10] Otto Stammer, "Aspekte der Totalitarismusforschung." In Bruno Seidel and Siegfried Jenkner, eds., *Wege der Totalitarismus-Forschung* (Wissenschaftliche Buchgesellschaft, 1968); Peter Christian Ludz, "Entwurf einer soziologischen Theorie totalitaer verfasster Gesellschaft," ibid.; Oskar Anweiler, "Totalitaere Erziehung," ibid.

[11] Ebenstein, *op. cit.,* p. 282; Friedrich and Brzezinski, *op. cit.,* pp. 11 (emphasis supplied) and 264.

That Friedrich and Brzezinski's work has been criticized for not being explanatory is at least partially the consequence of their disposition to talk about possessing a "descriptive theory" and a "model." The fact that they modify the term "theory" with the adjectival qualifier "descriptive" should have been enough to suggest that what they were attempting was not to produce a "model" or a "theory," but was rather an effort at *typologizing* or *taxonomizing*. It was not an attempt at "theorizing" in any strict empirical sense. Their use of the word "model" to identify their account was unfortunate. The word "model" is generally used in empirical science to suggest that some lawlike assertions characteristic of some range of inquiry can be successfully mapped over another (less well understood) range—one theory is imagined as "modeling" another. Since, as Frederic Fleron suggests, there is "a general lack of integrative theory" about specific Communist societies and totalitarianism in general, the use of the terms "theory" or "model" is confusing and misleading.[12] In treating "totalitarianism" we are not dealing with "theories" or "models," but with a problem in concept formation; employing a set of linguistic strategies designed to begin to sort some relatively stable constants out of the wealth of experience. Concept formation, in fact, begins characteristically with "initial vagueness" and is subject to "consequent frequent redefinition."[13] At the commencement of our work

----

[12] Frederic J. Fleron, Jr., "Soviet Area Studies and the Social Sciences: Some Methodological Problems in Communist Studies." *Soviet Studies,* 1968, 19/3: 313; cf. Patrick Suppes, "A Comparison of the Meaning and Uses of Models in Mathematics and the Empirical Sciences." In Hans Freudenthal ed., *The Concept and the Role of the Model in Mathematics and Social Sciences* (Reidel, 1961).

[13] May Brodbeck, "The Philosophy of Science and Educational Research." *Review of Educational Research,* 1957, 27/5: 429.

we begin to note, in an unselfconscious and nondeliberative way, some things that strike us as "hanging together"—what Friedrich and Brzezinski refer to as "a cluster of inter-related traits . . . ." [14] For recall and storage convenience we give such a trait-complex a name—in this case "totalitarianism." The cluster of traits may, or may not, suggest a number of vague and painfully unspecific researchable problems.

All of this indicates that we are not dealing with "theories" or "models" of totalitarianism. Fleron is obviously correct in stating that "the studies in the large literature on totalitarianism cannot, with few exceptions be viewed as building blocks in the construction of an empirical theory of totalitarianism. Rather, they have contributed to the formation of a conceptual scheme . . . ." [15] What Friedrich and Brzezinski have provided is, at its best, a "descriptive syndrome of discernible characteristics" that seemingly "hang together" in historic space.[16] Friedrich himself indicates that even with the availability of such a conceptual schema, there has been no "significant advance in causal explanation of the totalitarian phenomenon." [17] We have, in effect, no "general empirical theory" or "model" of totalitarianism. What we have is a preliminary criterial definition of a political construct composed of an indeterminate set of vaguely

---

[14] Friedrich and Brzezinski, *Totalitarian Dictatorship,* p. 9.

[15] Fleron, "Soviet Area Studies," p. 326.

[16] Zbigniew K. Brzezinski, *Ideology and Power in Soviet Politics* (Praeger, 1967), chap. 1; Carl Friedrich, "The Evolving Theory and Practice of Totalitarian Regimes." In Carl J. Friedrich, Michael Curtis, and Benjamin R. Barber, *Totalitarianism in Perspective: Three Views* (Praeger, 1969), p. 127.

[17] Friedrich, "The Evolving Theory," p. ix.

defined traits.[18] The possession of at least *one* of those traits would seem to be *logically* necessary for entry into the class "totalitarian." We are not sure, given the account provided by Friedrich and Brzezinski, whether they are content with such a modest admission requirement. Do they imagine that a political system must display *all* or *some* of the traits to qualify as "totalitarian"? If only *some* are required, *which* ones?

Problems of Prediction and Distinction

If we consider the trait-complex that characterizes totalitarian systems, it becomes obvious immediately that what we have is no more than a set of programmatic suggestions intended to serve as preliminary guides to inquiry. To be told, for example, that in "totalitarian" systems we can anticipate an "official ideology" that "covers" all "vital aspects of man's existence to which everyone living in that society is supposed to adhere" is not to tell us how to specifically or exhaustively distinguish totalitarian from nontotalitarian ideologies. To say that such ideologies are "chiliastic" and anticipate a "perfect final state of mankind"—that such a system of beliefs entertains a "radical rejection of the existing society and conquest of the world for the new one"— does not significantly distinguish, in principle, Leninism, or Fascism from the political system advocated by Plato, Calvin, Mao, Castro, or Nkrumah. There is no hard or precise distinction that one could argue with any objective conviction. To talk of a "technologically conditioned near complete monopoly of control . . . of all the means of effec-

----

[18] Benjamin R. Barber, "Conceptual Foundations of Totalitarianism." In Friedrich, Curtis, and Barber, p. 3.

tive mass communication . . . , of effective armed combat . . . , [and] the entire economy" [19] is not to tell us how to rigorously distinguish the controls effected by nontotalitarian as distinct from totalitarian systems. We are provided no "cutoff points and threshold levels" [20] that might distinguish "near complete monopoly of control" from any other control. The property traits of totalitarianism cannot be *qualitatively* characterized (that is to say, for example, we are not informed what *degree* of policy control would qualify as "terroristic" and what measure of formal and organizational support must be accorded an ideology to make it count as "official").[21] Only if such programmatic suggestions are given specific (at best, quantitative) reference, can one begin to undertake theoretically significant typological distinctions.

The fact that the principal work on totalitarian systems, that of Friedrich and Brzezinski, is a preliminary conceptual schema, rather than an effort to produce a scientific taxonomy or a *specific* guide to empirical research, much less a "general theory of totalitarianism," seems to have confused most commentators. Thus even as astute a commentator as Fleron suggests that Friedrich and Brzezinski should have provided "explicit definitions" [22] for their construct, when everything we know about such preliminary conceptual schemata suggests that they could not, and to be effective should not, attempt such closure. Explicit definitions specifically identify the *necessary* and *sufficient conditions* for the employment of a term—and as such are gen-

----

[19] Friedrich and Brzezinski, *Totalitarian Dictatorship,* p. 10.

[20] Burrowes, "Totalitarianism," p. 287.

[21] Gregor, *Metapolitics,* pp. 131ff.

[22] Fleron, "Soviet Area Studies," p. 328.

erally the exclusive product of closed or formal systems of thought—most characteristically mathematics and logic, or a formally developed science like physics that employs calculi to carry out its research.[23] The concepts in a quasi-experimental and informal science are not and, in general, cannot be other than "porous" or "open-textured" in order to accommodate the openness of on-going empirical inquiry. At the moment we simply do not know what the measure of "near monopoly control" might be that would explicitly and effectively distinguish totalitarian and non-totalitarian systems. We do not, on the basis of best evidence, know if such systems are to be plotted on a continuum from "open," or "constitutional," systems to "closed" or "totalitarian" systems, or if such systems can be discretely characterized in terms of mutually exclusive and exhaustive categories. To attempt to provide anything like an "explicit," or as another commentator states it "connotative," definition is to pretend to possess information we simply do not have.[24] The "ambiguity"[25] to which critics allude is intrinsic to such preliminary and essentially cataloging efforts. Burrowes seems to intuit as much. He maintains that "despite the illusion of theory it conveys, the totalitarian syndrome is perhaps most appropriately viewed as a set of general categories in terms of which a vast amount of data can be cataloged."[26] Until such time as social science has developed a defensible body of theory, which will permit the fairly rigorous distinctions required to support explicit and stipulative typologies or taxonomies, totalitarianism can

----

[23] Gregor, *Metapolitics*, pp. 127ff.

[24] Burrowes, "Totalitarianism," p. 283.

[25] Ludz, "Entwurf einer soziologischen theorie . . . ," pp. 533, 535.

[26] Burrowes, "Totalitarianism," p. 288.

only be assessed in terms of open-textured categories that are regularly revised, amplified, and explicated. To attempt closure at this point would be counterproductive.

In this sense most of Benjamin Barber's extended critique of the construct "totalitarian" misses the point.[27] Preliminary efforts like that of Friedrich and Brzezinski invariably either summarize and/or prompt the production of a vast body of work characterized by different perspectives, varying assessments, diffuse meanings, and frequently mutually incompatible claims. One could hardly have developed, for example, an explicit and rigorous taxonomy of organic life until one had at his disposal the vast amount of detailed empirical evidence, the rudiments of a generally accepted theory of organic evolution, and the relatively precise empirical theory concerning the transmission of genetic particles that we now possess. Before all those elements were available one could only produce preliminary and corrigible taxonomies like those of Aristotle or Linnaeus, schematic and general categories in which information that was available could be conveniently stored and retrieved. One could not talk about the "essential," "real," or "defining" properties of any species until one had the solid substance of an empirically viable theory on the basis of which one could effectively make such distinctions. Without such theoretical leverage on political life, one can allude, as Barber does, to "the barrenness of the assumptions about political life that underlie" the preliminary concept of "totalitarianism," but to no purpose. Preliminary conceptual schemata in informal disciplines are generally the products of commonplace assumptions. That is why they are preliminary. But one must begin somewhere—until one has reasonably well-confirmed theory at his disposal—and com-

---

[27] Barber, "Conceptual Foundations of Totalitarianism," p. 5.

monly accepted wisdom seems as good a place as any to start.

All commentators agree that we possess little in the way of defensible theories about political life in general, much less about a particular form of political life. Thus Herbert Spiro[28] in his summary discussion of "totalitarianism" indicates that we have various proposed interpretations of totalitarianism, but none of them are, in any systematic sense, competent. All of which is perfectly true. Friedrich and Brzezinski are clear in their judgment: the conceptual schema they suggest is, in and of itself, incapable of affording explanatory or predictive leverage. The question is whether such abstract and general cataloging and sorting strategies are productive of anything other than loose typologizing and discursive, incomplete, and partial explanation sketches. The only way to answer that would be to survey the literature of which the construct "totalitarianism" is a summary and the purposes to which it has subsequently been put. The construct summarizes, at a high level of abstraction, much of the material that found its way into the literature devoted to revolutionary political systems between 1930 and 1950. Almost all commentators we have reviewed —who have considered Fascism as a specific interpretive problem—have alluded to a class of political systems that shared with it certain general species properties. We have seen that Marxists and non-Marxists alike have identified, at a discursive and general level, attributes shared by the Soviet Union, National Socialist Germany, and Fascist Italy. A conceptual schema that conveniently summarizes these kinds of discursive judgments obviously has pedagogical and mnemonic merit. The question is, can this kind of cog-

----

[28] Herbert Spiro, "Totalitarianism." In David Sills, ed., *International Encyclopedia of the Social Sciences,* XVI (Macmillan, 1968).

nitive effort lead to more specific and consequently empirically significant results in the effort to produce defensible empirical explanations and reasonably competent predictions? The fact is that Friedrich and Brzezinski's initial work has generated attempts at more rigorous and inclusive taxonomies,[29] as well as efforts aimed at producing "theories of middle range"—that is to say, for example, an empirical theory of how "bureaucratic controls" might operate in particular socioeconomic environments (and then it might be part of a more inclusive "organization theory"). The efforts to produce such theories have been spoken of as moving from the "static and classificatory" character of the original conceptual schema via the "operationalization" of critical terms to the level of "dynamic" or "causal" accounts.[30] Such efforts at theory construction, both rigorously taxonomic, self-consciously experimental, quasi-experimental, and historically detailed, necessarily feedback and modify the loosely characterized formulations of the preliminary schema. All of this is both expected and salutary, and is the reaction to the availability of the original preliminary formulation. That is, apparently, how a social science proceeds.

When Michael Curtis warns that one should not expect to predict political and historic trends on the basis of conceptual typologies, particularly of the kind we are dealing with, he is perfectly, and obviously, correct.[31] One can only

[29] Robert C. Tucker, "Towards a Comparative Politics of Movement-Regimes," *American Political Science Review,* 1961, 55/2: 281–289.

[30] Stammer, "Aspekte der Totalitarismusforschung," pp. 430, 432; Peter Christian Ludz, "Offene Fragen in der Totalitarismusforschung." In Seidel and Jenkner, eds., *Wege der Totalitarismus-Forschung,* pp. 470, 473.

[31] Michael Curtis, "Retreat from Totalitarianism." In Friedrich, Curtis and Barber, p. 55.

deplore the fact that Friedrich and Brzezinski permitted their minor interest in prediction to confuse the essential character of their enterprise. The schema they proposed affords little, if any, predictive leverage. If a typology or a taxonomy has predictive capabilities it is because, by and large, it rests on a body of competent theory. Since neither Friedrich nor Brzezinski claimed to possess such a body of theory, their "predictions" could be no more substantial than the theories they entertained. Most of their suggestive judgments about the "future" of totalitarian systems are so vague and general that almost anything would be compatible with them. They generally did qualify all their explanatory and predictive suggestions with allusions to vague causes of error, historical contingencies and personality factors. We are "uncertain" as to the "real effect of ideological motivation upon the actual policymaker"; "it is difficult to prove" that a consensus has been established in one or another totalitarian system; the "historical record" "suggests" that there are cycles of intensification and relaxation of "autocratic power"; we have no "satisfactory general genetic theory which would truly explain why totalitarianism appeared in the twentieth century." It is clear that at best "we are moving on the rather abstract level." We are dealing with a construct which like most political terms is "surrounded by a haze of vaguer and conflicting notions . . . ." [32] The principal business of their work is not prediction mongering or explanation fobbing—it is the provision of a preliminary conceptual schema that has didactic, storage and retrieval, and perhaps heuristic, utility.

---

[32] Friedrich and Brzezinski, *Totalitarian Dictatorship,* chap. 27; Friedrich, "The Evolving Theory," pp. 123, 130, 131, 139, 140, 124.

Defining Totalitarianism

Once this is granted, we are left with the very complicated question of heuristic utility. Does a term like "totalitarian" identify some collection of phenomenological or observable traits with sufficient open-textured specificity to permit "a reasonable degree of correspondence" [33] with available evidence? Most commentators agree that "totalitarianism" is a heuristic construct, an "ideal type" that suggests something about the empirical reality of some loosely characterized class of political systems. Every science begins with such schemata which, at best, are calculated to summarize, store, and efficiently retrieve whatever funded information we have about our universe of inquiry.[34] A science needs points of view and problems to be solved. From that initial point the research scientist, concerned with a variety of issues that may overlap with those imbedded in the conceptual schemata made available in the literature at his disposal, may disaggregate a general construct (such as "totalitarianism") into a variety of dimensions. He may develop categories devoted to "freedom of political opposition," measured in terms of a voting system or "vulnerability of elites"; or to the means available in any political system for "interest aggregation" and "interest articulation"; or to techniques for the "transfer of effective political power"; or he may undertake a content analysis of published political literature to determine some measure of "ideological rigidity."

It is obvious that the disaggregation of such a construct

---

[33] Ibid., p. 125.

[34] Karl Popper, *The Logic of Scientific Discovery* (Basic Books, 1961), pp. 106ff.

can take a multiplicity of forms and will give rise to a variety of alternative empirical theories of varying degrees of generality. Factor analytic work might inform the research scientist if any of these constituents "load" on any more general factor and how much of the variance in any political system is to be attributable to any specific factor or cluster of factors. Professional interest in the history of ideas, on the other hand, may produce accounts that attempt to provide a catalog of argument forms that seem to characterize "totalistic" ideologies. These can range from loosely argued literary treatments that identify Plato or Aristotle as articulating a "totalitarian belief system" to more systematic, scholarly exegeses identifying totalitarian currents in "democratic" thought.[35] A preliminary schema such as the one in which the concept "totalitarianism" is housed can serve as a goad to research, a cataloging convenience, a suggestion of the multidimensionality of political systems, and a point of departure for academic scholarship.[36]

One question seems to be obscured by all this. Does the concept "totalitarian" refer, with any degree of plausibility, to an identifiable collection of observable traits displayed by some past or present political systems? Are there, or have there been, political systems that are, or were, individually animated by a reasonably formal collection of ideas that might, with some legitimacy, be called "official"? Are there, or were there, political systems in which executive responsibilities are, or were, discharged by a "charismatic" or

---

[35] J. L. Talmon, *The Origins of Totalitarian Democracy* (Secker and Warberg, 1952).

[36] A. James Gregor, "Classical Marxism and the Totalitarian Ethic," *Journal of Value Inquiry*, 1968, 2/1: 58–72, *Contemporary Radical Ideologies: Totalitarian Thought in the Twentieth Century* (Random House, 1968).

"pseudocharismatic" leader who was, or is, identified as "a world historical genius," a "telluric force," or some such hyperbolic characterization? Are there, or were there, political systems that do not, or did not, permit formal and voluntary "opposition"? Are there, or were there, political systems that "control" information flow? that develop an elaborate "bureaucratic infrastructure"? that "control" in "significant" measure the educational, productive and distributive processes? that have the potential for the exercise of "violence" and/or "terror" against their own citizens without providing them with institutionalized agencies of defense and/or redress? that seek to "inculcate" uniform and general political and moral opinions among their citizenry? that legitimize rules by appealing to an identifiable body of social, political and economic argument?

The answer is obviously yes, but the information such an account affords is clearly insufficient. We need fairly rigorous operational definitions, for example, of what might count as "official," "charismatic," "opposition," "control," "bureaucratic infrastructure," "significant," "violence" or "terror," and "inculcation." We need reliable and stable intersubjective indices that might be appropriate for measurement. We need competent content analyses and surveying strategies, systematic data collection and adequate sampling procedures. We require the formulation of testable generalizations, and the discharge of subsequent verificational studies. We need, in effect, rigorously formulated empirical theories that begin to provide defensible generalizations about some of the issues central to the problems suggested by the preliminary conceptual schema. All this will be constrained by a lack of creditable data, the passing of some of the historic exemplars of the class of "totalitarian systems" (Mussolini's Fascism among them), and our inability to conduct any serious research in most of them (our lack of research access to systems such as those in the Soviet Union, China, or Cuba). Under such constraints, much of our inquiry will be the consequence of rank speculation couched in the ordinary language of the intelligent layman. As a consequence, we probably will not be in the possession of viable theories of totalitarianism for the foreseeable future. For the time being what we have are reasonably competent historical and discursive accounts of various systems that can be spoken of with some cognitive merit as "totalitarian." Such accounts are not "theoretical" in any serious empirical sense. They are classificatory and typological and, at best, invoke vague and ambiguous low order generalizations. One cannot pretend to reliably explain how such systems arose nor what course they might subsequently follow.

We know enough, for example, about "convergent evolution" in organic development to know that entities that share a number of observable traits might be substantially, if not radically, different in any number of ways. But in order to transfer such insights into the realm of "totalitarianisms" we would have to possess theoretical knowledge about the genesis, the determinant variables, and the lawlike generalizations that characterize the developmental processes of political systems. We do not possess such knowledge. As a consequence, we neither know which traits of totalitarianism might be "essential" or "necessary," nor can we argue with any confidence that the shared similarities between totalitarianisms mean anything "significant." We do not have a body of theory by virtue of which such distinctions might be made.

Most of the criticism that has collected around the discussion of "totalitarianism" is, in fact, devoted to the ventilation of competitive *explanatory* efforts. Robert Burrowes, for instance, is convinced that *"modernization"* and *"industrialization"* are perhaps somehow crucial to the "understanding" of "totalitarian systems," while Michael Curtis seems to deny their significance.[37] Robert Tucker, in turn, suggests that under critical conditions it is the *psychology* of "charismatic leaders" that is of overriding significance.[38] Alexander Groth, on the other hand, maintains that it is the *analysis of groups,* in terms of their economic interests and political strength, that is critical.[39] All of these accounts are alternative attempts at theory construction, and they are undertaken under the spur of the work provided by Friedrich and Brzezinski. Many simply attempt to provide theoretical propositions to flesh out the totalitarian schema. Some tighten up the lexical definitions of critical terms. In fact, the bulk of the "criticism" directed against the concept of "totalitarianism" constitutes evidence that the concept has significant heuristic merit.

The notion "totalitarianism" finds a place in a pretheoretical conceptual schema that at its best summarizes, for recall convenience, a large body of funded material of a wide variety of sorts. The notion, and the schema it inhabits, attempt to suggest broad lines of historical, experimental and quasi-experimental research. One would hardly expect a pretheoretical schema to tell us more about Fascism or "totalitarianism" that we already know, for Friedrich and Brzezinski's clear intention was to summarize at a rather "abstract level" the substance of the literature devoted to Fascism, National Socialism, and Bolshevism produced over

----

[37] Burrowes, "Totalitarianism," pp. 267, 277; Curtis, "Retreat from Totalitarianism," pp. 84ff.

[38] Robert C. Tucker, "The Dictator and Totalitarianism." *World Politics,* 1965, 17/4: 555–583.

[39] Groth, "The 'isms' in Totalitarianism."

a thirty-year period. In this sense the recent discussion by Herbert Spiro and Benjamin Barber,[40] concerning the "ideological uses" to which the concept "totalitarianism" has been put, is quite beside the point. The concept "totalitarianism" was not coined during the "cold war" to satisfy some political or ideological interests. The concept "totalitarianism" was a summary of the judgments contained in the bulk of literature devoted to Fascism, National Socialism, and Bolshevism. In effect, the concept "totalitarianism" was not minted to serve "counterideological" purposes (however the concept was used by those who attempted to exploit it). It was articulated to serve primarily as a storage convenience, a mnemonic aid, and a pedagogical tool. As a consequence it *reflected* antecedent work.[41] In the original work of Friedrich and Brzezinski, the concept "totalitarianism" served primarily as a *pretheoretical* convenience. There was little pretense that what was being advanced constituted an explanatory "theory."

Since such is the case, the "interpretation" of Fascism as a "totalitarianism" does not provide any new leverage on coming to "understand" Fascism. Since the concept summarizes the expert opinion with which specialists have been long familiar, it serves as a storage and recall convenience rather than as a new interpretive insight. At best the concept "totalitarianism" serves heuristic purpose by suggesting that analysts recognize sustained similarities among a variety of intuitively "different" political systems, and search out common generic causes that might account for the rise

---

[40] Herbert Spiro and Benjamin Barber, "Counter-Ideological Uses of 'Totalitarianism.'" *Politics and Society,* 1970, 1/1: 3–22.

[41] Rodolfo Mondolfo, "Il fascismo in Italia." In Renzo De Felice, ed., *Il fascismo e i partiti politici Italiani* (Cappelli, 1966); Giuseppe Prezzolini, "Ideologia e sentimento," ibid.

of totalitarianisms of whatever specific or subspecific variety. There can be little doubt that Friedrich and Brzezinski accomplished what they had set out to do. They provided a storage, recall, and pedagogical aid of no mean significance—and they precipitated a great deal of interesting discussion. They have left us richer as a consequence.

It is hard to suppress the conviction that any reading of the literature devoted to Fascism, National Socialism, and Stalinism could have done anything other than produce a generic concept "totalitarianism" to refer to the prevailing similarities that characterize the overt behaviors of these regimes. The informal and discursive evidence that prompted such judgments provides the public warrant upon which the notion of "totalitarianism" must ultimately rest. The task of contemporary social scientists is to attempt to provide a reasonably competent theory in which such funded and discursive evidence can be rendered more precise and systematically housed. The work requires the collaborative effort of historians patient enough to scour the tons of documentary evidence now available. For that purpose they will require relatively clear selective criteria as to what they should seek out in that mass of material. All selective reporting requires fairly specific criteria of relevance and significance. A collaborative effort between historians, empirically oriented analysts, and generalizing social scientists is required, if we are ever to lift our comprehension of totalitarianism and Fascism above the level of commonplaces and ordinary language interpretation.

It is clearly not enough to say that Mussolini's Fascists had near-monopoly control over the Italian economy. One needs to know what "near-monopoly" might be taken to mean and how one might begin to measure it. It is not enough to suggest that Fascism was a "syncratic" system in which established agricultural and industrial elites "collaborated" with the Fascist movement in order to produce the kinds of surface features to which the concept "totalitarianism" alludes. We must search the documentary and statistical evidence to attempt to establish, with some degree of empirical plausibility, the nature and intensity of elite interests and how they were, in fact, negotiated. When we receive judgments that the Fascists *did not* "tame" established elites other judgments that they *did,* and still others that Fascists *sometimes did* and at other times *did not,*[42] one can only hope to have more documentary and empirical evidence to make a reasonably probative judgment. When we learn on the one hand, that "genuine economic growth during the years of Fascism was quite small," and on the other, that "some industries [in Fascist Italy] did experience a very rapid rate of growth: steel industries [for example] doubled their production . . . ," we obviously need reasonably precise definitions of what "genuine economic growth" might mean as well as a more adequate statistical and inclusive economic analysis.[43]

We obviously need to know a great deal more about Fascism as a totalitarianism if we are to pretend to have a competent "interpretation" of Fascism. We can make some judgments now, based on a considerable amount of historic evidence, that reveal the faulted character of many of the candidate interpretations we have inherited. What we do

----

[42] Groth, "The 'isms' in Totalitarianism," pp. 890ff.; Friedrich and Brzezinski, *Totalitarian Dictatorship,* p. 17; Roland Sarti, *Fascism and the Industrial Leadership in Italy: 1919–1940* (University of California Press, 1971).

[43] Charles F. Delzell, ed., *Mediterranean Fascism, 1919–1945* (Harper & Row, 1970), p. 138; S. Lombardini, "Italian Fascism and the Economy." In S. J. Woolf, ed., *The Nature of Fascism* (Random House, 1969), p. 157; A. James Gregor, "Fascism and Modernization: Some Addenda." *World Politics* (to be published in April 1974).

not have is a general theory of Fascism (much less a general theory of totalitarianism). We can dismiss, given the contemporary information and theoretical tools at our disposal, interpretations of Fascism as the consequence of moral crisis, those accounts that exploit the hopeless strategies of psychoanalytic interpretation, as well as the simplistic versions of the interpretation of Fascism as the product of "amorphous masses." The more sophisticated accounts to be found in contemporary Marxist or "neo-Marxist" literature seem more promising. That interpretation which unites elements of an empirically oriented analysis of mass behaviors, economic growth, and the putative dispositional properties entailed in such processes, seems at the moment, most likely to yield the best results. Should such accounts provide a body of theory that entails the appearance of descriptive properties like those employed by the concept "totalitarianism," such an effort might provide the rudiments of a more general and inclusive theory. We might then not only have a serious theory of Fascism, we might even aspire to a general theory of totalitarianism.

CHAPTER EIGHT

Conclusion

For almost half a century historians and social scientists have attempted to provide a comprehensive and compelling account of Mussolini's Fascism. The collective effort has produced a number of notable historical works, particularly those of Renzo De Felice—but all historical works, good and bad alike, inevitably exploit social science generalizations upon which, in the final analysis, "understanding" must rest. Moreover, such generalizations provide sorting criteria for the selective reporting of information in historical narratives. De Felice, for instance, feels not only that it is significant to report that "business interests" provided some financial support for Mussolini's efforts to bring Italy into World War I, but he also provides an account of the motives which animated that support.[1] Interred in such a recital are a number of low-level and commonsense generalizations: men act as a consequence of motives, some motives are financial in character, businessmen can be understood to be moved by profit concerns, intervention in World War I necessarily implied increased armaments production and the possibility of increased profits, therefore some businessmen were disposed to aid Mussolini's efforts. Laced together by some commonsense logic, the account furnishes a measure of "understanding" on why there was business support for Mussolini's publication that advertised itself as a "socialist daily." A more adequate understanding of such a sequence would require a review of the empirical regularities governing decision making under conditions of cross-pressure—in which political actors are moved by conflicting impulses, attitudes, interests and/or cognitive appraisals. Intervention in World War I, it might be argued, may have had a higher immediate salience among the mul-

---

[1] Renzo De Felice, *Mussolini il rivoluzionario* (Einaudi, 1965), p. 277.

tiple interests that animate businessmen than opposition to
"socialism"—an argument that would rest on further empirical generalizations.

The Search for Explanatory Strategies

Historians pursue their narratives with minimal concern
for unearthing the empirical generalizations upon which
their accounts ultimately rest. At best, historians will weave
their accounts together with commonsense generalizations
and the logic of ordinary language. Social science interpretations, on the other hand, generally and self-consciously
invoke relatively broad-gauged empirical generalizations. A
typical social science account might read, "The masses liberated in the last century to a literate existence—have remained intellectually illiterate. Motion pictures are their
chief agent of entertainment. Even the books they read are
written in a movie-like manner. Impressionistic and full of
action, they appeal to the senses more than to the brain." [2]
Knowing this, "demagogic propaganda" has made good use
of those psychological disabilities. "The modern demagogue
realizes that what the mass man longs for is an emotional
outlet for active participation" in order to satisfy the senses
and dissipate the "fear" that ignorance and isolation breed
in him. "The suppression of fear is, in fact, the chief aim of
dictatorial organization. The introduction of uniforms ful-
fills this purpose, as does the observance of strict discipline."
Finally, rituals are equally "good outlets for anxiety feelings." [3] What obtains in such accounts is a collection of

---

[2] Sigmund Neumann, *Permanent Revolution: The Total State in a
World at War* (Harper & Row, 1965), p. 222.

[3] Ibid., p. 228.

broad descriptive and theoretical generalizations about some vaguely characterized range of concerns. Taken all together—loose definitions, low-level generalizations, broad-gauged empirical claims, putative functional relationships between behavioral dispositions and overt behavior—such collections constitute common instances of "social science explanations." Often historians employ such accounts not only as the substructure of their own narratives, but also as a guide to selective reporting. Fortunately different historians select different "perspectives" in undertaking their respective accounts and the differential focus, each with different selective criteria, provides a relatively independent data base against which social science generalizations can be assessed and revised.

However one chooses to approach the Fascist phenomenon—as a historian or as a social scientist—one's enterprise directly or indirectly, immediately or upon analysis, turns on the hub of "theory." This is as true for the treatments of paradigmatic Fascism as it is for generic fascism. Most accounts, of course, are not specifically "unitheoretical." They tend to be *eclectic* insofar as they employ elements from a variety of "perspectives" in order to produce a connected discussion. In such accounts we might be told, for example, that the "revolt of the masses is the core of modern [revolutionary] dynamism"—that the "dissolution of social groups" produces "lonely," "frightened," "amorphous masses" that are then "institutionalized" to provide the "real background of Fascism." But more than that, we are told that the revolutionary elite pursues a policy of economic development and rationalization in order to attain industrial self-sufficiency and military preparedness and the "*stato corporativo* [of Fascism] is a technician's concept of politics. A council of experts by their essential limitations as experts necessitates dictatorship, i.e., the coordinating apex of the experts' pyramid. A 'managerial revolution' can thus easily get out of the control of the great economic engineers and be diverted into the stream of . . . professional revolutionaries . . . ." Thus while appeal to "amorphous masses" constitutes the "core" of the explanation, programmatic economic policies explain Fascism's special appeal and function. But more than that, some provision must be made for the presence in the system of "stable groups" that are composed of anything other than "amorphous masses." Revolutionary appeals must address themselves to the real, proximate interests of viable and active population elements organized into self-conscious associations. Added to all this is the conviction that the politics of revolution can be, at least in part, conceived as a "conflict of generations." The "young war generation" that survived World War I was joined by a postwar generation of "restless youth which had lacked fatherly guidance in its childhood." Conjoined to all that, the explanation of fascism also makes further and final recourse to the fact that "Germany and Italy" had a "different historic fate and national traditions." [4]

In effect, the most common "explanations" of Fascism available to students appeal to all but the entire collection of explanatory strategies available in social science literature: the thesis of the role and disposition of "amorphous masses"; the requirements of stages of economic development and industrial growth; intergenerational conflict; primary socialization; and finally, but not exhaustively, "national character." Such eclectic accounts are prevalent and popular because they are maximally insulated against counterevidence and disconfirmation. If some part of the interpretation is faulted, emphasis can be readily shifted to some other

----

[4] Ibid., pp. 97, 101, 108, 115, 164, 214, 251.

aspect of the complex "explanation." The burden of explanation can be readily lifted from a fragile support to those that seem more substantial. One can move artfully from some vague theory of "mass behaviors," to "primary socialization," to the function of special interest groups, and finally, if all else fails, to the notion that Fascism was the product of a peculiar national tradition.

Eclectic accounts can always escape serious scrutiny by failing to invest any specific interpretation with full responsibility. What they produce are plausibilities, and that seems what, by and large, we must be content with in the interpretation of Fascism.

Moralistic Accounts of Fascism

The cognitively least satisfying accounts of Fascism are those that conceive it to have been the simple consequence of "evil," "brutality," and "inhumanity." Few contemporary social scientists would be content with a similar interpretation of Bolshevism, Maoism, or Castroism. When Ludwig von Mises provides us with an account of "communism" that pretends to inform us that the "militant communists are to be found only in the ranks of those who make a living from their communism or expect that a revolution would further their personal ambitions," and that the "real significance of the Lenin revolution is to be seen in the fact that it was the bursting forth of the principle of unrestricted violence and oppression . . . the negation of all the political ideals that had for three thousand years guided the evolution of Western civilization,"[5] we are

---

[5] Ludwig von Mises, *Planned Chaos*, pp. 43, 63.

prepared to dismiss such "explanations" as a tissue of banalities. The fact that Stalin massacred millions of Russians, that Maoists launched a reign of terror throughout China for years after the founding of the "People's Republic," and that Castro has forced almost ten percent of the population of Cuba to flee, would hardly be enough, for most historians and social scientists, to license an "embodiment of evil" interpretation as adequate. Those interpretations that pretend to see in Fascism a "conflict of ideals" or "the moral crisis of the West" are no more adequate as explanations when applied to Fascism than when they are applied to "communism."

The attempted explanations of Fascism in terms of "irrationality" and "evil" are frequently supported by claims that Fascists made no attempt to provide normative arguments in support of their revolution or in support of their system—claims faulted by the available body of Fascist literature dedicated precisely to the "moral substance" of Fascism. Anglo-American analysts have shown themselves to be singularly unfamiliar with an enormous body of Fascist literature. For some curious reason few have seen fit to undertake a serious appraisal of Fascist argument. Similar treatment of "Marxist" literature and "Marxist" political systems immediately would disqualify one as an "authority." Similar ignorance of Fascist literature, however, rarely has been considered a disability.

Recently David Ingersoll has lamented that "we have surprisingly little scholarship on fascism as an ideology" [6] —a sad commentary on the quality of fascist studies. We have been studying fascism for half a century and the

----

[6] David Ingersoll, *Communism, Fascism and Democracy* (Merrill, 1971), p. 92.

number of competent works devoted to the ideology of Mussolini's Fascism could be counted on one hand. Given the paucity of competent scholarship in the area, the interpretation that understands Fascism to have been the consequence of a "conflict of ideas" or a "crisis" in the "moral principles" of the West can hardly recommend itself.

The Need for an Adequate Classificatory Schema

The fact of the matter is that we have no generally accepted social science characterization of generic fascism. Social science has still to generate an adequate classificatory schema by virtue of which serious comparative studies of contemporary revolutionary movements can be undertaken. Without comparative studies and regularity analysis it is difficult to understand how it might be possible to produce and subsequently confirm even low-order generalizations, much less articulate a compelling theoretical interpretation. Leonard Schapiro recently has complained that if "fascism" is to be an object of serious study "the first essential would seem to be to specify the particular regimes and movements to which alone the term . . . is, by definition, to be applied." [7] The difficulty with this kind of recommendation is that definitions are invariably by-products of some kind of theoretical generalizations. To attempt to provide definitions before one has a body of viable theoretical propositions at one's disposal seems to be counterproductive. The definition of fascism as "the politically or-

---

[7] Leonard Schapiro, "What is Fascism?" *New York Review of Books,* February 12, 1970, p. 13.

ganized expression of the average human character structure . . ." [8] is clearly parasitic on neo-Freudian theoretical
speculations. Nolte's quaint definition of Italian Fascism as
"an anti-revolutionary revolution of subversive conservatives" [9] exploits an inventory of generalizations about group
and individual behavior and the putative motives which
animate it. S. J. Woolf's identification of fascism as "a mass
movement of reaction" is clearly predicated on comparative
generalizations governing a variety of systems. Fascism did
not "nationalize the means of production," for Woolf, while
Soviet Russia did; fascism was "brutally authoritarian" in
its control over workers organizations, while Soviet Russia
was not. Fascism, in fact and as a consequence of these
comparative judgments, was "typical of a type of development of capitalism in its 'final phase.' " [10] To which Schapiro
could only reply:

> What does the abstraction about "nationalizing the means
> of production" mean in reality? Is there so very much dif-
> ference between Nazi control over the means of production
> and Communist control over the means of production, ex-
> cept that in the one case the benefits go to both the pro-
> prietors . . . and the Nazi bosses, while in the other the
> main benefits go to the Communist party bosses? The pop-
> ulation has no say in either case. Was Stalin less "brutally
> authoritarian" to workers than Hitler—let alone Musso-

---

[8] Wilhelm Reich, *Mass Psychology of Fascism* (Orgone, 1946),
p. ix.

[9] Ernst Nolte, *Three Faces of Fascism* (Holt, Rinehart and Winston,
1966), p. 64.

[10] S. J. Woolf, "Introduction." In S. J. Woolf, ed., *European Fascism*
(Random House, 1968), p. 9, "Did a Fascist Economic System Exist?"
In S. J. Woolf, ed., *The Nature of Fascism* (Random House, 1969), pp.
142ff.

lini? And in what sense is fascism capitalism in its final phase? [11]

The interpretation of fascism as a generic or specific political phenomenon abounds in paradox and seeming confusion. All of which suggests the lack of serious theoretical substance in most accounts. We cannot unambiguously identify "fascist" movements or regimes because we have no adequate classificatory strategy. We seem to have no suitable classificatory schema because we do not have a defensible theoretical system that might support it.

Flaws in Psychoanalytic Interpretations of Fascism

There is a complex relationship between efforts at classification, some discrete set of empirical generalizations, and the theoretical matrix in which they are lodged. The objections to psychoanalytic interpretations of fascism in general, and Fascism in particular, turn on the very poverty of the theoretic substructure that supports the classification of such phenomena as "homosexual movements of sadomasochists." Such a characterization has been employed to identify not only Fascism and National Socialism, but Stalin's Bolshevism as well. One would imagine that no less could be said of Castro's Cuba or Mao's China, among a host of other possible candidates.

The resistance to psychoanalytic interpretations arises not because its classificational system is so inclusive, but because its serious methodological and theoretical deficiencies conspire to make empirical confirmation or disconfirma-

---

[11] Schapiro, "What is Fascism?" p. 13.

tion of its specific claims impossible. All "general interpretations" of "fascism" suffer something of the same disabilities, but the psychoanalytic treatment seems singularly deficient.

Flaws in the Socioeconomic Interpretations

The interpretation of Fascism as the product of a "society of mass," or as a function of a stage of economic growth produce classifications that are almost as general as that of psychoanalysis, and most of the critical concepts in such accounts are vexatiously vague. The distinction between them and the psychoanalytic interpretation seems to lie in their potential for resolving some of their classificatory and research problems, while psychoanalytic interpretations retreat further and further into the recesses of "unconscious intentions" and "symbolic interpretations" forever insulated from empirical scrutiny.

The interpretation of Fascism as the consequence of the "rise of amorphous masses" provides a toehold on explanation in so far as a "mass-mobilizing movement" requires masses for its mobilization. Unhappily, we have only begun to attempt to isolate the conditions that might be necessary or sufficient to render "masses" mobilizable. We have some indirect evidence concerning the properties of "mass-man," drawn from the nonrandom and consequently nonrepresentative samples of individuals that could be so characterized. How confidently we can project such findings over whole populations is quite another matter. How much of this information is applicable to the Italian population of 1919 through 1922, or to that same population from 1922 to 1945, is difficult to establish with any credibility. We have few lawlike assertions that could cover mass behaviors or that might competently explain the recruitment successes of the Fascist movement for the period of its rapid, unprecedented, and all but totally unexpected growth, for example, during 1921 and 1922. We seem to have a general plausibility at our disposal, but little that could count as hard evidence in support of the omnibus claims that give the account substance. Moreover, using the unrestricted claims concerning the species properties of "mass-man," it is very difficult to explain specific historic or political occurrences that seem central to the actual sequence of events. The interpretation of Fascism as the product of politics in a society of masses very frequently sounds as though its protagonists were attempting to explain the manifest behavior traits of Fascism by projecting the putative traits of "mass-man" over the entire phenomenon. We know very little about the dispositional properties of "mass-man"—certainly far too little to provide us with an empirical basis for a general interpretation.

Marxists of whatever persuasion and whatever competence have been prepared to grant that "masses" functioned in a critical manner throughout the history of Fascism. They generally have recognized that "masses" have "resonated" to Fascist propaganda,[12] but they were equally quick to insist that one is compelled to attempt an explanation of why Fascist, and not "revolutionary socialist," propaganda attracted mass support and assent. Marxists and "neo-Marxists" have even been prepared to accept not only a qualified version of the "amorphous masses" thesis, but psychoanalytic accounts of the "sado-masochistic latent homosexual" appeals of Fascism as well.[13] They have generally insisted, however, that such insights be coupled with

----

[12] R. Osborn, *Psychology of Reaction* (Gollancz, 1938), Preface.

[13] Reinhard Kuehnl, *Formen buergerlicher Herrschaft: Liberalismus-Faschismus* (Rowolt, 1971), p. 95.

a rendering that affords an assessment of Fascism's socio-economic and political "functions." For such analysts, Fascism's "function" was to defend the system of privilege—to defend the ensconced economic agrarian and industrial elites from the threat of "revolution from below." The psychosocial insights provided by the notion of Fascism as the product of a society of masses or of individual psychodynamic impairments are joined to an analysis of socio-economic and political functions attributable to Fascism. Such formulations appear more inclusive, internally consistent, and applicable to specific cases—and consequently more plausible. The classifications they produce turn on the "conservative" or "revolutionary" functions attributable to various movements.

The difficulty with such treatments is that they generally seem to suggest that Fascism would be the predictable consequence of crisis in industrially advanced economic systems: the product of the "decay" of "monopoly capitalism." As a matter of fact, generic fascism first manifested itself, and ultimately was most widespread, in *underdeveloped* economic systems most notably those of Italy, Spain, Portugal, and Rumania. Moreover, even when fascism appeared in an advanced industrial system, Germany, it clearly seemed more concerned with politically controlling the privileged classes than providing them with a defense against "revolution from below." [14] Most contemporary Marxists are prepared to grant that fascist movements acted with considerable autonomy vis-à-vis the economic elites. Fascism could not plausibly be construed as anything more than the product of decaying monopoly capital or the

---

[14] Iring Fetscher, "Faschismus und Nationalsozialismus: Zur Kritik des sowjetmarxistischen Faschismusbegriffs," *Politische Vierteljahresschrift* (March, 1962), 3/1: 42–63.

"armed defense" of privilege—even if such an account were supported by whatever other insights.

Flaws in the Theory of Italian Fascism as a Consequence of "Delayed Industrialization"

The most contemporary efforts at interpretation attempt to account for all the features, alluded to by antecedent "theories," that seem to have attended fascism. In general, contemporary interpretations attempt to understand Italian Fascism as a political system that arose characteristically in an environment characterized by "delayed industrialization." In order to create a system that could effectively compete in the twentieth century, Fascists charged themselves with the obligation of creating a viable and advanced industrial enterprise. Fascism drove Italy into a period of intensive capital accumulation. Capital was required in order to provide the resources for "social overhead," the development of modern educational, communications, road and rail systems, the development of scarce power resources, and the insulation of essential, but noncompetitive, local industries. The most immediate, effective, and least dislocating way of accomplishing those ends was a system of "class collaboration" in which wages and consumption were stringently controlled to provide for massive savings and capital accumulation. Capitalists served as the transmission belts for capital investment—high profits insured a high rate of savings and savings provided the funds for directed capital investment. During the Fascist period the rate of savings and fixed asset formation reached levels that were not to be surpassed until Italy's postwar "economic miracle." Conceivably, "class collaboration" was a strategy calculated not only to provide for intensive capital

accumulation, but to protect and maintain the pool of enterprisory and entrepreneurial talent to be found among the
"bourgeoisie" of Italy as well. To protect the system from
the massive dislocations that "socialist revolution" might
introduce, Fascism insulated "property" and "functional
elites" from jeopardy and insured a propitious investment
climate for the expanding industrial system. As the system
expanded, Fascism developed bureaucratic controls that
insured its political dominance. By 1938 Fascism effected
more controls over the economic system than did any
country outside the Soviet Union. The "masses" that were
involved in the process were politically mobilized in order
to inure them to a system that would require massive controls over consumption and "nonproductive expenditure."
Wage levels had to be kept at the lowest tolerable levels.
Tolerance was sustained by noneconomic benefits: pageantry, histrionics, posturing, uniforms, and the entire
choreography of Fascism. By making common cause with
ensconced elites for its own purposes, Fascism could capture
"masses" that had initially been displaced by war and
economic dislocation. Having captured restive masses Fascism could keep them "socially demobilized" and manage-
able by techniques of careful orchestration that dissipated
their frustrations and made austerity tolerable.

The interpretation of Fascism as a product of an economic and social system in the process of a sustained drive
to economic maturity strikes one as maximally plausible
because it accounts for all the overt features of Fascism
alluded to by other efforts at interpretation in a consistent,
mutually supportive, and integral fashion. Systems undergoing intensive economic development would be expected
to be characterized by high emotional salience and restiveness. Large numbers of persons are being displaced, re-
located, retrained; established patterns of interpersonal

behavior are being eroded and significantly modified; and urban populations expand. We have suggestive empirical evidence that such circumstances breed restiveness, a high order of free floating hostility, and appreciable measures of insecurity. The restiveness is dissipated in marches and posturing, the hostility is geared up against outgroups, "the plutocratic democracies" that "surround" and "threaten" the "Fatherland." The insecurity is offset by the provision of a leadership that is "infallible" and "invincible." We have suggestive evidence from surveys and interviews undertaken with those who lived through fascist systems that a sense of personal identity, security, and self-respect was, in fact and at least in part, generated by such population management techniques. The availability of mass support, as well as the extensive bureaucratic controls developed by the expanding system, provided Italian Fascism an appreciable amount of independence—sufficient to make foreign policy, for example, the consequence of the decisions of the "infallible" "Leader." Moreover, the "nonfascist allies" of the system could be effectively managed—until military defeat all but totally alienated both mass and elite support.

For all that, such an account cannot provide anything like testable generalizations concerning threshold levels beyond which "dislocated masses" can be effectively mobilized or socially demobilized populations managed. We have no index that would suggest at *what point* "delayed" or "thwarted" industrialization or economic dislocation provides leverage on predicting political change. In effect, what the most plausible contemporary interpretations of Fascism provide are *discursive generalizations* that, because of their intrinsic vagueness and ambiguity, are nontestable. There is no conceivable immediate "verification study" that can grow out of the plausible explanation of Fascism as a function of an episode in modernization. We are a long way from making a compelling theory of such plausibilities and credibilities. This is made transparent when one recognizes, with most specialists, that the term "fascist" has no clearly defined reference class. Such terms have specific reference only in the body of rigorously formalized theory. Since we have no theory of generic fascism we can hardly expect the term to have specific reference. Contemporary discussions of "fascism" will continue to provide evidence of the vagueness of the reference class. There is no generally accepted range of phenomena over which the term can be applied.

Any effort at interpretation that attempted to make "fascism" exclusively the product of "thwarted" or "delayed" industrialization would have to face the problem of how one might classify Hitler's National Socialism. Certainly National Socialism shared many traits with Mussolini's Fascism, and Germany, at the time of Hitler's advent to power could hardly be characterized as suffering thwarted or delayed industrialization. Because of this particular anomaly, a number of social scientists have attempted to invoke the concept "totalitarianism" to cover a more inclusive class of political systems that would include Fascism, National Socialism, Stalin's Bolshevism and, perhaps, Mao's China and Castro's Cuba. In such a construal Fascism was subsumed under the more inclusive "fascism," and "fascism" was considered a subspecies of "totalitarianism." "Totalitarianism," which included Stalin's Bolshevism, was conceived as a species of the genus "authoritarianism." There have been any number of variations on such a schematization. Robert Tucker has suggested a variation that would subsume "revolutionary mass-movement regimes under single-party auspices" under the class "authoritarianism," with "totalitarianism" a subset of such "mass-movement regimes." "Totalitarianism" would be but one of the forms that the members of the genus might take on. It is interesting to note in this regard that Fascist theoreticians such as Mihail Manoilescu early identified a class of political movements that were novel to the twentieth century as products of a "revolutionary mass-mobilizing unitary party." [15] For both Tucker and Manoilescu, the suggestion is, that the genus can be divided into several species, among which are those that develop or "devolve" into "totalitarian forms." All the distinctions within the genus are made in terms of various sorting criteria. All members of the genus share certain "family traits," and the distinctions between them are "not fully distinct." For example, in attempting to characterize "fascist movement regimes," Tucker alludes to a feature that seems to function, in his judgment, as a defining trait: in "fascism" ". . . the psychology, or more accurately the psychopathology, of the leader becomes the driving force of the political mechanism. The regime is shaped into a highly complicated instrumentality for acting out the needs of the paranoid leader-personality, whose psychodynamics are politicalized, i.e., expressed in political action." [16] In so doing Tucker seems to have identified Stalinism as a "fascism." We immediately find ourselves puzzled. Is Maoism animated by a system in which the "psychology . . . of the leader becomes the driving force of the political mechanism"? [17] What of Castroism? Are these both fascisms? If so, then where are the "communisms"? If Maoism and Castroism are not fascisms, why not?

Peter Wiles has rehearsed some of these difficulties —and recognizes that Tucker's classificatory efforts threaten

----

[15] Mihail Manoilescu, *Die Einzige Partei* (Stollberg, 1941).

[16] Robert C. Tucker, "Towards a Comparative Politics of Movement Regimes." *American Political Science Review,* 1961, 55/2: 288.

[17] R. J. Lifton, *Revolutionary Immortality: Mao Tse-tung and the Chinese Cultural Revolution* (Random House, 1968).

to make Mao Tse-tung a "fascist"—and that strikes Wiles as straining language "well beyond its breaking point." [18] Irrespective of Wiles's misgivings, if generic fascism is to be defined as a mass-mobilizing movement under single-party auspices that acts out the "psychological needs" of the "leader" then, irrespective of its counterintuitive impression, Maoism may well be a variant of fascism. That it is difficult to characterize "psychological" or "paranoid" needs, and to specify how a mass movement might "act out" those needs, constitute *empirical* and *research problems,* not embarrassments for the speakers of ordinary language. A scientific classificatory system is not required to satisfy the common sense of ordinary language. Whales are not fish, although ordinary language users may continually so identify them. The identification of whales as mammals may appear counterintuitive to "common sense"—so much the worse for "common sense." The sense of science need not be common.

Classifications of complex phenomena invariably constitute a form of "experimental naming." They are suggestive and stenographic renderings of hypotheses entertained, and are ultimately based on empirical generalizations. As one pursues empirical inquiry—historical, experimental, or quasi-experimental in character—hypotheses are more rigorously formulated and ultimately influence effective definition. As the body of well-formulated and well-confirmed generalizations are articulated into more coherent and integral accounts, the preliminary definitions that may have initiated inquiry are transformed into more precise formulations that can be lodged in relatively rigorous classificatory schemata. Such schemata may, in turn, reveal redundancies

----

[18] Peter Wiles, "Comment on Tucker's 'Movement-Regimes.' " *American Political Science Review,* 1961, 55/2: 293.

and draw out implications, precipitate a review of funded theory, and generate new hypotheses and verification studies.

The Existing Theoretical Base for the Study of Fascism

What we seem to have at our disposal, for the time being, is a theoretical base that is largely discursive in character, but which provides some initial insight into the interpretation of fascism. Fascist systems seem to be those hierarchically ordered systems that utilize mass mobilization to organize collective energies behind extensive programs of national rehabilitation, industrialization or renovation. Their mobilization strategy normally exploits reactive nationalism in order to win for their respective national communities a "place in the sun." They seem invariably to involve a massive effort at industrial expansion and/or economic modernization in order to service goals that include effective defensive and/or aggressive capabilities to restore "national dignity," "lost territories," provide a resource base for economic insulation or "autarchy," or defeat the "international imperialist enemy," "the international Jewish conspiracy," or the "plutocratic powers." In the course of their enterprise such movements tend to develop an infrastructure of "capillary" or "cellular" organizations under the direction of a unitary or single-party under the hierarchical and centralized control of a "central committee" and typically a "charismatic leader." Such a general and vague characterization would not distinguish between Mussolini's Fascism, Hitler's National Socialism, Stalin's Bolshevism, Mao's or Castro's "communism," Nasser's Arab "socialism," or Nkrumah's "conscienscism."

Distinctions might be made through an analysis of the

recruitment base of each such revolutionary mass-mobilizing nationalist movement. In environments suffering massive
"power deflation," for example, in which traditional power
sources are significantly undermined—the army has suffered
total defeat, the landed gentry or aristocracy is discredited,
or the capitalist class is weak or nonexistent, and the
church is no longer viable—such movements might rest on
the "masses" without compromise with established socioeconomic, institutional, or political elites. In some cases,
on the other hand, the movement might be compelled to
negotiate with "nonmovement allies"—Mussolini's Fascism
and Hitler's National Socialism being immediate cases in
point. The resistance capabilities of such allies might be
subsequently destroyed or neutralized by the movement, and
the movement might then be able to act out its specifically
ideological purpose—the process surrounding Hitler's "final
solution" of the "Jewish question" might constitute a case in
point. Much the same might be said of Castro's accession
to absolute control in Cuba. Castro came to power with
the assistance of "nonmovement allies." Massive support
from the Soviet Union permitted him to neutralize and
ultimately to exile all potential political resistance. Mussolini's Fascism, in turn, was freed from its "nonmovement
allies" in the monarchy, the business community, and the
Church by their defection in the course of the military defeat that took place in 1943. At that point Fascism could
embark on its belated "socialization" of the Italian economy.

Such movements, on the other hand, might fall captive
to nonmovement allies and become "extinct." Franco
Spain seems to be a case in point. Alternatively, the movement might be destroyed—Nkrumah's "African socialism"
might constitute just such a case.

Among such mass-mobilizing movements some might

be clearly developmental in character, and might under the pressure of circumstances, or from intention, devolve into "totalitarianism." Other movements of the same species or subspecies might conceivably be "antimodernizing" in character or intention. They might equally well constitute another subset of "totalitarianisms." Any such movement might be successful or unsuccessful; it might recruit from one or another class or stratum of the population; it might employ nonmovement allies or not. In effect, there are any number of permutations that might provide a preliminary classificatory schema for "mass-mobilizing movements under single-party auspices." Such a schema might effectively relate some "crisis," "modernizing," or "developmental" regimes to "totalitarianism"—and thereby maximally exploit the interpretive capabilities of several contemporary social science concepts.

The best we could expect from such efforts, at this stage, are "heuristic conceptual schemata"—suggestive strategies for further inquiry. They might suggest a form of "experimental naming" that might, for instance, conceive peripheral and nonviable aspirant mass-mobilizing movements such as the (now all but defunct) Black Panthers to be variants of "fascism," rather than any alternative. Hugh Seton-Watson, Michael Curtis, and the authors in Norman Hill's collection have suggested as much.[19] If such a construal is anything other than polemical, it alludes to a family of criterial traits that identify the Black Panthers, or similar political groups, as members of a relatively specific class of

----

[19] Hugh Seton-Watson, "Fascism, Right and Left." *Journal of Contemporary History,* 1966, 1/1: 197; Michael Curtis, "Retreat from Totalitarianism." In Carl J. Friedrich, Michael Curtis, and Benjamin R. Barber, *Totalitarianism in Perspective: Three Views* (Praeger, 1969), p. 112; Norman Hill, ed., *The Black Panther Menace: America's Neo-Nazis* (Popular Library, 1971).

political movements. The characterization, when it is applied to aspiring movements, refers to the mass-mobilizing, paramilitary, developmental, and aggressive self-assertiveness of a hierarchically organized movement led by "charismatic" leaders who conceive violence as having some special therapeutic merit in restoring "manhood" to status-deprived populations. The enemy in such circumstances are "imperialist pigs," "Zionists," and/or "the Man." That the prospects of success for such movements are nil cannot militate against the analysis. Again, the distinctions between such movements would have to be made in terms of their political intentions, their recourse to "nonmovement allies," and their respective recruitment bases.[20]

Such movements, irrespective of their developmental or "antimodern" intentions, or the initial influence of their nonmovement allies or differential recruitment sources, might, under special socioeconomic and political circumstances, develop into the "totalitarianisms" to which Friedrich and Brzezinski allude. When all potential opposition and all erstwhile nonmovement alliances are neutralized—primary and secondary socialization, interest aggregation and articulation, information flow and communications, economic and political decision-making processes fall under the tutelary and pedagogical control of the single party and ideally under the dominance of a "charismatic" leader—we could legitimately speak of "totalitarianism."

Obviously, empirical indices are required to flesh out such discursive generalizations and stenographic characterizations. We need defensible generalizations that can be mapped over historic sequences—an identification of

----

[20] Cf. Eugen Weber, "The Men of the Archangel," *Journal of Contemporary History*, 1966, 1/1: 101–126; Robert J. Soucy, "The Nature of Fascism in France," *Journal of Contemporary History*, 1966, 1/1: 27–55.

thresholds above which mass mobilization can be successful, for example, or some technique for identifying "crises,"
isolating viable socioeconomic, political, and cultural elites;
competent characterization of specific ideological commitments; adequate definitions of "developmental" or "antimodern"; and generalizations covering the "logic" of individual and collective decision-making processes. It is
equally obvious that social science, at the moment, can provide us with very little of this. In effect and at best, we can
claim only a measure of "insight" into the Fascist phenomenon. We have succeeded in gaining some foothold on generic fascism and we can make some allusions to comparative studies of the mass-mobilizing revolutionary movements
that seem so abundant in our century.

We cannot claim, however, to have a compelling theory of Fascism, much less a compelling interpretation of
"fascism" or "totalitarianism." We have some considerable
body of hard data about a variety of revolutionary mass-
mobilizing movements, some significant biographical and
historical accounts, and a catalog of discursive and literary
treatments of entire sequences. What we do not have is a
body of viable theory to give support to all this. We do have
a great number of negative insights. We know, for example,
that many popular accounts of Fascism are hopelessly
inadequate.

There is little prospect that the near future will deliver
a fully competent theory of Fascism. We will have to be
content with plausibilities and detailed historical accounts.
The best efforts will be "eclectic," attempting to weave together the most defensible of plausibilities into a narrative
in which we can invest some confidence. Historians will
continue to analyze available actuarial and archival materials; survey specialists will continue to collect data; psychologists, sociologists and political scientists will continue

to attempt low-order, middle-range or unrestricted generalizations to deductively lace together substantive findings and disinter the generalizations that provide the cognitive foundations of historical writings and hypotheses formation. Social science is a collaborative enterprise, ideally tolerant of promising novelty, rigorous in its demand for intersubjective evidence and internal consistency, and eminently and unalterably corrigible in its substantive and normative judgments. The study of Fascism, and of generic fascism, requires nothing less.

BIBLIOGRAPHY

T. W. Adorno, Else Frenkel-Brunswik, D. J. Levinson, and R. N. Sanford, *The Authoritarian Personality*. Harper, 1950.

Paolo Alatri, *Le origini del fascismo*. Riuniti, 1963.

Gilbert Allardyce, ed., *The Place of Fascism in European History*. Prentice-Hall, 1971.

Giovanni Ansaldo, "Il fascismo e la piccola borghesia technica." In Costanzo Casucci, ed., *Il fascismo*. Mulino, 1961.

Oskar Anweiler, "Totalitaere Erziehung." In Bruno Seidel and Siegfried Jenkner, eds., *Wege der Totalitarismus-Forschung*. Wissenschaftliche Buchgesellschaft, 1968.

Alberto Aquarone, *L'organizzazione dello stato totalitario*. Einaudi, 1965.

Giulio Aquila, "Il fascismo Italiano." In Renzo De Felice, ed., *Il fascismo e i partiti politici Italiani*. Cappelli, 1966.

Hannah Arendt, *The Origins of Totalitarianism*. Harcourt, Brace, 1951.

Max Ascoli and Arthur Feiler, *Fascism for Whom?* Norton, 1938.

Paul A. Baran and Paul M. Sweezy, *Monopoly Capital*. Monthly Review, 1966.

Benjamin R. Barber, "Conceptual Foundations of Totalitarianism." In Carl J. Friedrich, Michael Curtis, and Benjamin R. Barber, *Totalitarianism in Perspective: Three Views*. Praeger, 1969.

Otto Bauer, "Der Faschismus." In Wolfgang Abendroth, ed., *Faschismus und Kapitalismus*. Europa Verlag, 1967.

Heinrich Bennecke, *Wirtschaftliche Depression und politischer Radikalismus: Die Lehre von Weimar*. Olzog, 1968.

Antonio Stefano Benni, "Lo sviluppo industriale dell'Italia fascista." In T. Sillani, ed., *Lo Stato Mussoliniano*. La Rassegna Italiana, 1930.

Robert F. Berkofer, *A Behavioral Approach to Historical Analysis*. Free Press, 1969.

Aldo Bertele, *Aspetti ideologici del fascismo*. Druetto, 1930.

Franz Borkenau, *World Communism*. University of Michigan, 1962.

————, "Zur Soziologie des Faschismus." In Ernst Nolte, ed., *Theorien ueber den Faschismus*. Kiepenheuer & Witsch, 1967.

Guido Bortolotto, *Die Revolution der jungen Voelker*. Kittlers Verlag, 1934.

Karl D. Bracher, *The German Dictatorship*. Praeger, 1970.

Y. S. Brenner, *Theories of Economic Development and Growth*. George Allen and Unwin, 1966.

May Brodbeck, "The Philosophy of Science and Educational Research." *Review of Educational Research,* 1957, 27/5: 427–440.

Roger Brown, *Social Psychology*. Free Press, 1965.

Zbigniew K. Brzezinski. *Ideology and Power in Soviet Politics,* rev. ed. Praeger, 1967.

Robert Burrowes, "Totalitarianism: The Revised Standard Version." *World Politics,* 21/2 (January, 1969), 272–294.

John M. Cammett, "Communist Theories of Fascism, 1920–1935." *Science and Society,* 1967, 31/2: 149–163.

Alan Cassels, *Fascist Italy*. Crowell, 1968.

Costanzo Casucci, ed., *Il fascismo*. Mulino, 1961.

Pietro Chimienti, "L'individuo e la massa." *Gerarchia,* 1935, 13/6: 479–483.

R. Christie and Marie Jahoda, eds., *Studies in the Scope and Method of "The Authoritarian Personality."* Free Press, 1954.

G. Ciano, *Ciano's Hidden Diary: 1937–1938.* Dutton, 1953.

———, *The Ciano Diaries: 1939–1943.* Doubleday, 1946.

George D. H. Cole, *The Meaning of Marxism.* University of Michigan Press, 1964.

———, *Socialism and Fascism, 1931–1939.* St. Martin's, 1960.

Richard Collier, *Duce! A Biography of Benito Mussolini.* Viking, 1971.

Benedetto Croce, "Chi è 'fascista'?" *Pagine politiche.* Laterza, 1945.

———, "Il fascismo come pericolo mondiale," and "La libertà italiana nella libertà del mondo." *Per la nuova vita dell'Italia.* Ricciardi, 1944.

———, "Il fascismo come parentesi." In Costanzo Casucci, ed., *Il fascismo.* Mulino, 1961.

Michael Curtis, "Retreat from Totalitarianism." In Carl J. Friedrich, Michael Curtis, and Benjamin R. Barber, *Totalitarianism in Perspective: Three Views.* Praeger, 1969.

Giuseppe De Falco, "Il fascismo milizia di classe." In Renzo De Felice, ed., *Il fascismo e i partiti politici Italiani.* Cappelli, 1966.

Renzo De Felice, *Le interpretazioni del fascismo.* Laterza, 1969.

———, *Mussolini il fascista: la conquista del potere, 1921–1925.* Einaudi, 1966.

———, *Mussolini il fascista: l'organizzazione dello Stato fascista, 1925–1929.* Einaudi, 1968.

———, *Mussolini il rivoluzionario.* Einaudi, 1965.

————, *Storia degli ebrei Italiani sotto il fascismo.* Einaudi, 1962.

Charles F. Delzell, ed., *Mediterranean Fascism, 1919–1945.* Harper & Row, 1970.

Julius Deutsch, *Die Fascistengefahr.* Wiener Volksbuchhandlung, 1923.

Isaac Deutscher, *Russia in Transition,* rev. ed. Grove Press, 1960.

Peter Drucker, *The End of Economic Man: The Origins of Totalitarianism.* Harper & Row, 1969.

Rajani Palme Dutt, *Fascism and Social Revolution.* International, 1934.

————, *Fascism: An Analysis.* India Publishing House, 1943.

William Ebenstein, "The Study of Totalitarianism." *World Politics,* 1958, 10/2: 274–288.

Luigi Einaudi, *Il buongoverno.* Laterza, 1954.

Paul Einzig, *The Economic Foundations of Fascism.* Macmillan, 1933.

Iring Fetscher, "Faschismus und Nationalsozialismus: Zur Kritik des sowjetmarxistischen Faschismusbegriffs." *Politische Vierteljahresschrift,* 1962, 3/1: 42–63.

Frederic J. Fleron, Jr., "Soviet Area Studies and the Social Sciences: Some Methodological Problems in Communist Studies." *Soviet Studies,* 1968, 19/3: 313–339.

Carl J. Friedrich, "The Evolving Theory and Practice of Totalitarian Regimes." In Carl J. Friedrich, Michael Curtis, and Benjamin R. Barber, *Totalitarianism in Perspective: Three Views.* Praeger, 1969.

———— and Zbigniew Brzezinski, *Totalitarian Dictatorship and Autocracy.* Praeger, 1956.

Erich Fromm, *Escape from Freedom.* Avon, 1965.

————, *The Sane Society.* Rinehart, 1955.

Daniel Fusfield, *Fascist Democracy in the United States.* Union for Radical Political Economics, 1968.

A. Galkin, "Capitalist Society and Fascism." *Social Sciences: USSR Academy of Sciences,* 1970, 2: 128–138.

Ludovico Garruccio, "Let tre età del fascismo." *Il Mulino,* 1971, 213: 53–73.

————, *L'industrializzazione tra nazionalismo e rivoluzione.* Mulino, 1969.

Giovanni Gentile, "Origini e dottrina del fascismo." In Costanzo Casucci, ed., *Il fascismo.* Mulino, 1961.

Gino Germani, "Fascism and Class." In S. J. Woolf, ed., *The Nature of Fascism.* Random House, 1969.

Dante Germino, *The Italian Fascist Party in Power.* University of Minnesota Press, 1959.

Harold E. Goad, *What is Fascism?* Italian Mail & Tribune, 1929.

Dino Grandi, "Le origini e la missione del fascismo." In Renzo De Felice, ed., *Il fascismo e i partiti politici Italiani.* Cappelli, 1966.

A. James Gregor, "Classical Marxism and the Totalitarian Ethic." *Journal of Value Inquiry,* 1968, 2/1: 58–72.

————, *Contemporary Radical Ideologies: Totalitarian Thought in the Twentieth Century.* Random House, 1968.

————, "Fascism and Modernization: Some Addenda." *World Politics,* to be published in April, 1974.

————, *The Ideology of Fascism.* Free Press, 1969.

————, *An Introduction to Metapolitics.* Free Press, 1971.

Alexander Groth, "The 'isms' in Totalitarianism." *American Political Science Review,* 1964, 58/4: 888–901.

Daniel Guerin, *Fascism and Big Business.* Pioneer, 1939.

——, *Fascismo e gran capitale.* Schwarz, 1956.

Elie Halevy, *The Era of Tyrannies.* Doubleday, 1965.

Norman Hill, ed., *The Black Panther Menace: America's Neo-Nazis.* Popular Library, 1971.

Eric Hoffer, *The True Believer: Thoughts on the Nature of Mass Movements.* Harper & Row, 1951.

Leo Huberman and Paul M. Sweezy, "Goldwaterism." *Monthly Review,* 1964, 16/5: 273–283.

David Ingersoll, *Communism, Fascism and Democracy.* Merrill, 1971.

H. Roderick Kedward, *Fascism in Western Europe, 1900–45.* New York University Press, 1971.

G. A. Kelly and C. W. Brown, "Editors' Comment." In G. A. Kelly and C. W. Brown, eds., *Struggles in the State: Sources and Patterns of World Revolution.* Wiley, 1970.

John F. Kirscht and Ronald C. Dillehay, *Dimensions of Authoritarianism: A Review of Research and Theory.* University of Kentucky Press, 1967.

G. Klaus and M. Buhr, eds., *Philosophisches Woerterbuch,* VEB, 1966.

N. Kogan, "Discussion—Fascism and the Polity." In S. J. Woolf, ed., *The Nature of Fascism.* Random House, 1969.

Hans Kohn, *Political Ideologies of the Twentieth Century.* Harper & Row, 1966.

——, *Revolutions and Dictatorships.* Harvard University Press, 1943.

William Kornhauser, *The Politics of Mass Society.* Free Press, 1959.

Reinhard Kuehnl, *Formen buergerlicher Herrschaft: Liberalismus-Faschismus.* Rowolt, 1971.

————, "Probleme einer Theorie ueber den internationalen Faschismus." *Politische Vierteljahresschrift,* 1970, 11/2–3: 318–341.

Harold D. Lasswell and Daniel Lerner, eds., *The World Revolutionary Elites.* M.I.T. Press, 1965.

Gustave Le Bon, *The Crowd.* Viking, 1960.

————, *The Psychology of Revolution.* G. P. Putnam, 1913.

Emil Lederer, *The State of the Masses: The Threat of the Classless Society.* Norton, 1940.

V. I. Lenin, "Imperialism: The Highest Stage of Capitalism." In James Connor, ed., *Lenin: On Politics and Revolution.* Pegasus, 1968.

R. J. Lifton, *Revolutionary Immortality: Mao Tse-tung and the Chinese Cultural Revolution.* Random House, 1968.

S. Lombardini, "Italian Fascism and the Economy." In S. J. Woolf, ed., *The Nature of Fascism.* Random House, 1969.

Boris R. Lopukhov, "Il problema el fascismo Italiano negli scritti di autori sovietici." *Studi storici,* 1965, 6/2: 240–255.

Peter Christian Ludz, "Entwurf einer soziologischen Theorie totalitaer verfasster Gesellschaft." In Bruno Seidel and Siegfried Jenkner, eds., *Wege der Totalitarismus-Forschung.* Wissenschaftliche Buchgesellschaft, 1968.

————, "Offene Fragen in der Totalitarismusforschung." In Bruno Seidel and Siegfried Jenkner, eds., *Wege der Totalitarismus-Forschung.* Wissenschaftliche Buchgesellschaft, 1968.

Angus Maddison, *Economic Growth in the West: Comparative Experience in Europe and North America.* Twentieth Century Fund, 1964.

Mihail Manoilescu, *Die einzige Partei.* Stollberg, 1941.

Filippo T. Marinetti, *Teoria e invenzione futurista.* Mondadori, 1968.

Masao Maruyama, *Thought and Behavior in Modern Japanese Politics.* Oxford University Press, 1969.

Mary Matossian, "Ideologies of Delayed Industrialization: Some Tensions and Ambiguities." In John H. Kautsky, ed., *Political Change in Underdeveloped Countries.* Wiley, 1962.

Giacomo Matteotti, *The Fascisti Exposed.* Fertig, 1969.

Nazareno Mezzetti, *Mussolini e la questione sociale.* Pinciana, 1931.

Robert Michels, *Sozialismus und Faschismus in Italien.* Meyer & Jensen, 1925.

Ludwig von Mises, *Planned Chaos.* Foundation for Economic Education, 1947.

Mario Missiroli, *Il fascismo e il colpo di stato dell'Ottobre, 1922.* Cappelli, 1966.

Rodolfo Mondolfo, "Il fascismo in Italia." In Renzo De Felice, ed., *Il fascismo e i partiti politici Italiani.* Cappelli, 1966.

Barrington Moore, Jr., *Social Origins of Dictatorship and Democracy.* Beacon, 1966.

Arnaldo Mussolini, *Panorami di realizzazioni del fascismo,* vols. 1–2, Cataldi, 1942.

Benito Mussolini, *Opera omnia,* vols. 1–36. La fenice, 1951–1963.

Agostino Nasti, "Civiltà collettivistica." *Critica fascista,* 1933, 11/16: 301–302.

Peter Nathan, *The Psychology of Fascism*. Faber, 1943.

Sigmund Neumann, *Permanent Revolution: The Total State in a World at War*. Harper, 1965.

Robert A. Nisbet, *Social Change and History*. Oxford University Press, 1969.

Ernst Nolte, *Three Faces of Fascism*. Holt, Rinehart and Winston, 1966.

————, *Die faschistischen Bewegungen*. Deutscher Taschenbuch Verlag, 1966.

————, ed., *Theorien ueber den Faschismus*. Kiepenheuer & Witsch, 1967.

D. C. North, *Growth and Welfare in the American Past: A New Economic History*. Prentice-Hall, 1966.

A. F. K. Organski, *The Stages of Political Development*. Knopf, 1965.

————, "Fascism and Modernization." In S. J. Woolf, ed., *The Nature of Fascism*. Random House, 1969.

Jose Ortega y Gasset, *The Revolt of the Masses*. Norton, 1932.

R. Osborn, *The Psychology of Reaction*. Gollancz, 1938.

Sergio Panunzio, *Che cos'è il fascismo*. Alpes, 1924.

————, "Teoria generale della dittatura." *Gerarchia*, 1936, 14/4: 228–236; 1936, 14/5: 303–316.

————, *Teoria generale dello Stato fascista*. Cedam, 1939.

Talcott Parsons, "Some Sociological Aspects of the Fascist Movements." In T. Parsons, *Essays in Sociological Theory*, rev. ed., Free Press, 1949.

Gustavo Pesenti, "Alcuni aspetti del mondo nuovo." *Gerarchia*, 1935, 13/5: 383–402.

Theo Pirker, ed., *Utopie und Mythos der Weltrevolution*. DTV, 1964.

Karl R. Popper, *The Logic of Scientific Discovery*. Basic Books, 1961.

Giuseppe Prezzolini, "Ideologia e sentimento." In Renzo De Felice, ed., *Il fascismo e i partiti politici Italiani*. Cappelli, 1966.

Emilio Radius, *Usi e costumi dell'uomo fascista*. Rizzoli, 1964.

Wilhelm Reich, *The Mass Psychology of Fascism*. Orgone, 1946. (Rev. ed. trans. by Vincent Carfago. Farrar, Strauss & Giroux, 1970.)

Bruno Rizzi, *Dove va l'U.R.S.S.?* La Prora, 1938.

———, *La lezione dello Stalinismo*. Opere Nuove, 1962.

Rosario Romeo, *Breve storia dell'industria Italiana*. Cappelli, 1963.

Arthur Rosenberg, "Der Faschismus als Massenbewegung." In Wolfgang Abendroth, ed., *Faschismus und Kapitalismus*. Europa Verlag, 1967.

M. Rosenthal and P. Yudin, eds., *A Dictionary of Philosophy*. Progress Publishers, 1967.

Jakob Rosner, *Der Faschismus*. Selbstverlag Jakob Rosner, 1966.

Ernesto Rossi, *Padroni del vapore e fascismo*. Laterza, 1966.

Walt W. Rostow, *Politics and the Stages of Growth*. Cambridge University Press, 1971.

———, *The Process of Economic Growth*, 2nd ed. Norton, 1962.

———, *The Stages of Economic Growth: A Non-Communist Manifesto*. Cambridge University Press, 1960.

G. Rumi, *Alle origini della politica estera fascista.* Laterza, 1968.

Luigi Salvatorelli, *Nazionalfascismo.* Gobetti, 1923.

———— and Giovanni Mira, *Storia d'Italia nel periodo fascista.* Einaudi, 1964.

Gaetano Salvemini, *Under the Axe of Fascism.* Gollancz, 1936.

Roland Sarti, *Fascism and the Industrial Leadership in Italy: 1919–1940.* University of California Press, 1971.

Leonard Schapiro, "What is Fascism?" *New York Review of Books,* February 12, 1970, pp. 13–15.

Carl Schmidt, *The Plough and the Sword.* Columbia University Press, 1938.

Luigi Scrivo, *Sintesi del Futurismo.* Bulzoni, 1968.

Renzo Sereno, "The Fascists: The Changing Elite." In Harold D. Lasswell and Daniel Lerner, eds., *The World Revolutionary Elites.* M.I.T. Press, 1965.

Hugh Seton-Watson, "Fascism, Right and Left." *Journal of Contemporary History,* 1966, 1/1: 183–197.

David Shermer, *Blackshirts: Fascism in Britain.* Ballantine, 1971.

S. M. Slobodskoi, *Storia del fascismo.* Riuniti, 1962.

J. Solé-Tura, "The Political 'Instrumentality' of Fascism." In S. J. Woolf, ed., *The Nature of Fascism.* Random House, 1969.

Robert J. Soucy, "The Nature of Fascism in France." *Journal of Contemporary History,* 1966, 1/1: 27–55.

Ugo Spirito, "Il corporativismo come liberalismo assoluto e socialismo assoluto." In Costanzo Casucci, ed., *Il fascismo.* Mulino, 1961.

Herbert Spiro, "Totalitarianism." In David Sills, ed., *International Encyclopedia of the Social Sciences,* vol. 16. Macmillan, 1968.

———— and Benjamin Barber, "Counter-Ideological Uses of 'Totalitarianism.' " In *Politics and Society,* 1970, 1: 3–22.

Otto Stammer, "Aspekte der Totalitarismusforschung." In Bruno Seidel and Siegfried Jenkner, eds., *Wege der Totalitarismus-Forschung.* Wissenschaftliche Buchgesellschaft, 1968.

Patrick Suppes, "A Comparison of the Meaning and Uses of Models in Mathematics and the Empirical Sciences." In Hans Freudenthal, ed., *The Concept and the Role of the Model in Mathematics and Social Sciences.* Reidel, 1961.

J. L. Talmon, *The Origins of Totalitarian Democracy.* Secker and Warburg, 1952.

Angelo Tasca, *Nascita e avvento del fascismo.* La Nuova Italia, 1950.

August Thalheimer, "Ueber den Faschismus." In W. Abendroth, ed., *Faschismus und Kapitalismus.* Europaeische Verlagsanstalt, 1967.

Palmiro Togliatti, "A proposito del fascismo." In Costanzo Casucci, ed., *Il fascismo.* Mulino, 1961.

H. R. Trevor-Roper. "The Phenomenon of Fascism." In S. J. Woolf, ed., *European Fascism.* Random House, 1968.

Leon Trotsky, *The Revolution Betrayed.* John Day, 1937.

————, *Fascism: What It Is—How to Fight It.* Pioneer, 1944.

Robert C. Tucker, "The Dictator and Totalitarianism." *World Politics,* 1965, 17/4: 555–583.

————, "Towards a Comparative Politics of Movement-Regimes." *American Political Science Review,* 1961, 55/2: 281–289.

Filippo Turati, "Fascismo, socialismo e democrazia." In Costanzo Casucci, ed., *Il fascismo*. Mulino, 1961.

H. A. Turner, "Fascism and Modernization." *World Politics,* 1972, 24: 547–564.

Mihaly Vajda, "The Rise of Fascism in Italy and Germany." *Telos,* 1972, 12: 3–26.

Pierre Vilar, "Développement historique et progrès social: les étapes et les critères." *Crecimiento y desarollo.* Ariel, 1964.

L. Villari, *Italian Foreign Policy Under Mussolini.* Devin-Adair, 1956.

Gioacchino Volpe, "Genesi del fascismo." In Costanzo Casucci, ed., *Il fascismo.* Mulino, 1961.

Eugen Weber, "The Men of the Archangel." *Journal of Contemporary History,* 1966, 1/1: 101–126.

William Welk, *Fascist Economic Policy.* Harvard University Press, 1938.

Peter Wiles, "Comment on Tucker's 'Movement-Regimes,' " *American Political Science Review,* 1961, 55/2: 290–293.

S. J. Woolf, "Did a Fascist Economic System Exist?" In S. J. Woolf, ed., *The Nature of Fascism.* Random House, 1969.

———, "Introduction." In S. J. Woolf, ed., *European Fascism.* Random House, 1968.

Clara Zetkin, "Der Kampf gegen den Faschismus." In E. Nolte, ed., *Theorien ueber den Faschismus,* Kiepenheuer & Witsch, 1967.

Fulvio Zugaro, "La produzione del suolo italiano." In *Annali di Economia,* 1924, 1: 280–289.

Index

1 2 3 4 5 6 7 8—COL—80 79 78 77 76 75 74